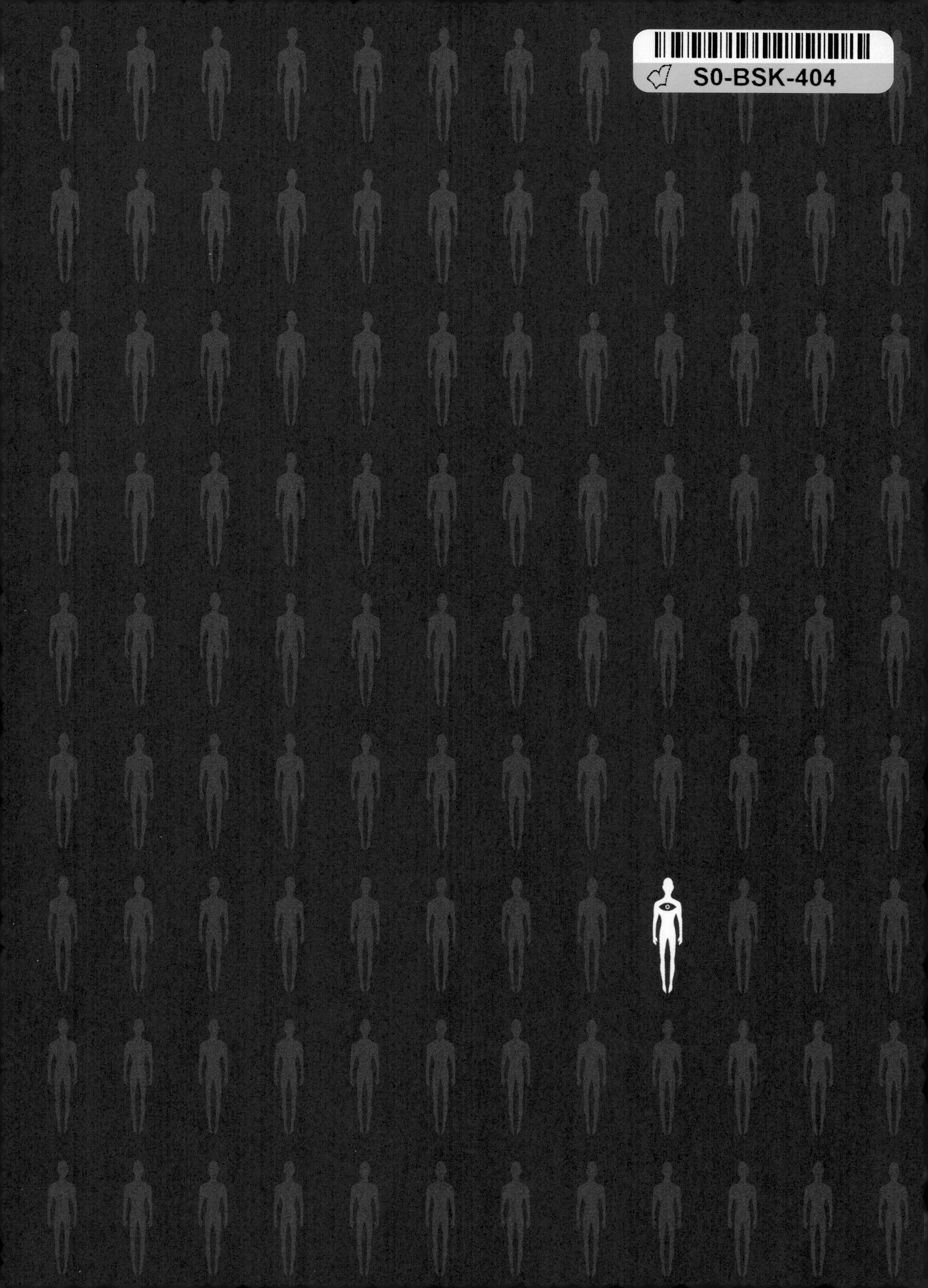

LAST DAYS OF AN IMMORTAL

Gwen De **Bonneval** & Fabien **Vehlmann**

ARCHAIA ENTERTAINMENT LLC
WWW.**ARCHAIA**.COM

LAST DAYS OF AN IMMORTAL™

Written by Fabien **Vehlmann**
Illustrated by Gwen De **Bonneval**

Rebecca Taylor, *Editor*
Didier Gonord, *French Edition Design*
Edward Gauvin, *Translator*
Deron Bennett, *Letterer*
Scott Newman, *Production Manager*

Archaia Entertainment LLC

PJ Bickett, *CEO*
Mark Smylie, *CCO*
Mike Kennedy, *Publisher*
Stephen Christy, *Editor-in-Chief*

Published by **Archaia**

Archaia Entertainment LLC
1680 Vine Street, Suite 1010
Los Angeles, California, 90028, USA
www.archaia.com

ARCHAIA™
NEW STORIES. NEW WORLDS.

LAST DAYS OF AN IMMORTAL Original Graphic Novel Hardcover. April 2012. FIRST PRINTING.

10 9 8 7 6 5 4 3 2 1

ISBN: 1-936393-44-1

ISBN 13: 978-1-936393-44-2

Printed in **Hong Kong**.

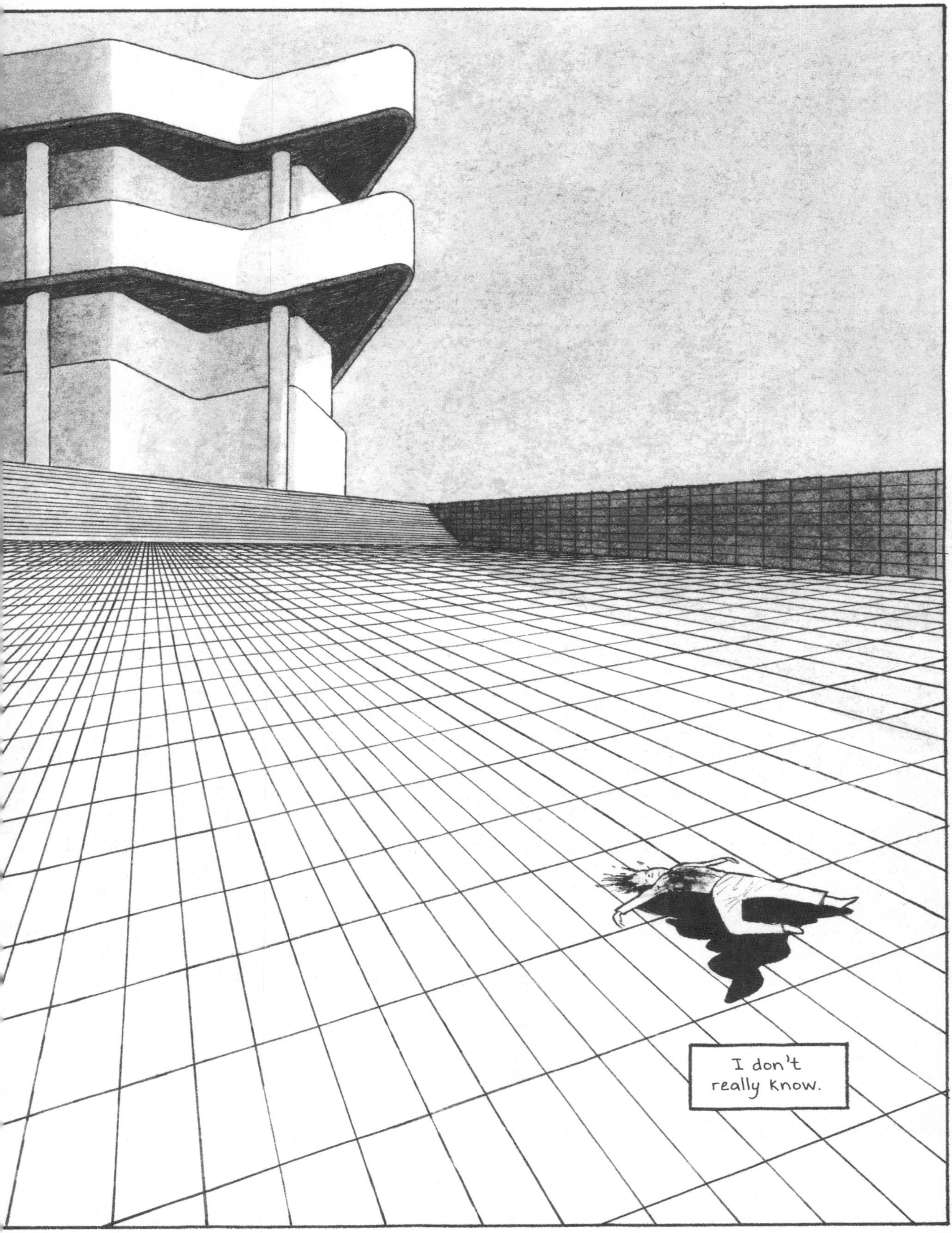
I don't really know.

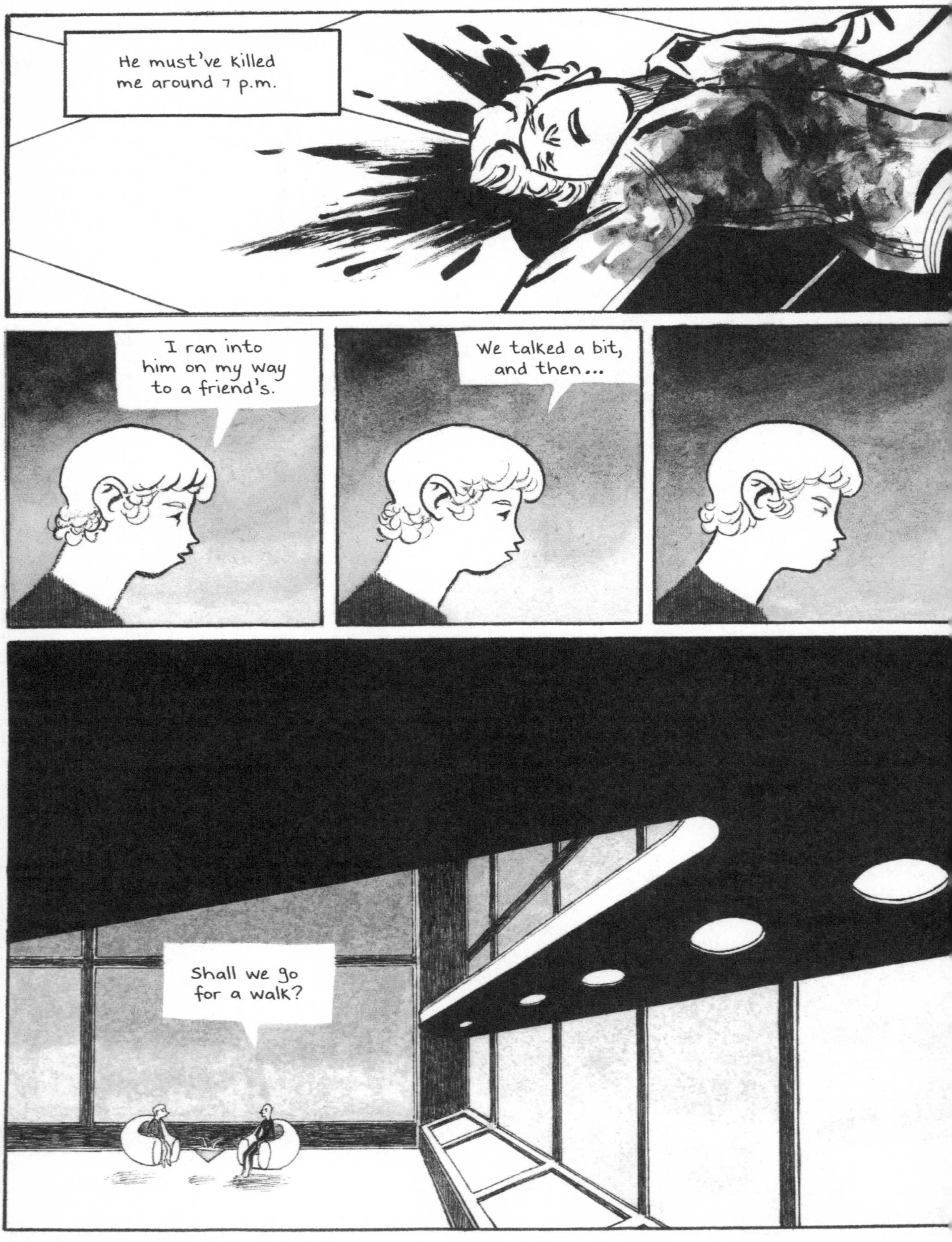
He must've killed me around 7 p.m.
I ran into him on my way to a friend's.
We talked a bit, and then...
Shall we go for a walk?

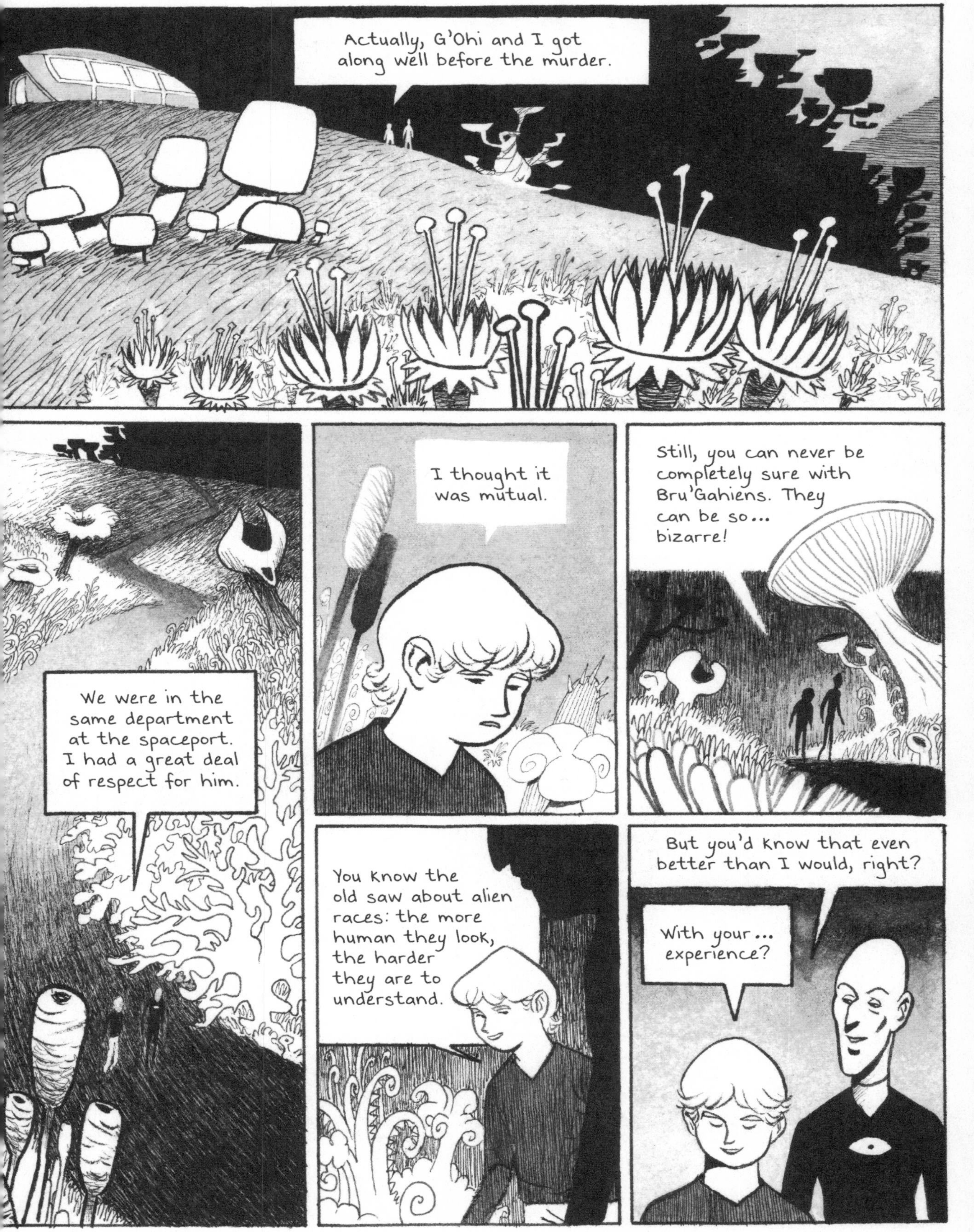
Actually, G'Ohi and I got along well before the murder.
We were in the same department at the spaceport. I had a great deal of respect for him.
I thought it was mutual.
Still, you can never be completely sure with Bru'Gahiens. They can be so... bizarre!
You know the old saw about alien races: the more human they look, the harder they are to understand.
But you'd know that even better than I would, right?
With your... experience?

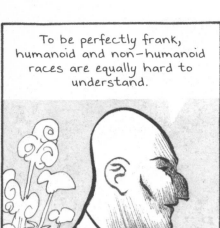

To be perfectly frank, humanoid and non-humanoid races are equally hard to understand.

What do affect us, however, are the expectations we bring to the encounter.

Part of us imagines contact will go more smoothly with aliens who look like us. In the end, our disappointed expectations are to blame for making it seem more difficult.

You're right: this kind of situation requires a certain watchfulness.

Yes... I thought as much.

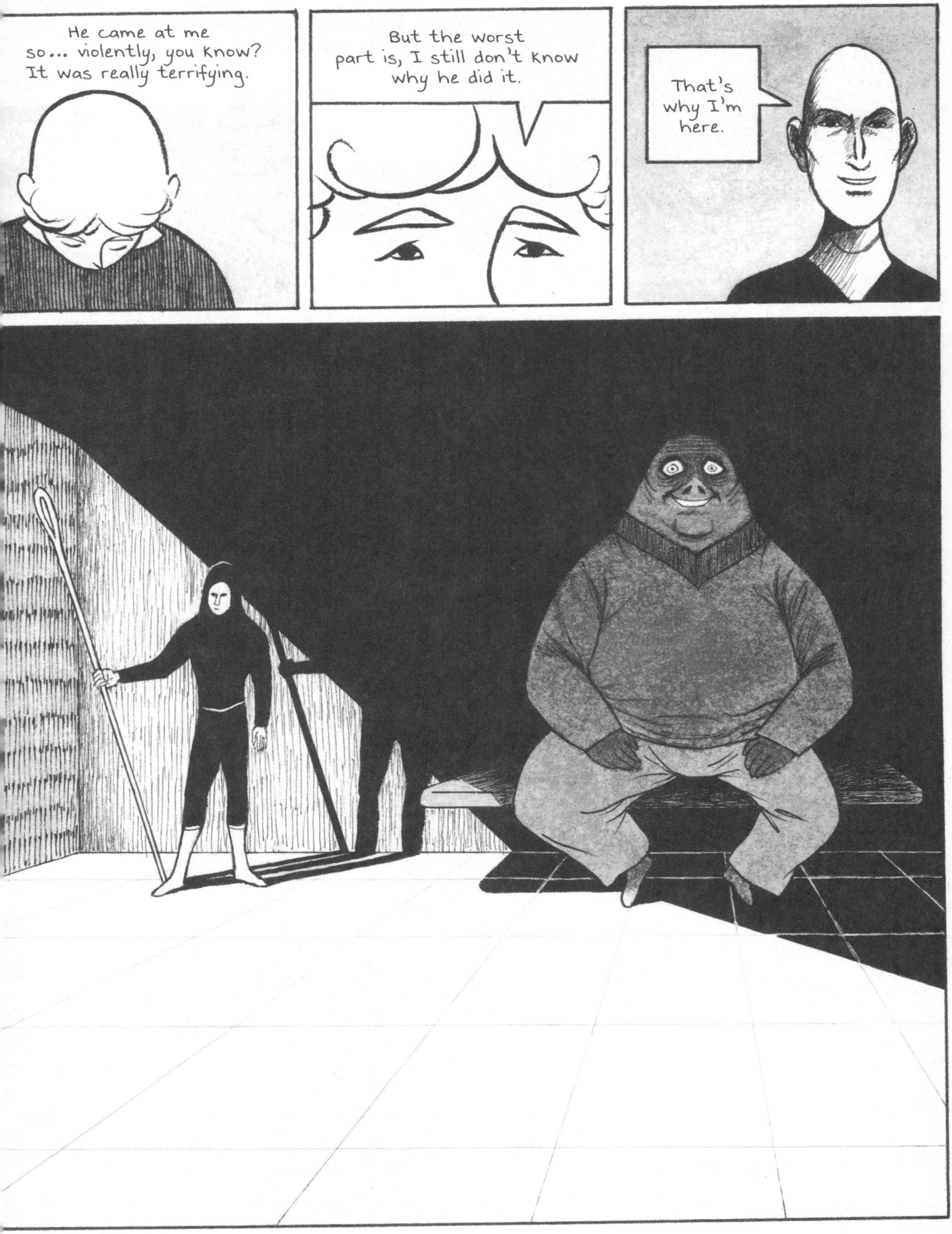
He came at me so... violently, you know? It was really terrifying.
But the worst part is, I still don't know why he did it.
That's why I'm here.

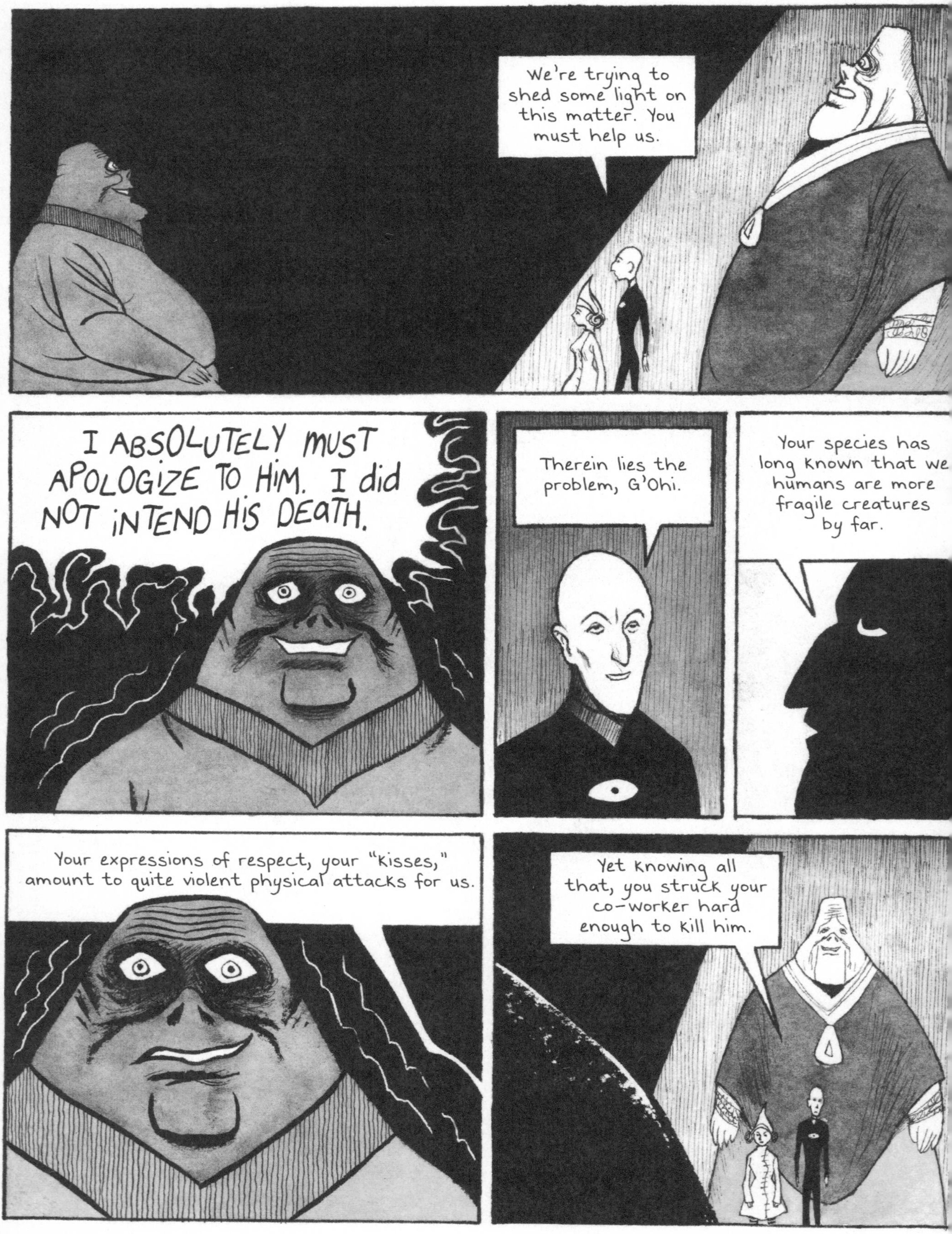
We're trying to shed some light on this matter. You must help us.
I ABSOLUTELY MUST APOLOGIZE TO HIM. I did NOT INTEND HIS DEATH.
Therein lies the problem, G'Ohi.
Your species has long known that we humans are more fragile creatures by far.
Your expressions of respect, your "kisses," amount to quite violent physical attacks for us.
Yet knowing all that, you struck your co-worker hard enough to kill him.

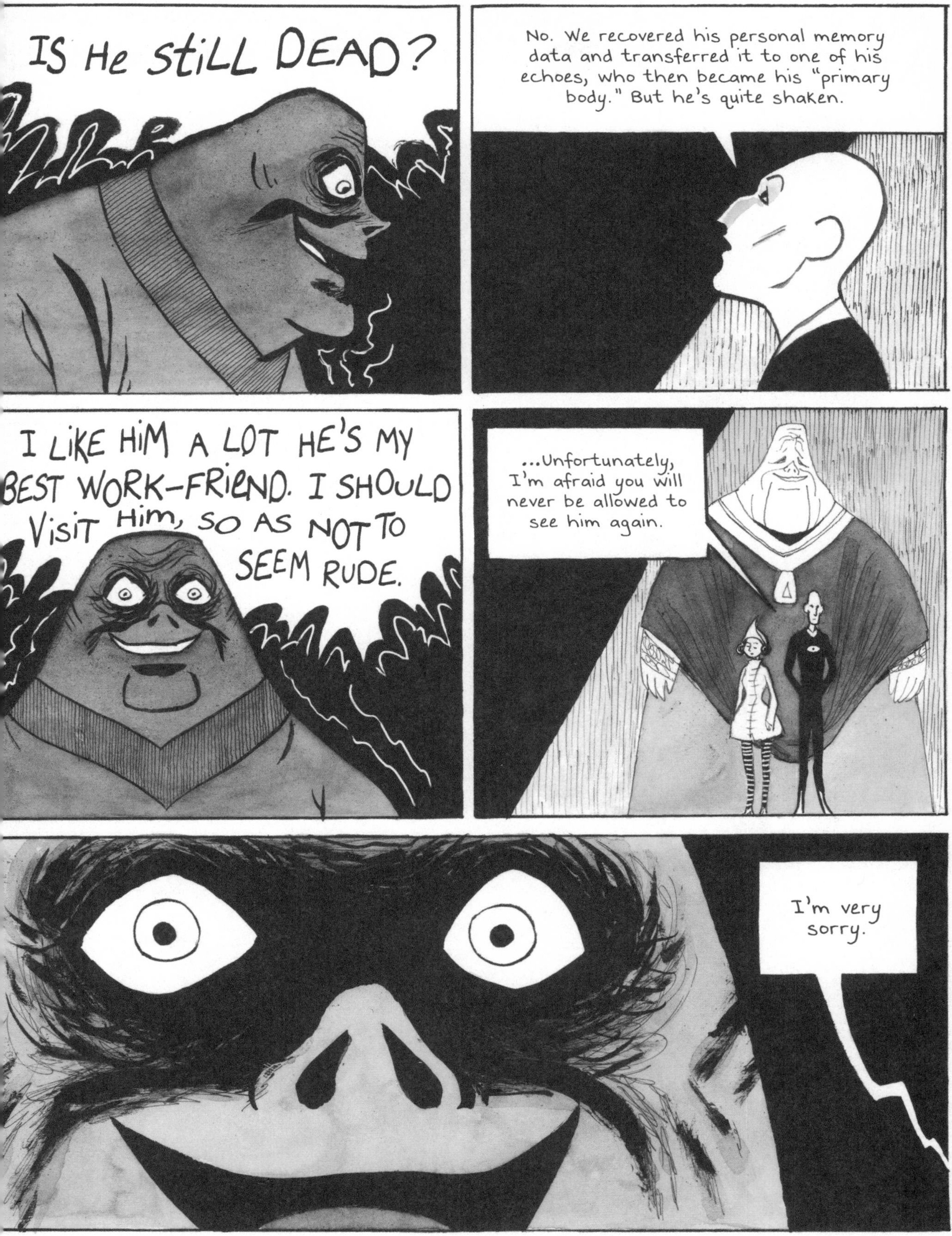
IS He stiLL DEAD?
No. We recovered his personal memory data and transferred it to one of his echoes, who then became his "primary body." But he's quite shaken.
I LIKE HIM A LOT HE'S MY BEST WORK-FRIEND. I SHOULD VISIT HIM, SO AS NOT TO SEEM RUDE.
...Unfortunately, I'm afraid you will never be allowed to see him again.
I'm very sorry.

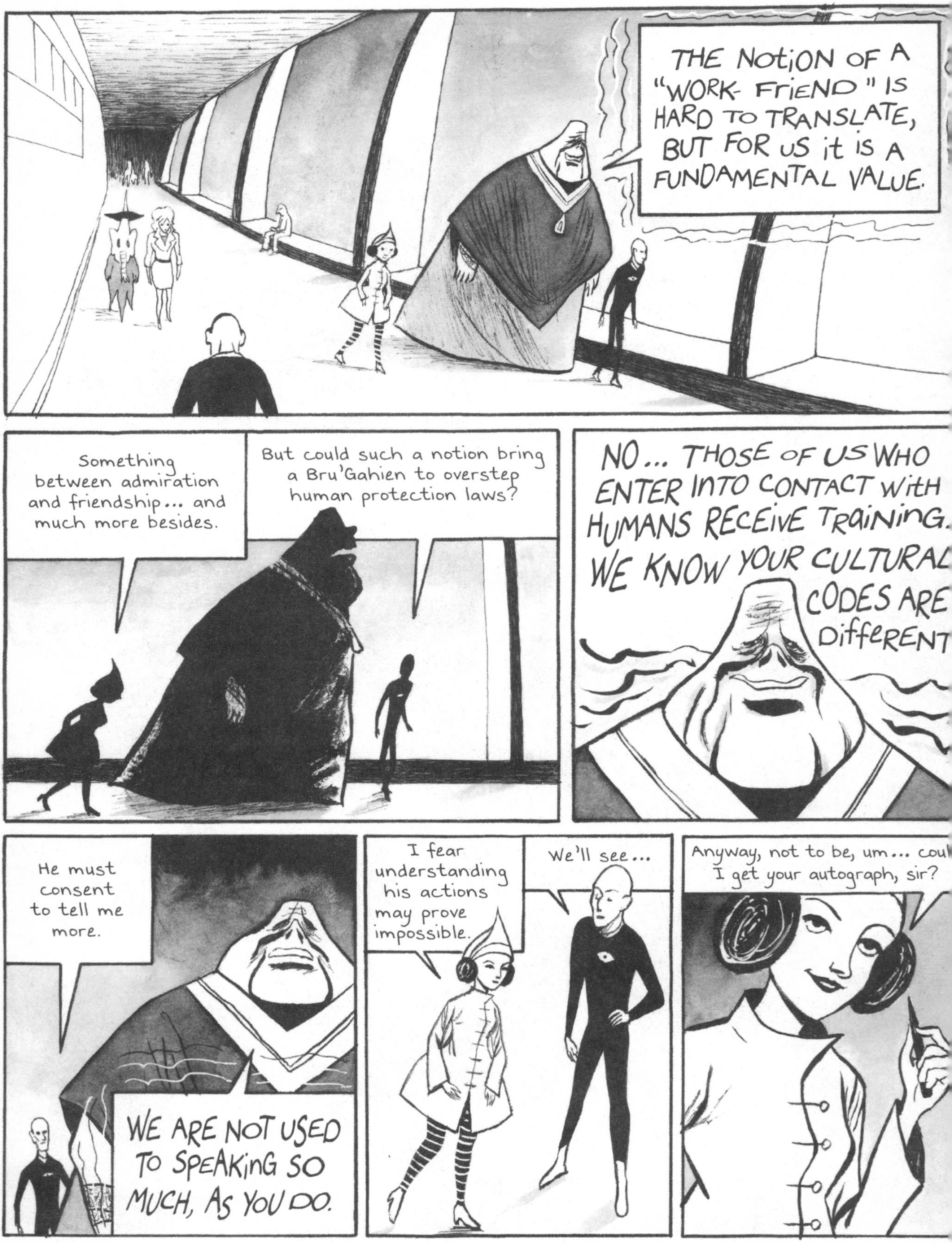
THE NOTION OF A "WORK-FRIEND" IS HARD TO TRANSLATE, BUT FOR US IT IS A FUNDAMENTAL VALUE.
Something between admiration and friendship... and much more besides.
But could such a notion bring a Bru'Gahien to overstep human protection laws?
NO... THOSE OF US WHO ENTER INTO CONTACT WITH HUMANS RECEIVE TRAINING. WE KNOW YOUR CULTURAL CODES ARE DIFFERENT
He must consent to tell me more.
WE ARE NOT USED TO SPEAKING SO MUCH, AS YOU DO.
I fear understanding his actions may prove impossible.
We'll see...
Anyway, not to be, um... coul
I get your autograph, sir?

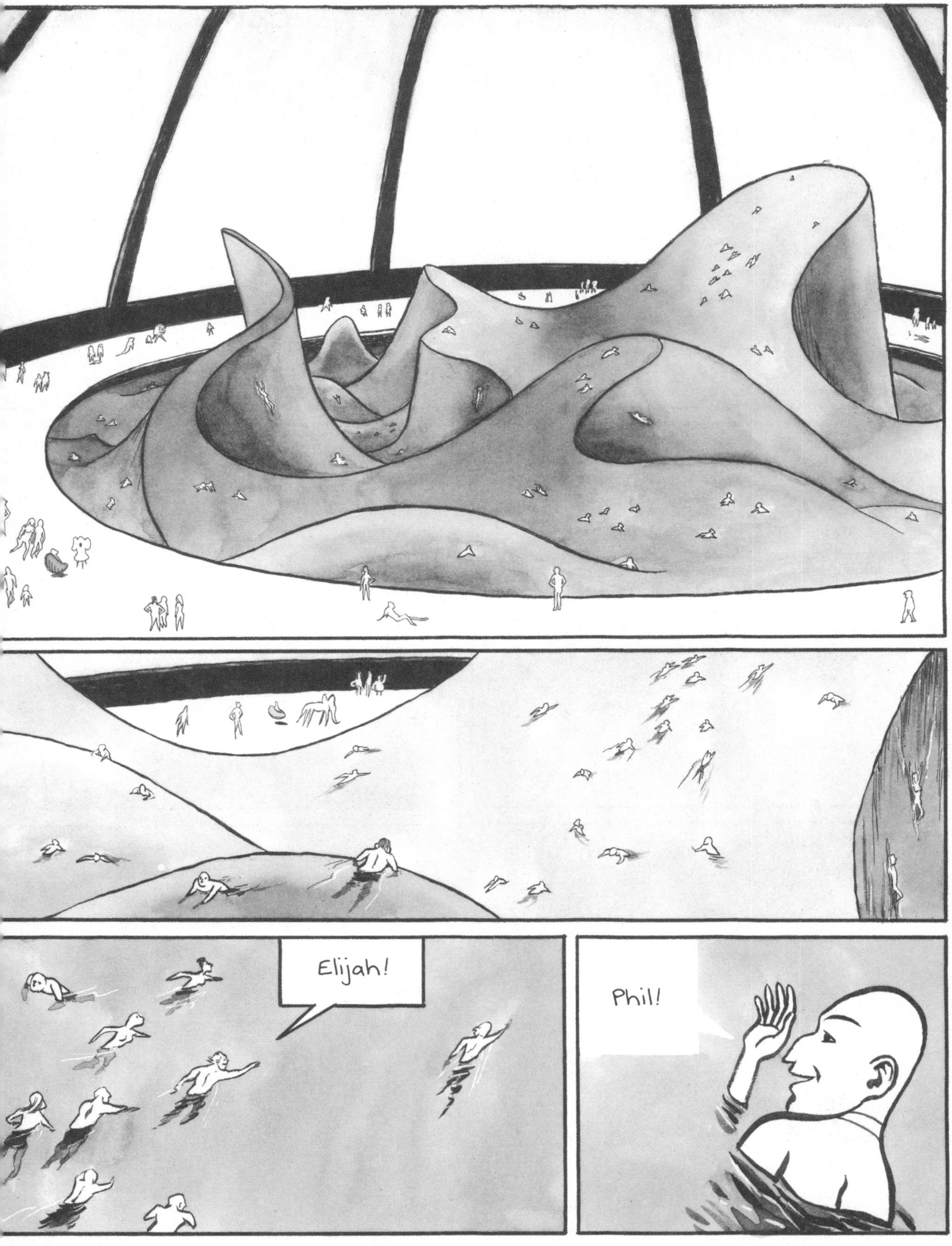
Elijah!
Phil!

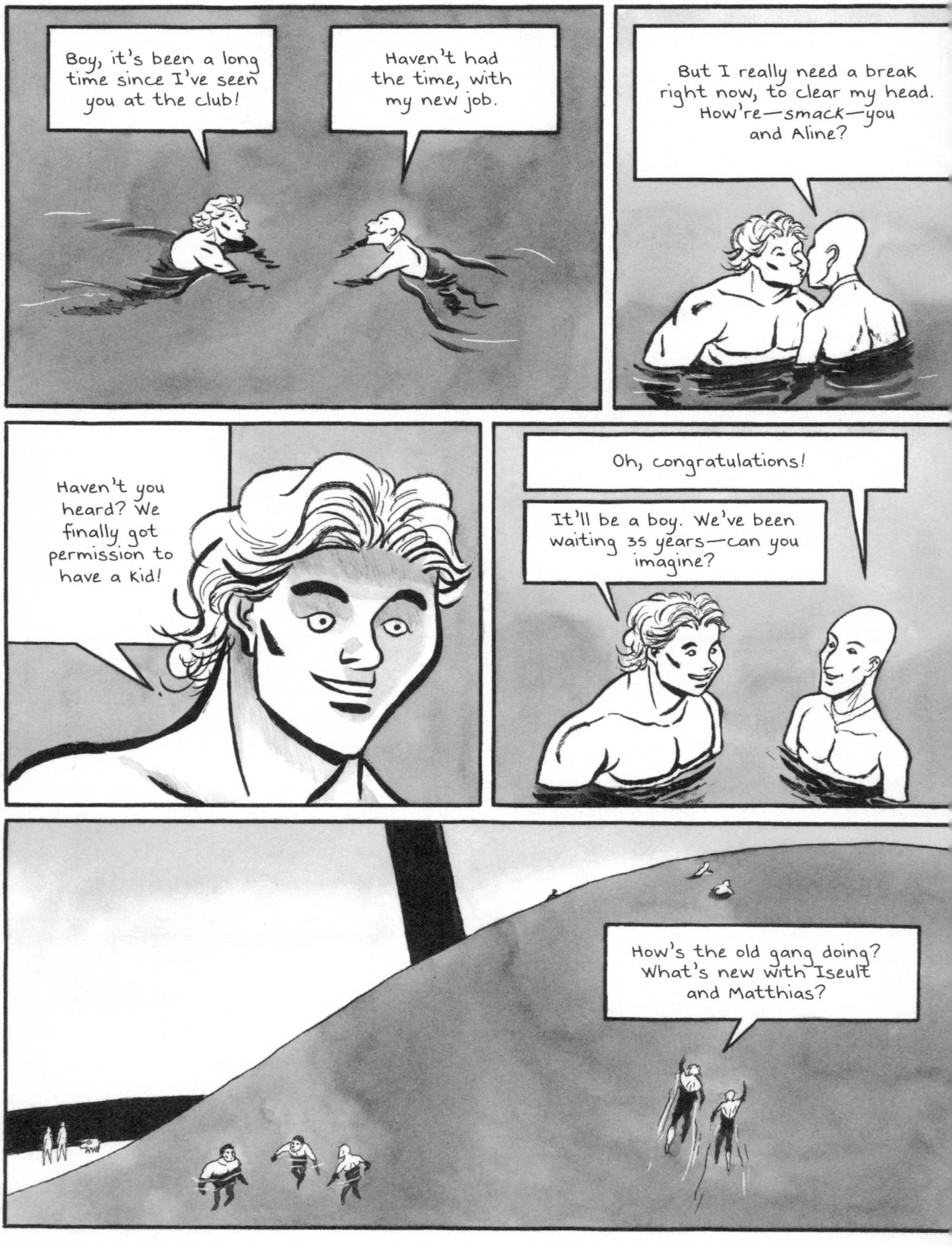

Boy, it's been a long time since I've seen you at the club!
Haven't had the time, with my new job.
But I really need a break right now, to clear my head. How're—*smack*—you and Aline?
Haven't you heard? We finally got permission to have a kid!
It'll be a boy. We've been waiting 35 years—can you imagine?
Oh, congratulations!
How's the old gang doing? What's new with Iseult and Matthias?

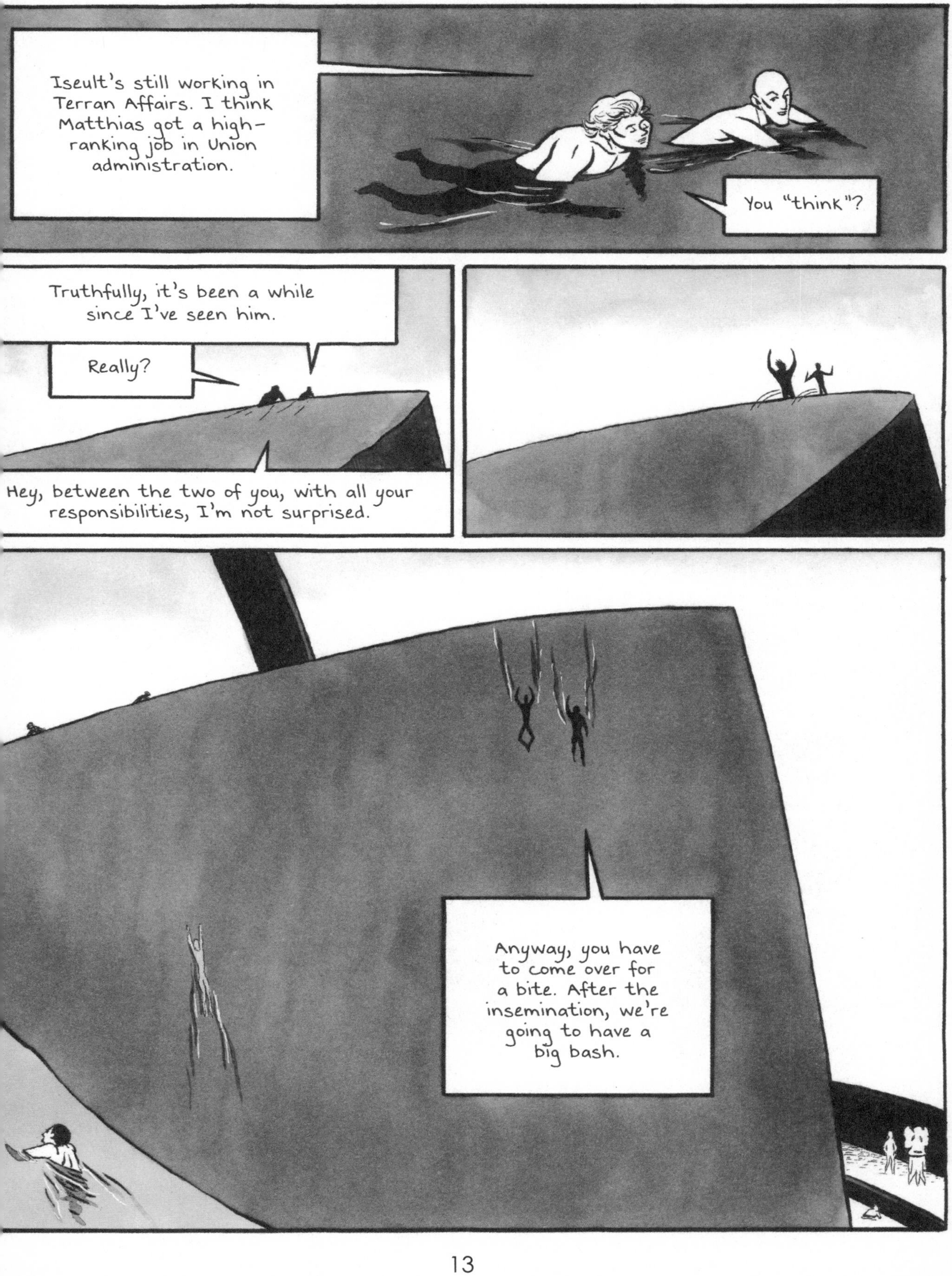
Iseult's still working in Terran Affairs. I think Matthias got a high-ranking job in Union administration.
You "think"?
Truthfully, it's been a while since I've seen him.
Really?
Hey, between the two of you, with all your responsibilities, I'm not surprised.
Anyway, you have to come over for a bite. After the insemination, we're going to have a big bash.

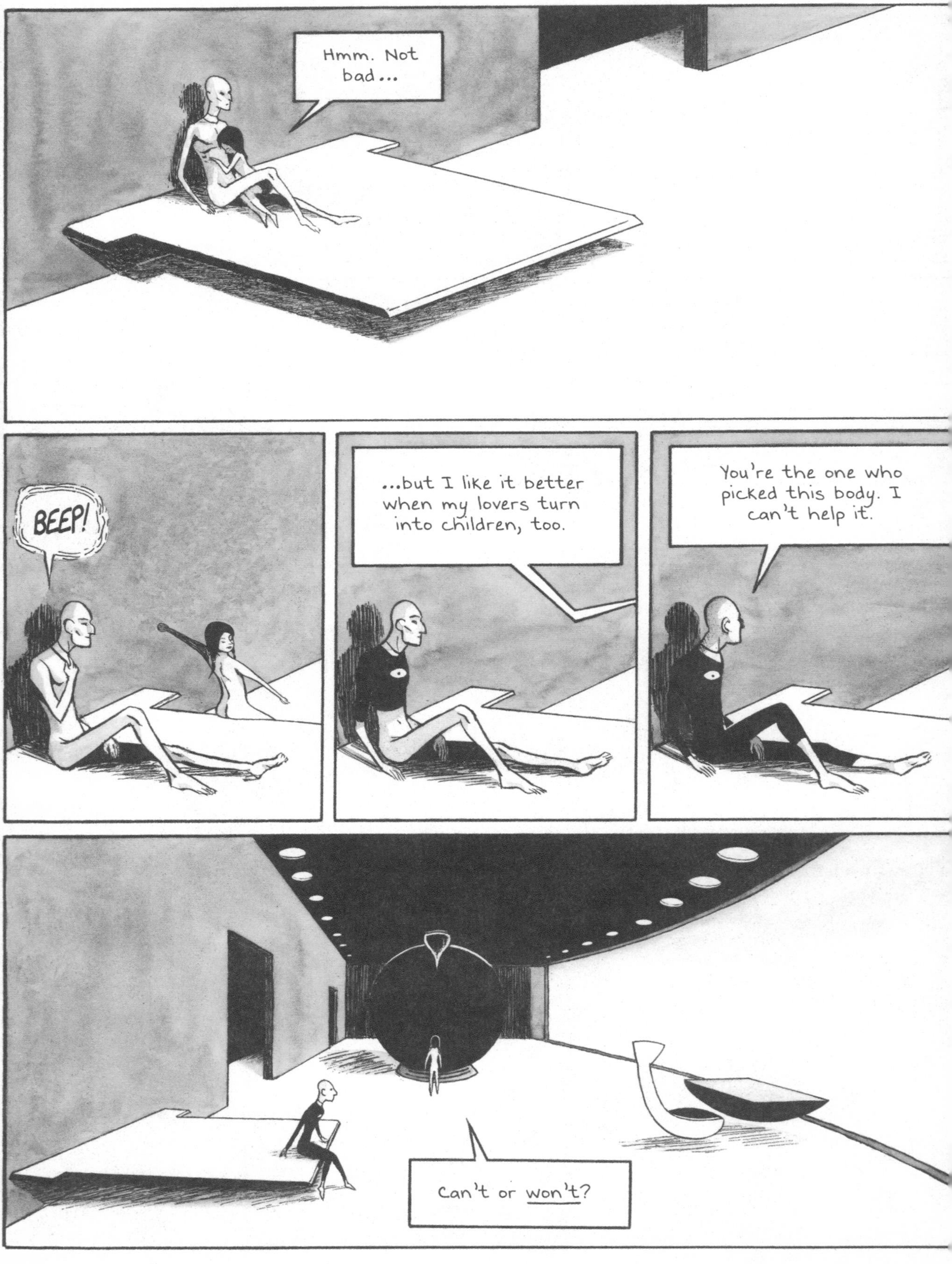
Hmm. Not bad...
BEEP!
...but I like it better when my lovers turn into children, too.
You're the one who picked this body. I can't help it.
Can't or won't?

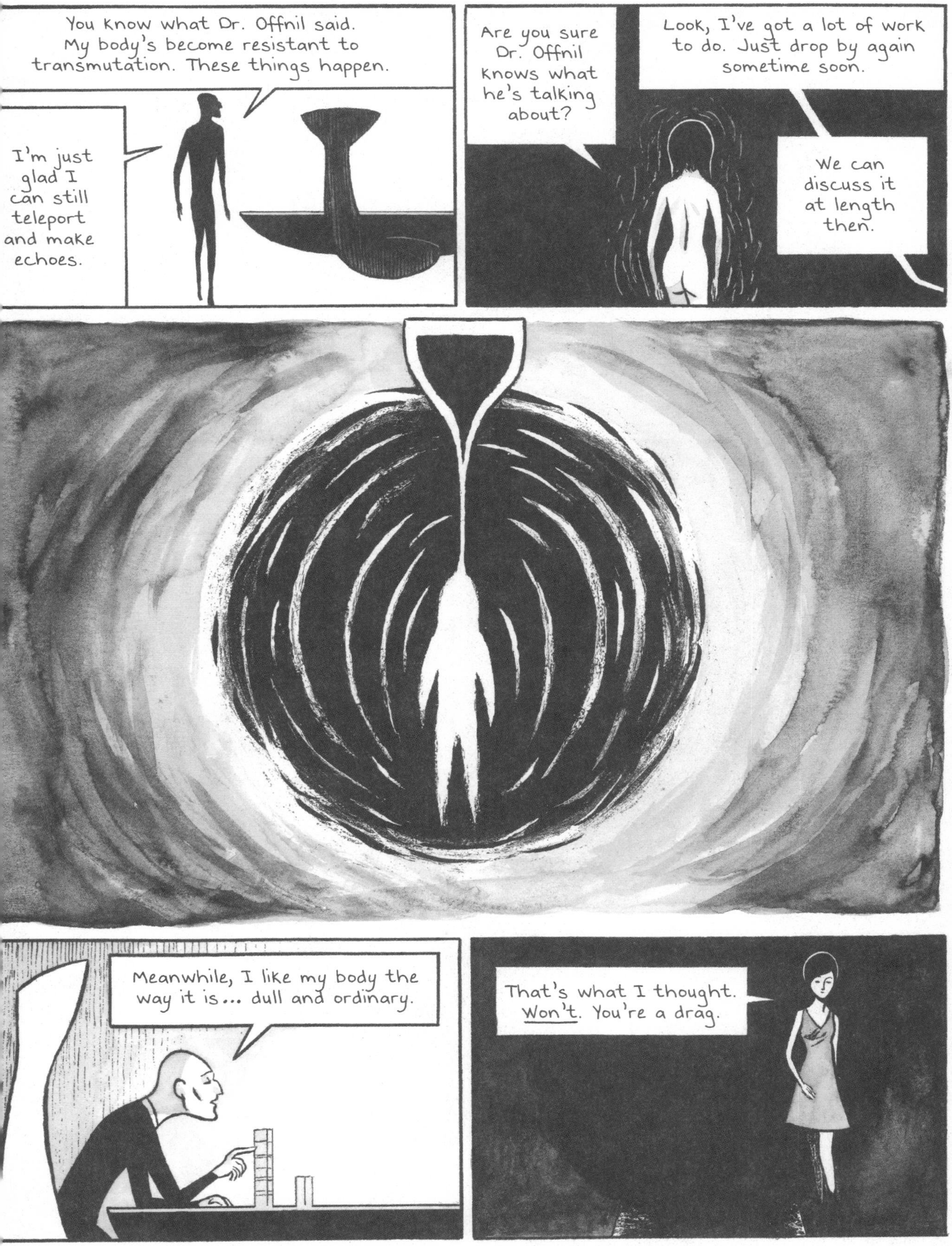
You know what Dr. Offnil said. My body's become resistant to transmutation. These things happen.
I'm just glad I can still teleport and make echoes.
Are you sure Dr. Offnil knows what he's talking about?
Look, I've got a lot of work to do. Just drop by again sometime soon.
We can discuss it at length then.
Meanwhile, I like my body the way it is... dull and ordinary.
That's what I thought. Won't. You're a drag.

20232450

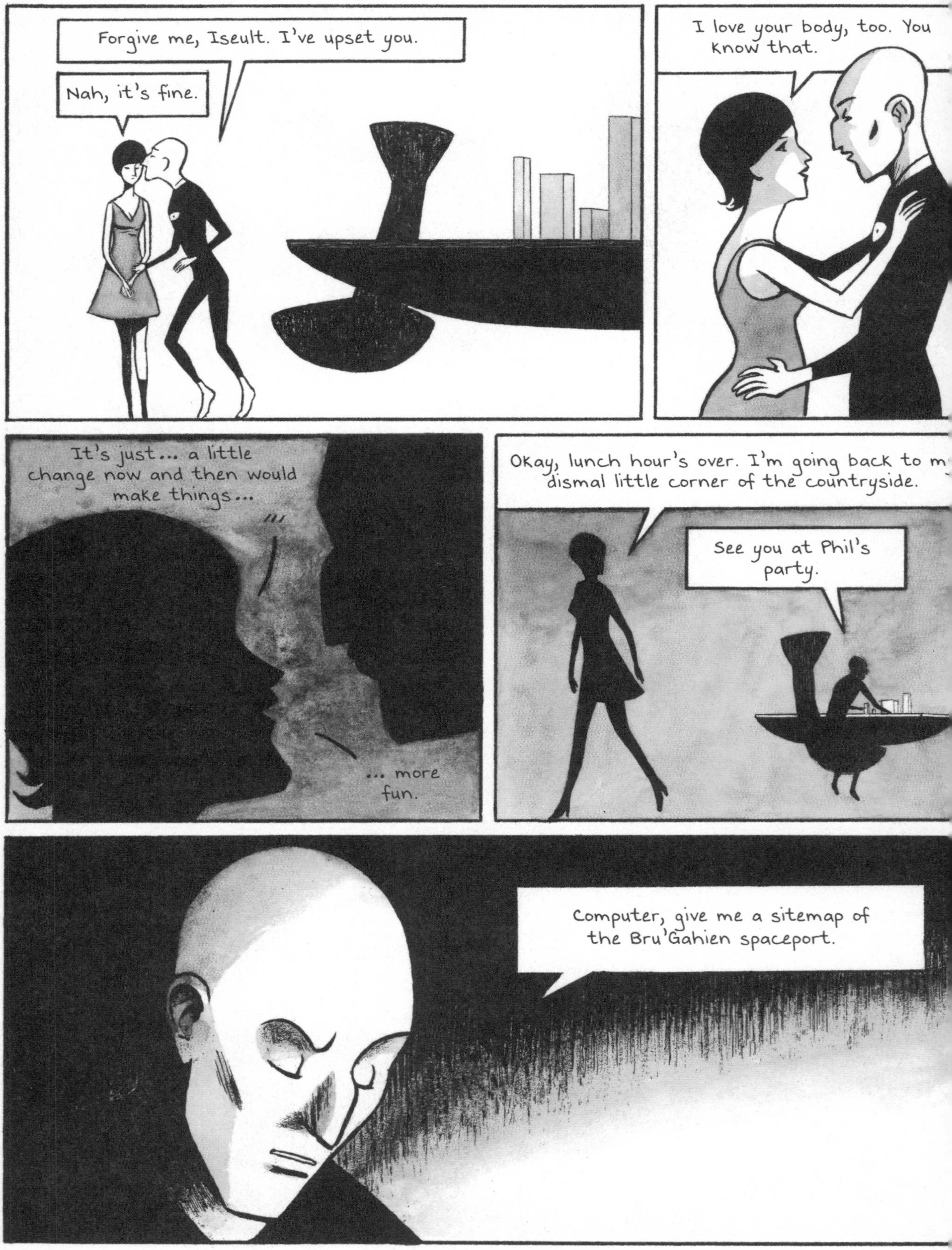
Forgive me, Iseult. I've upset you.
Nah, it's fine.
I love your body, too. You know that.
It's just... a little change now and then would make things...
... more fun.
Okay, lunch hour's over. I'm going back to my dismal little corner of the countryside.
See you at Phil's party.
Computer, give me a sitemap of the Bru'Gahien spaceport.

Heeeeey! Come on in!

Iseult! It's so good to see you!

I'm really glad you came. I know you're really busy!

Congrats on the kid!

Partaking?

Low frequency, maybe. I have to stay sober.

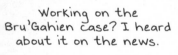

Working on the Bru'Gahien case? I heard about it on the news.

Yes, but I'm kind of stuck right now.

You'll figure it out. I have faith in you. You're the best.

May I?

Of course.

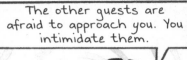

The other guests are afraid to approach you. You intimidate them.

Really?

With your status, some wonder if you're just another rich showboat. Y'know, the kind who buys thirty echoes just to be seen everywhere.

I don't want to put a damper on the party.

C'mon! Don't be ridiculous!

I'm going to go dance. That'll break the ice.

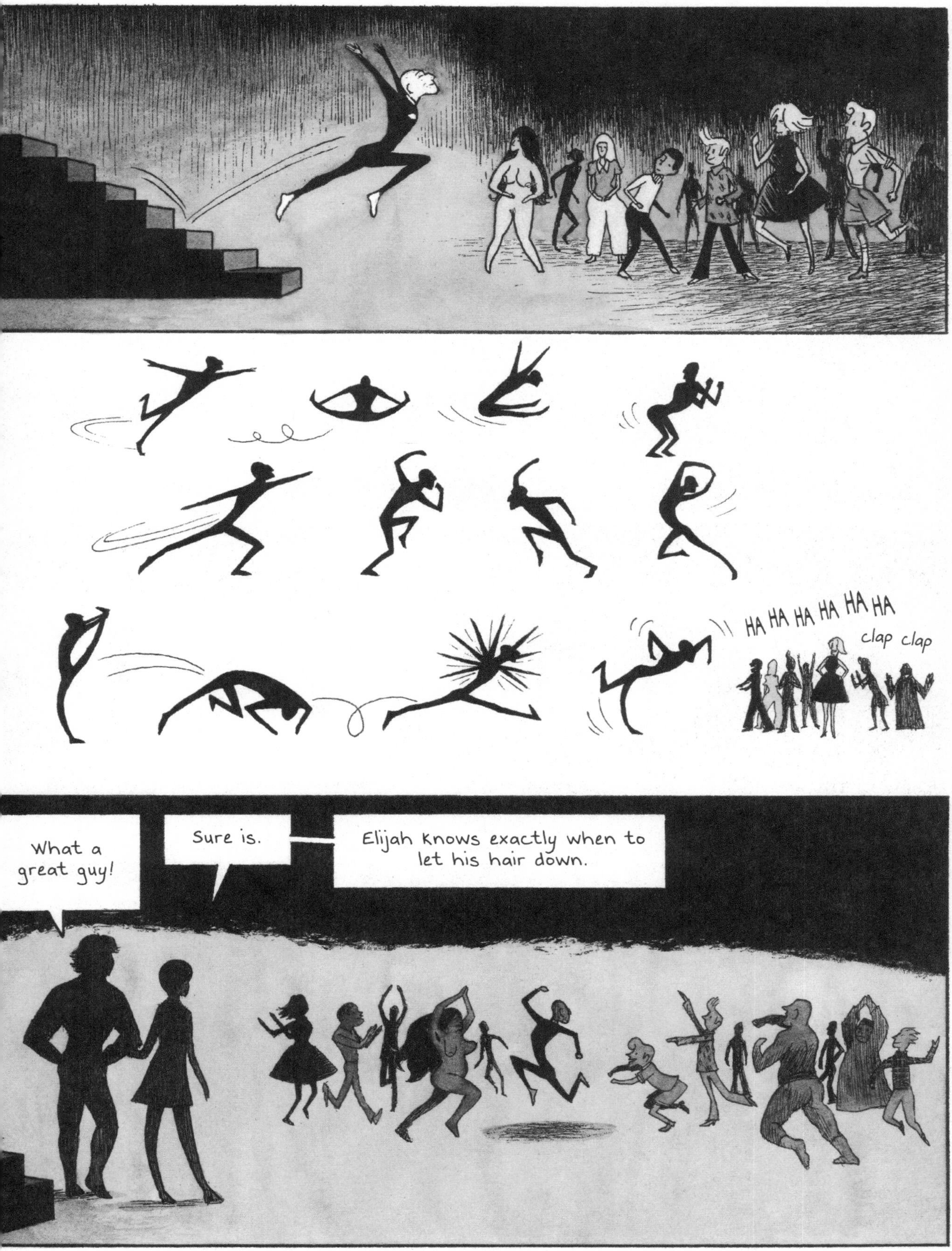
HA HA HA HA HA HA
clap clap
What a great guy!
Sure is.
Elijah knows exactly when to let his hair down.

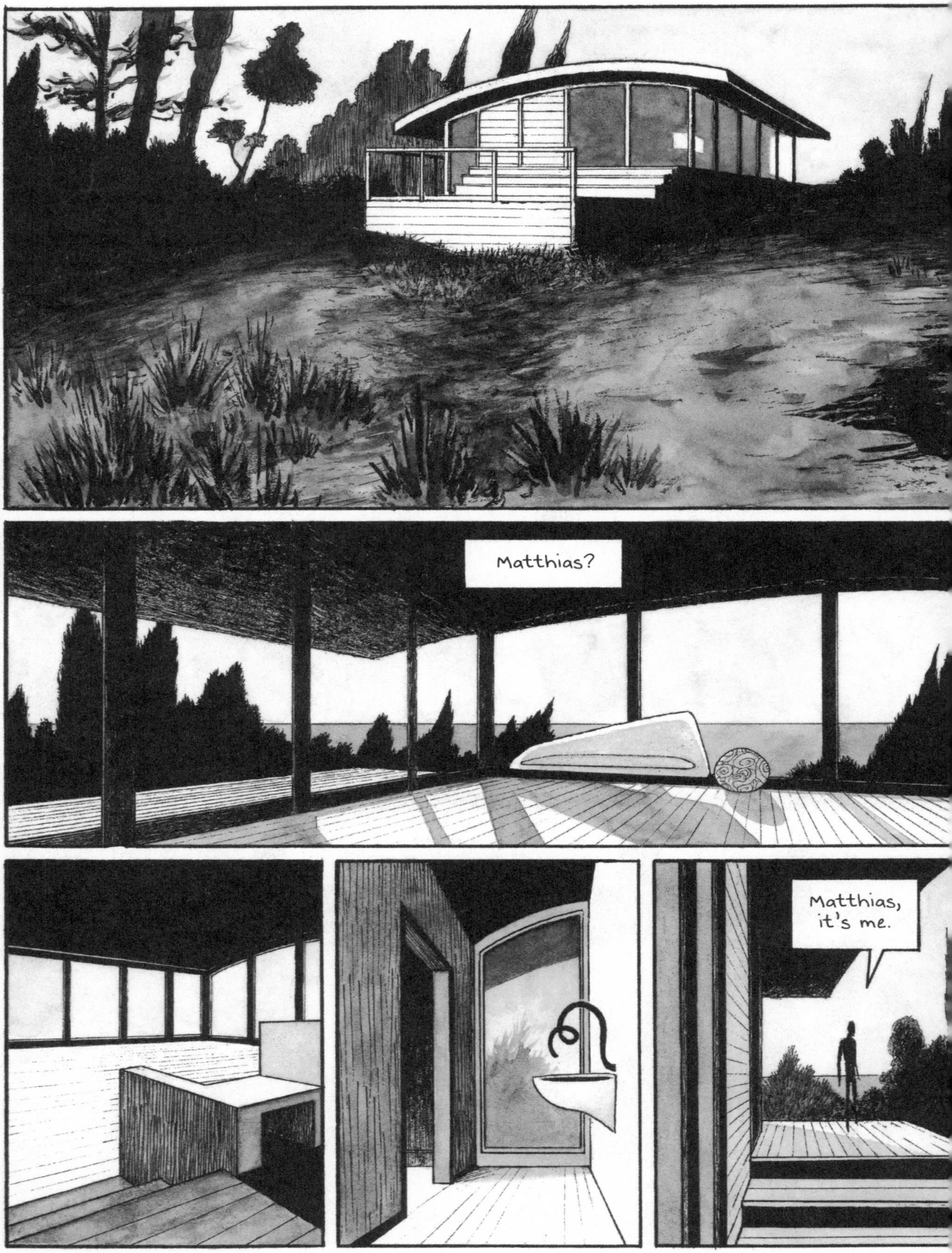
Matthias?
Matthias, it's me.

Well! Elijah!

I've been trying to reach you for weeks. Were you trying to avoid me?

Sorry. I've got a great many things to take care of right now.

I didn't tell you, but I ended my life a year ago.

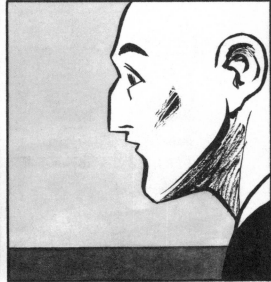

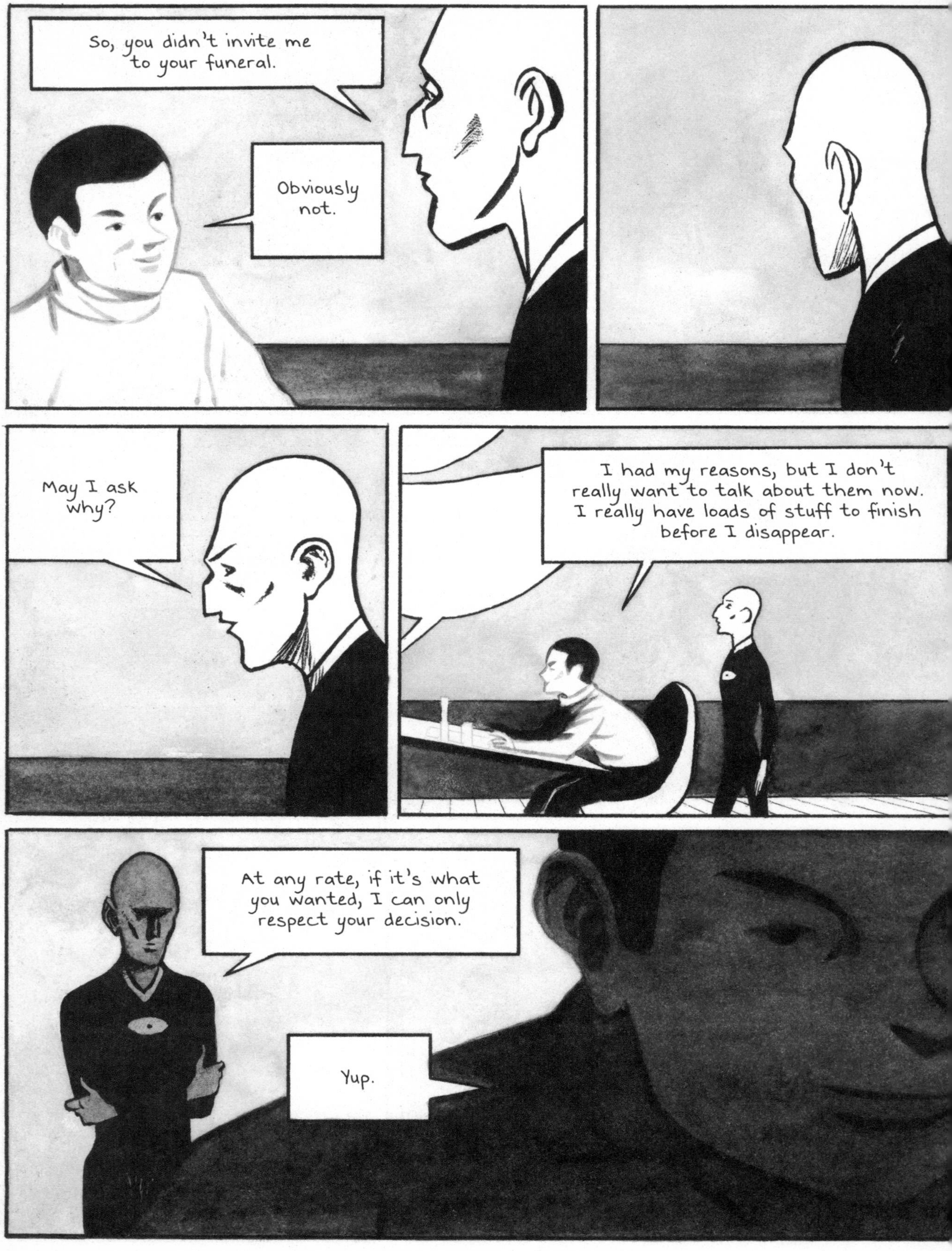
So, you didn't invite me to your funeral.
Obviously not.
May I ask why?
I had my reasons, but I don't really want to talk about them now. I really have loads of stuff to finish before I disappear.
At any rate, if it's what you wanted, I can only respect your decision.
Yup.

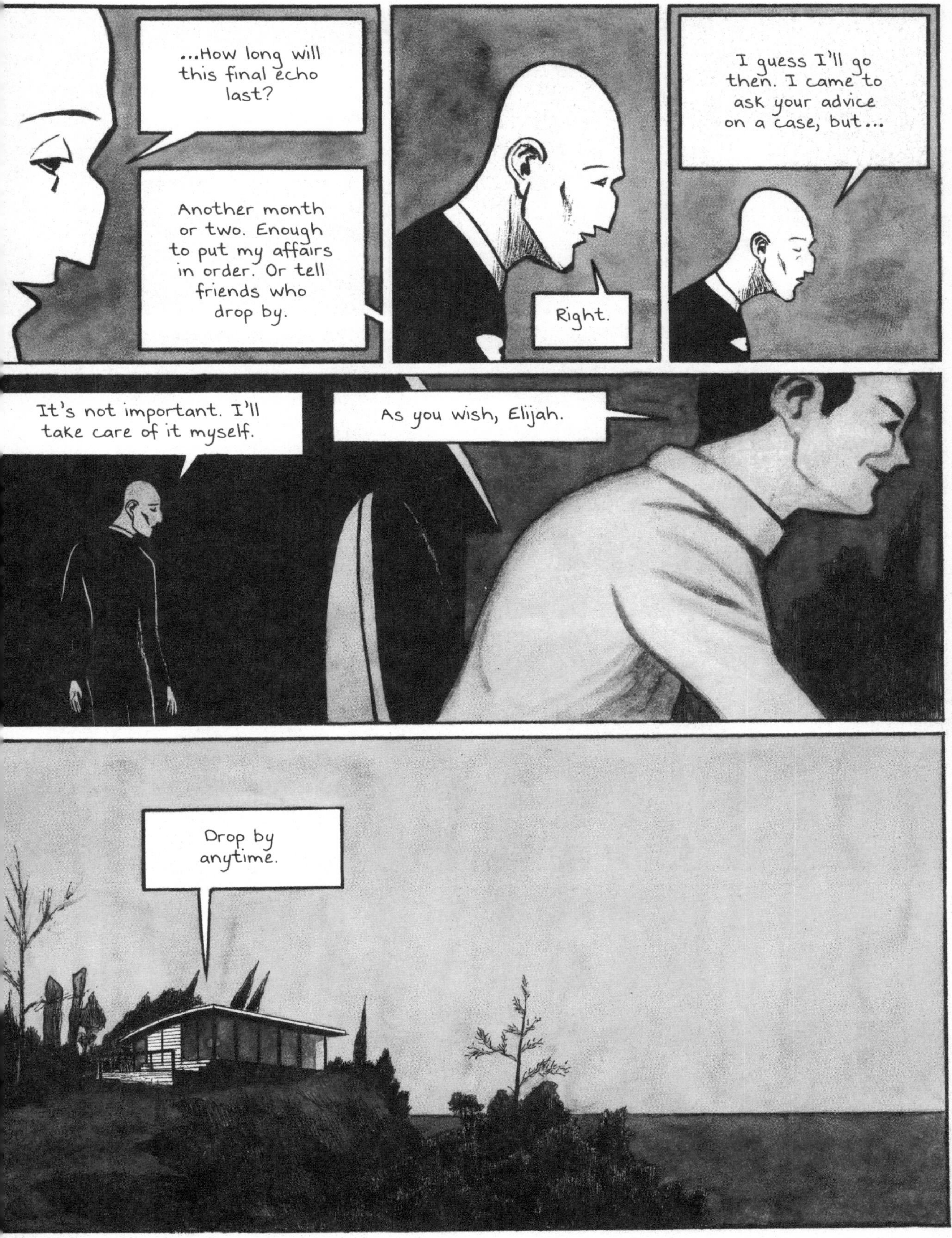
...How long will this final echo last?
Another month or two. Enough to put my affairs in order. Or tell friends who drop by.
Right.
I guess I'll go then. I came to ask your advice on a case, but...
It's not important. I'll take care of it myself.
As you wish, Elijah.
Drop by anytime.

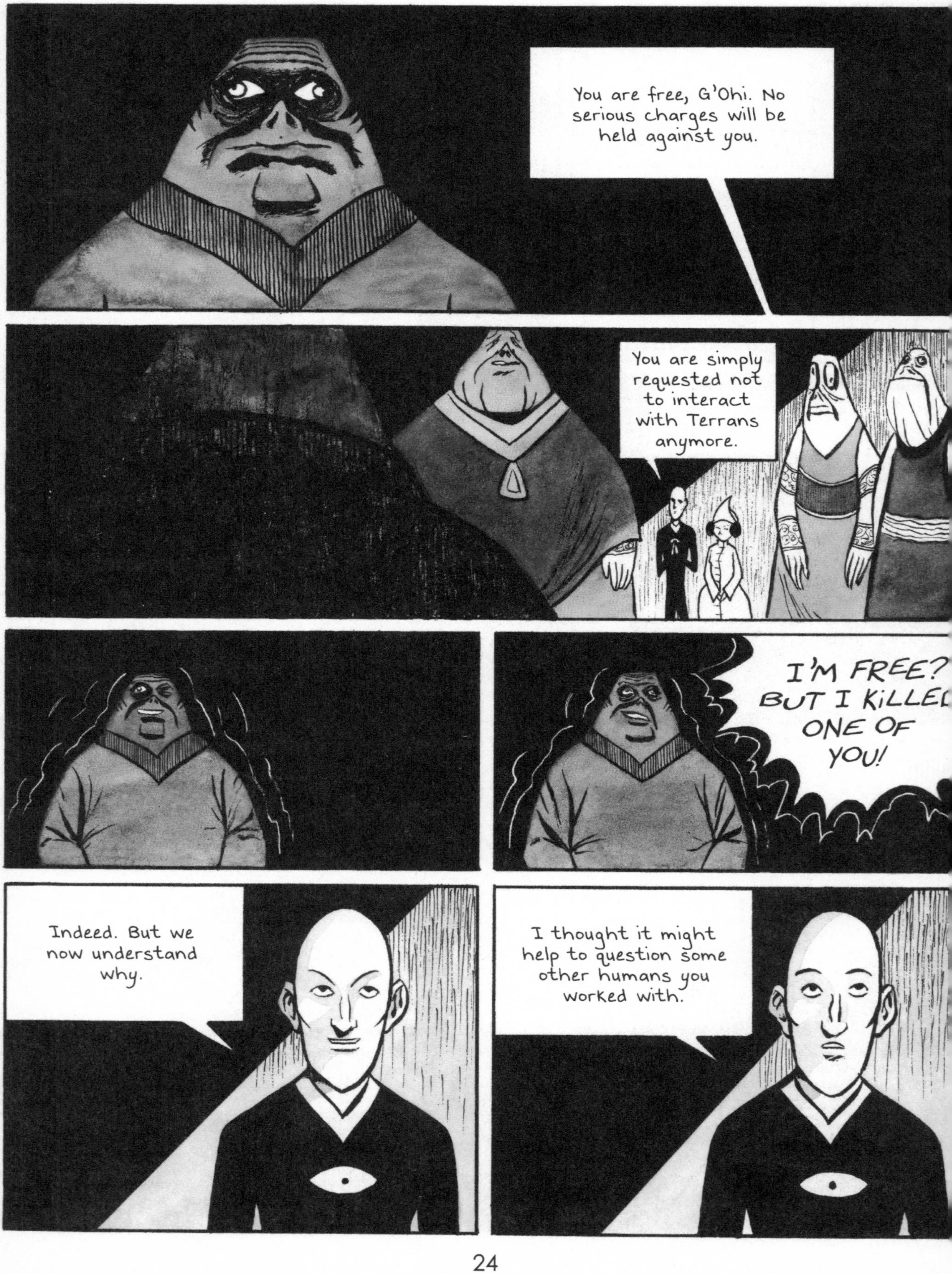

You are free, G'Ohi. No serious charges will be held against you.
You are simply requested not to interact with Terrans anymore.
I'M FREE? BUT I KILLED ONE OF YOU!
Indeed. But we now understand why.
I thought it might help to question some other humans you worked with.

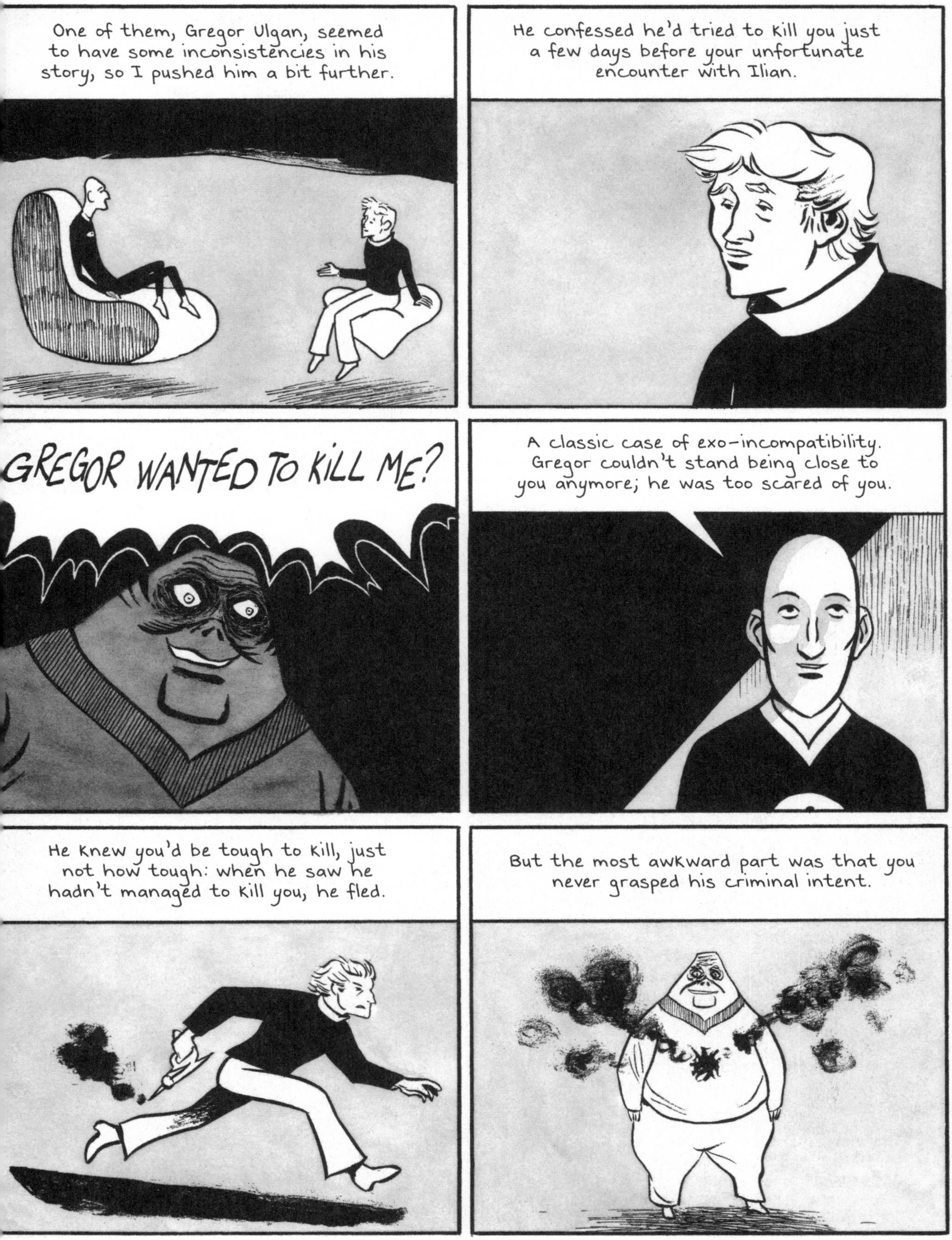
One of them, Gregor Ulgan, seemed to have some inconsistencies in his story, so I pushed him a bit further.
He confessed he'd tried to kill you just a few days before your unfortunate encounter with Ilian.
GREGOR WANTED TO KILL ME?
A classic case of exo-incompatibility. Gregor couldn't stand being close to you anymore; he was too scared of you.
He knew you'd be tough to kill, just not how tough: when he saw he hadn't managed to kill you, he fled.
But the most awkward part was that you never grasped his criminal intent.

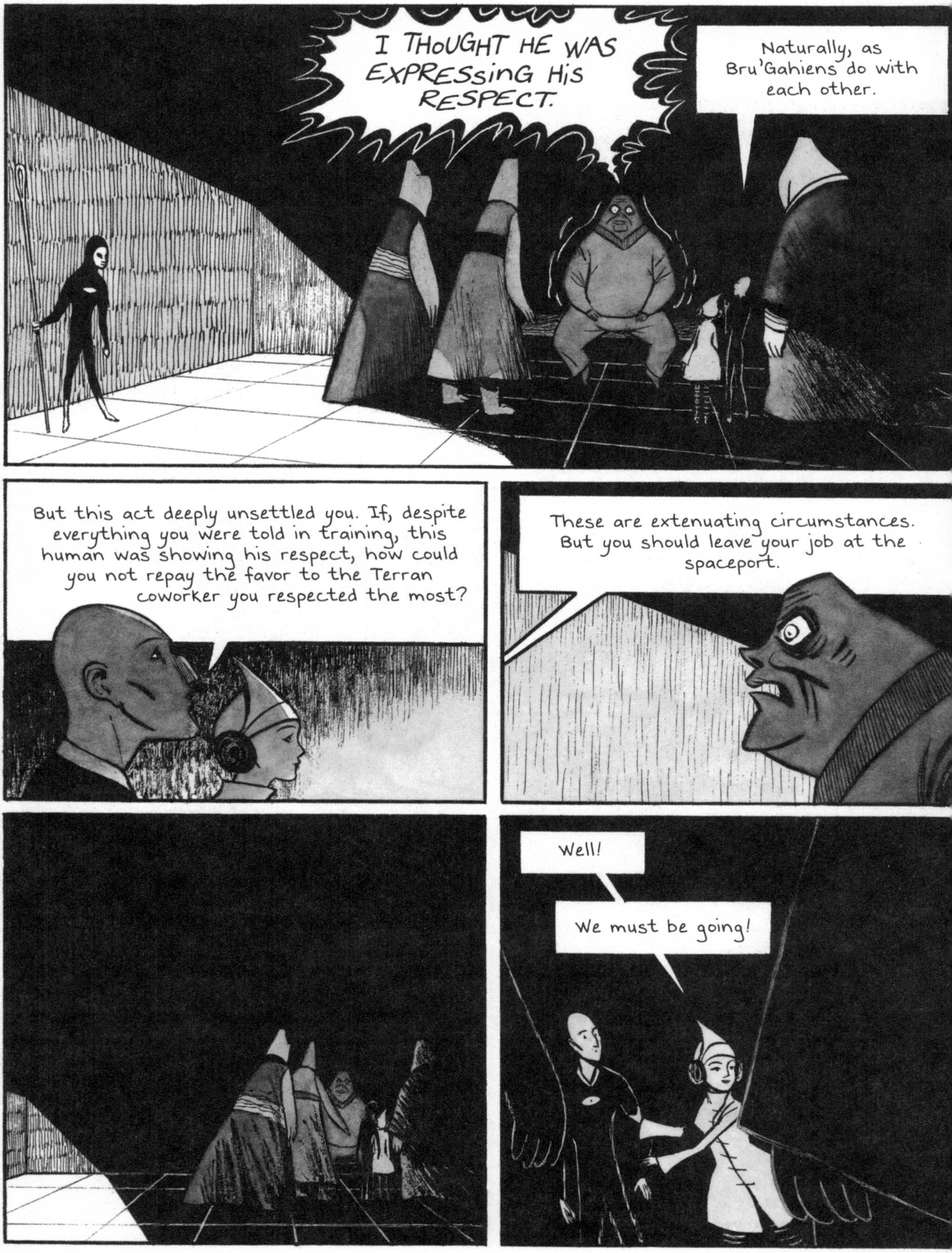
I THOUGHT HE WAS EXPRESSING HIS RESPECT.
Naturally, as Bru'Gahiens do with each other.
But this act deeply unsettled you. If, despite everything you were told in training, this human was showing his respect, how could you not repay the favor to the Terran coworker you respected the most?
These are extenuating circumstances. But you should leave your job at the spaceport.
Well!
We must be going!

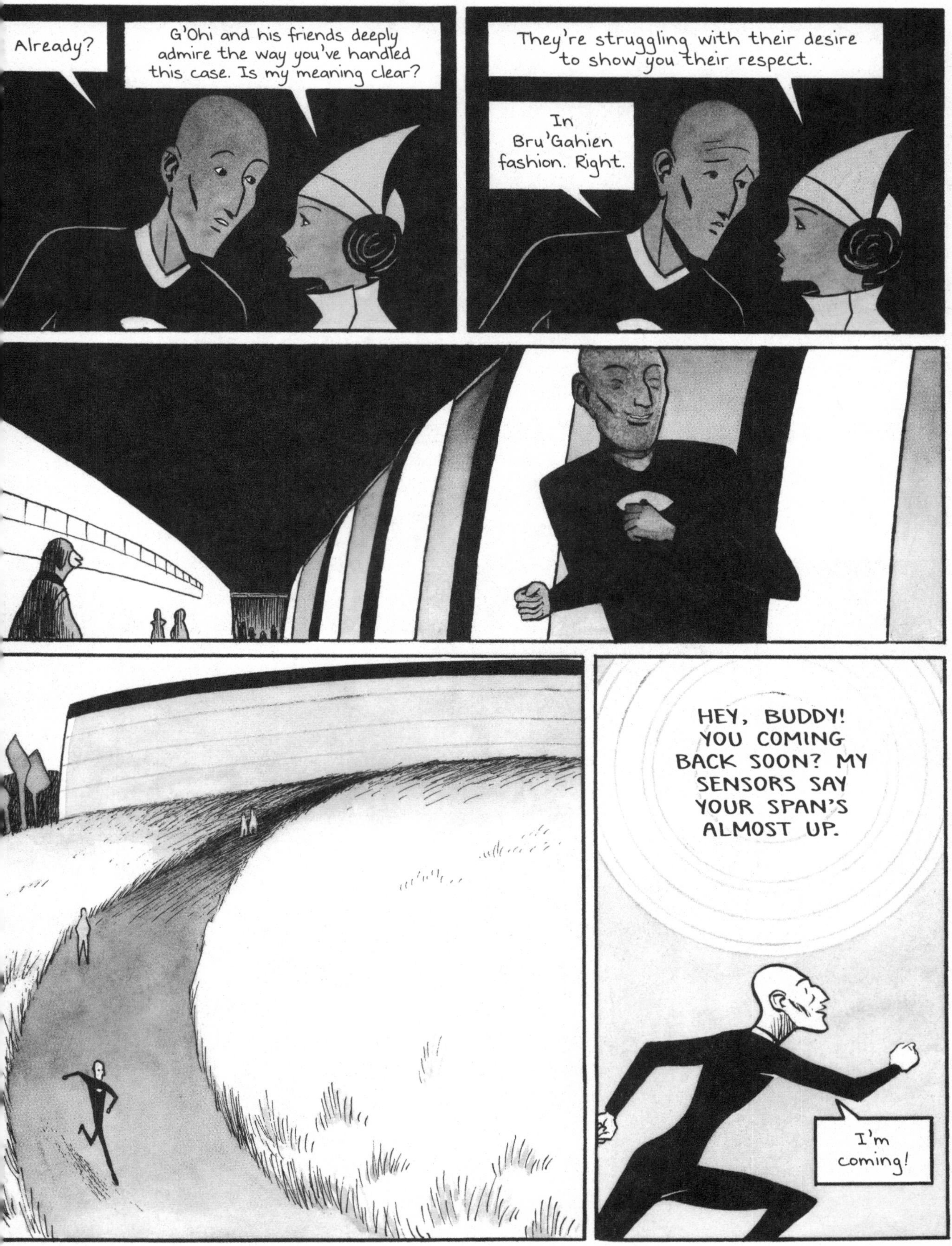
Already?
G'Ohi and his friends deeply admire the way you've handled this case. Is my meaning clear?
They're struggling with their desire to show you their respect.
In Bru'Gahien fashion. Right.
HEY, BUDDY! YOU COMING BACK SOON? MY SENSORS SAY YOUR SPAN'S ALMOST UP.
I'm coming!

Well? How'd it go?

The Bru'Gahiens were so happy I almost got mauled.

But you'll see for yourself in a minute.

Hey, you're all dressed up!

I just got summoned by the High Director of the 1st District.

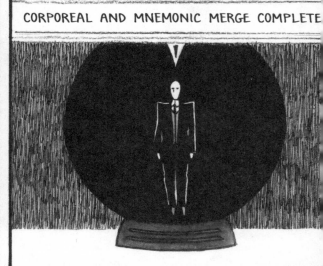

CORPOREAL AND MNEMONIC MERGE COMPLETE

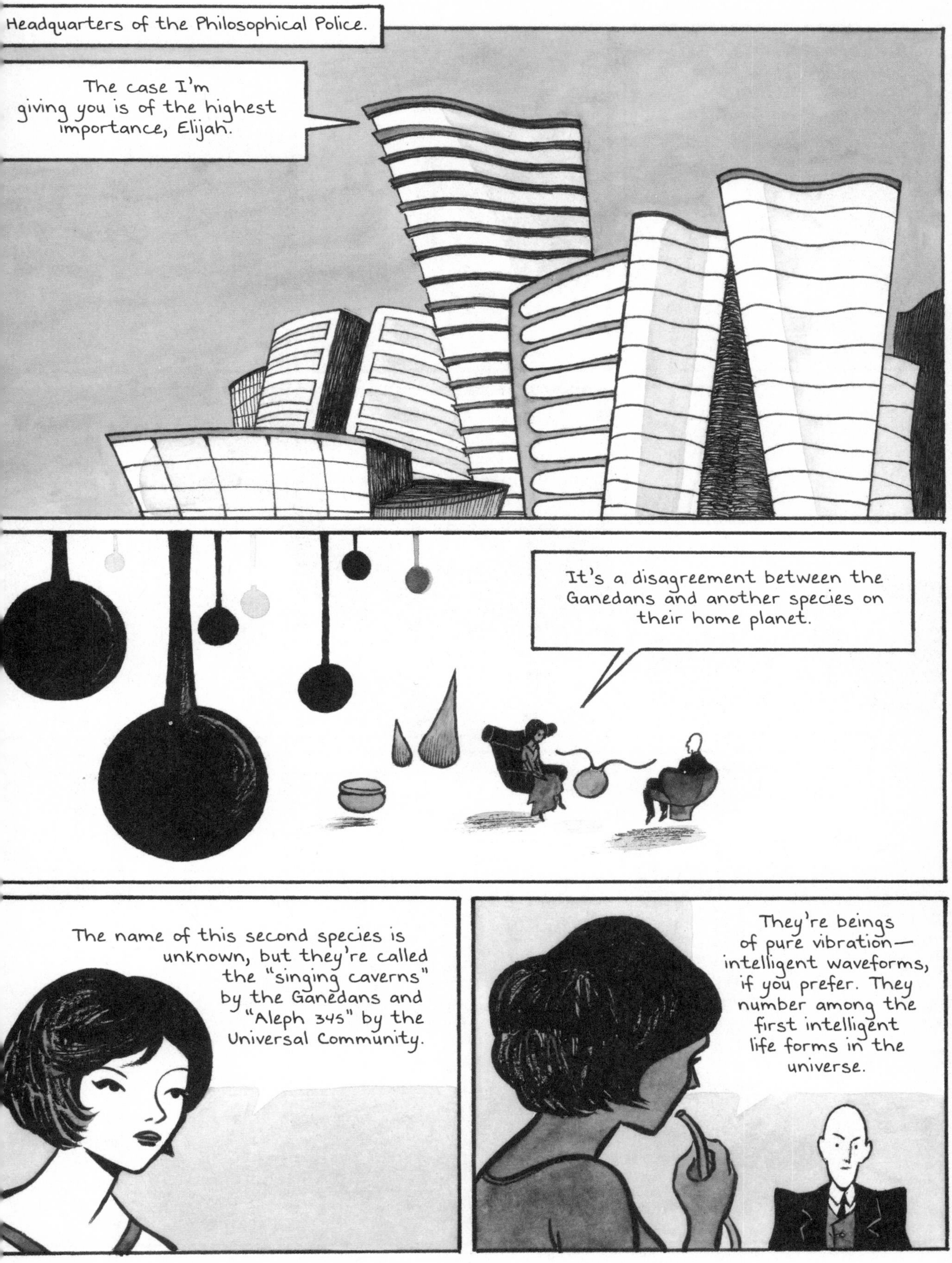
Headquarters of the Philosophical Police.
The case I'm giving you is of the highest importance, Elijah.
It's a disagreement between the Ganedans and another species on their home planet.
The name of this second species is unknown, but they're called the "singing caverns" by the Ganedans and "Aleph 345" by the Universal Community.
They're beings of pure vibration— intelligent waveforms, if you prefer. They number among the first intelligent life forms in the universe.

The Aleph 345 have been showing signs of intense anger for a century now. The Ganedans don't know why.

This anger is muted for now, but it's growing in strength and could wind up giving way to open war.

Such a conflict would have distressing consequences for the entire Community. The Ganedans have powerful political backing within the Union so their problems are our problems.

Shall we go for a walk? The Eloa roving sculpture exhibit will be passing through our sector. I've heard it's worth seeing.

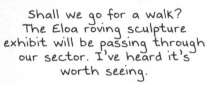

The Ganedans believe, quite rightly, that certain crises require the intervention of a mediator.

So they've asked our district to send them mediators.

A team to arbitrate the situation with the utmost impartiality.

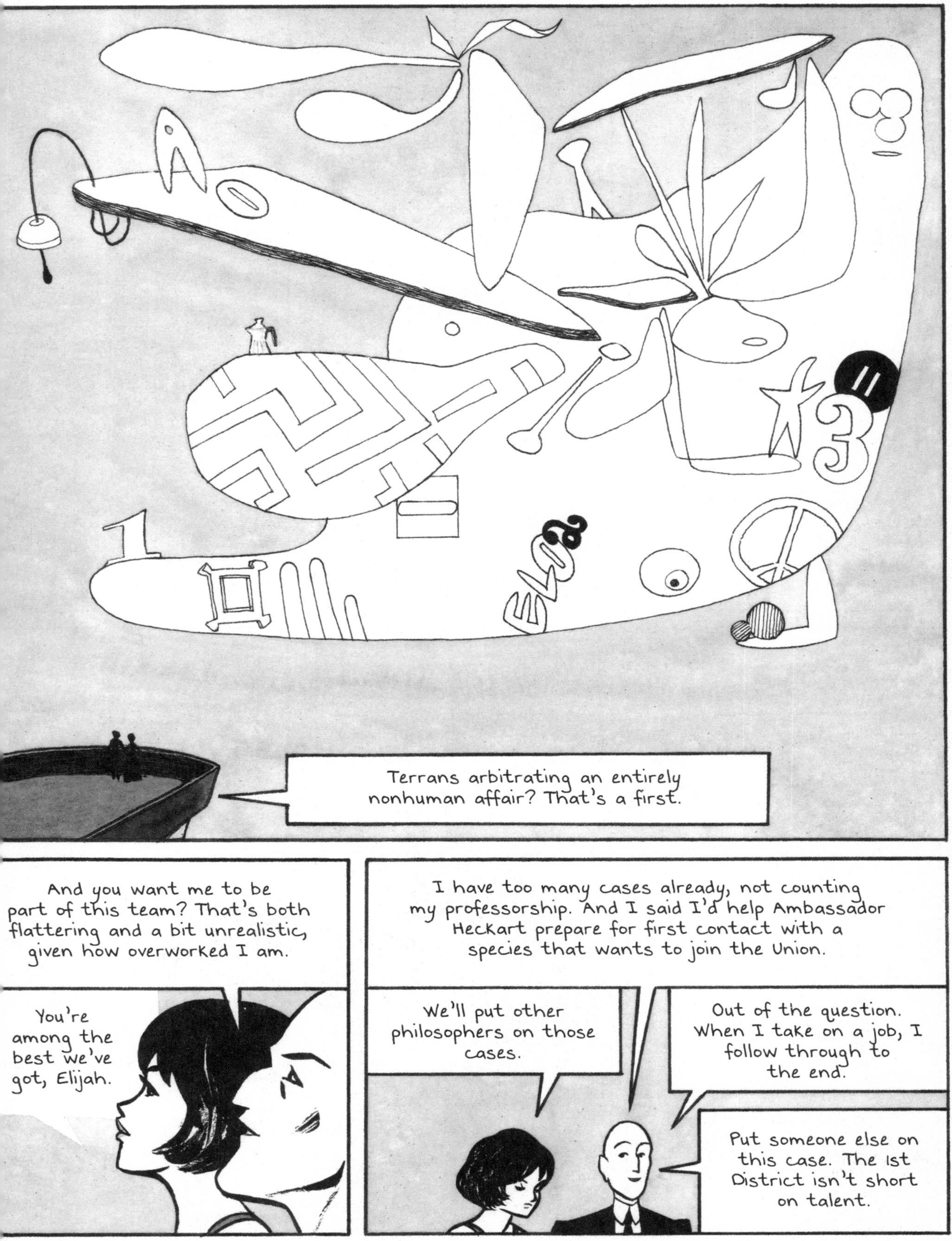
Terrans arbitrating an entirely nonhuman affair? That's a first.
And you want me to be part of this team? That's both flattering and a bit unrealistic, given how overworked I am.
You're among the best we've got, Elijah.
I have too many cases already, not counting my professorship. And I said I'd help Ambassador Heckart prepare for first contact with a species that wants to join the Union.
We'll put other philosophers on those cases.
Out of the question. When I take on a job, I follow through to the end.
Put someone else on this case. The 1st District isn't short on talent.

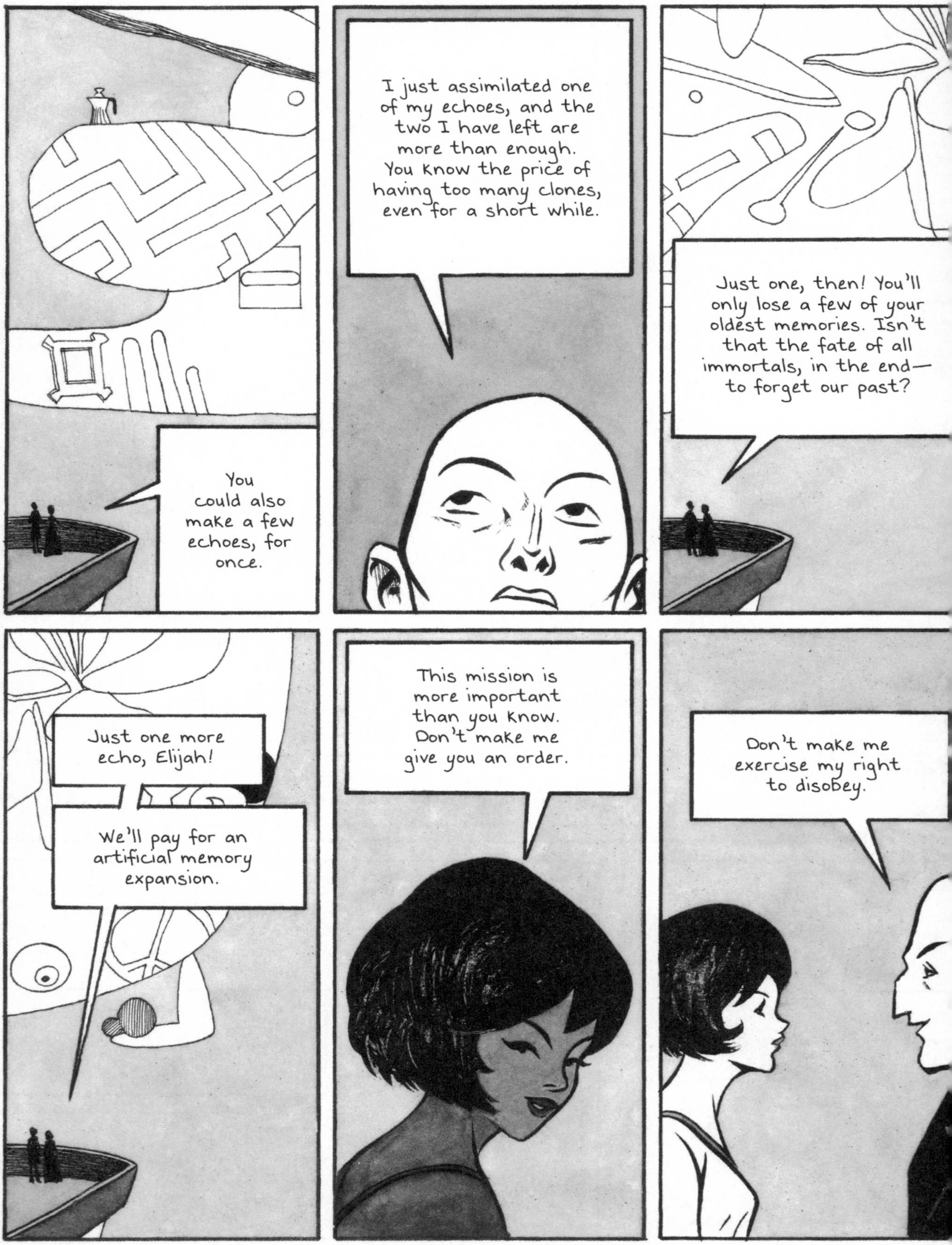
You could also make a few echoes, for once.
I just assimilated one of my echoes, and the two I have left are more than enough. You know the price of having too many clones, even for a short while.
Just one, then! You'll only lose a few of your oldest memories. Isn't that the fate of all immortals, in the end—to forget our past?
Just one more echo, Elijah!
We'll pay for an artificial memory expansion.
This mission is more important than you know. Don't make me give you an order.
Don't make me exercise my right to disobey.

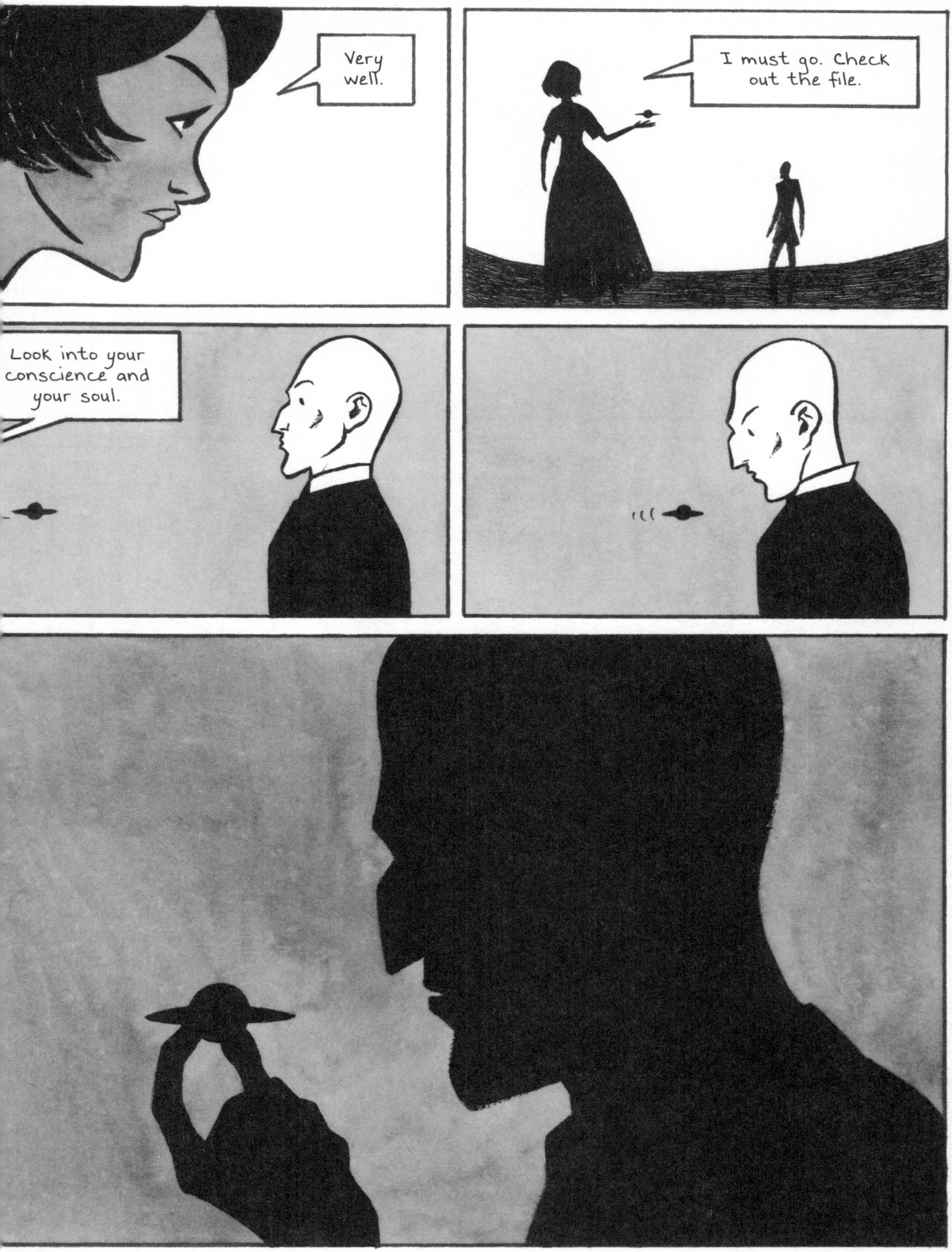

Very well.
I must go. Check out the file.
Look into your conscience and your soul.

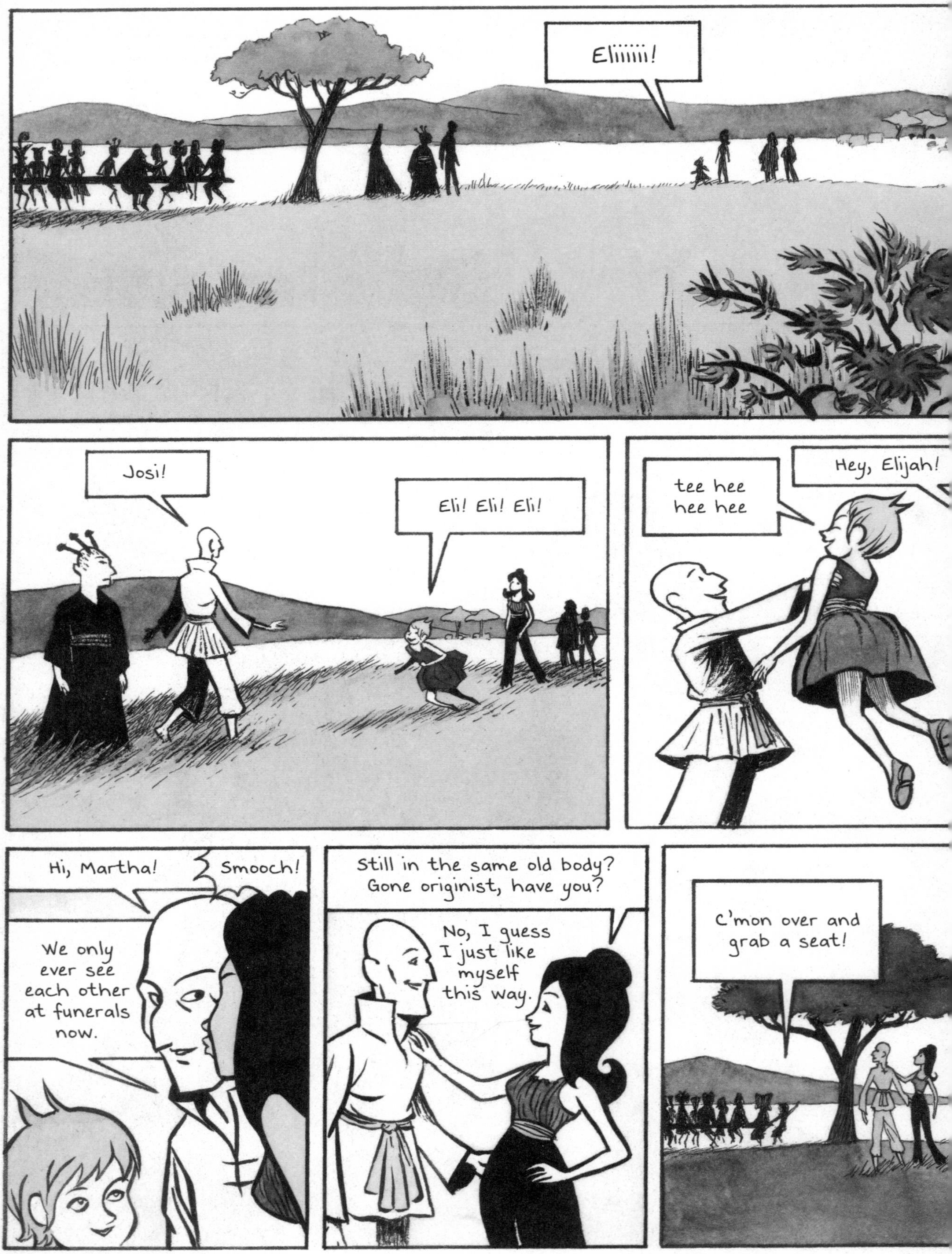
Eliiiiii!
Josi!
Eli! Eli! Eli!
tee hee
hee hee
Hey, Elijah!
Hi, Martha!
Smooch!
We only ever see each other at funerals now.
Still in the same old body? Gone originist, have you?
No, I guess I just like myself this way.
C'mon over and grab a seat!

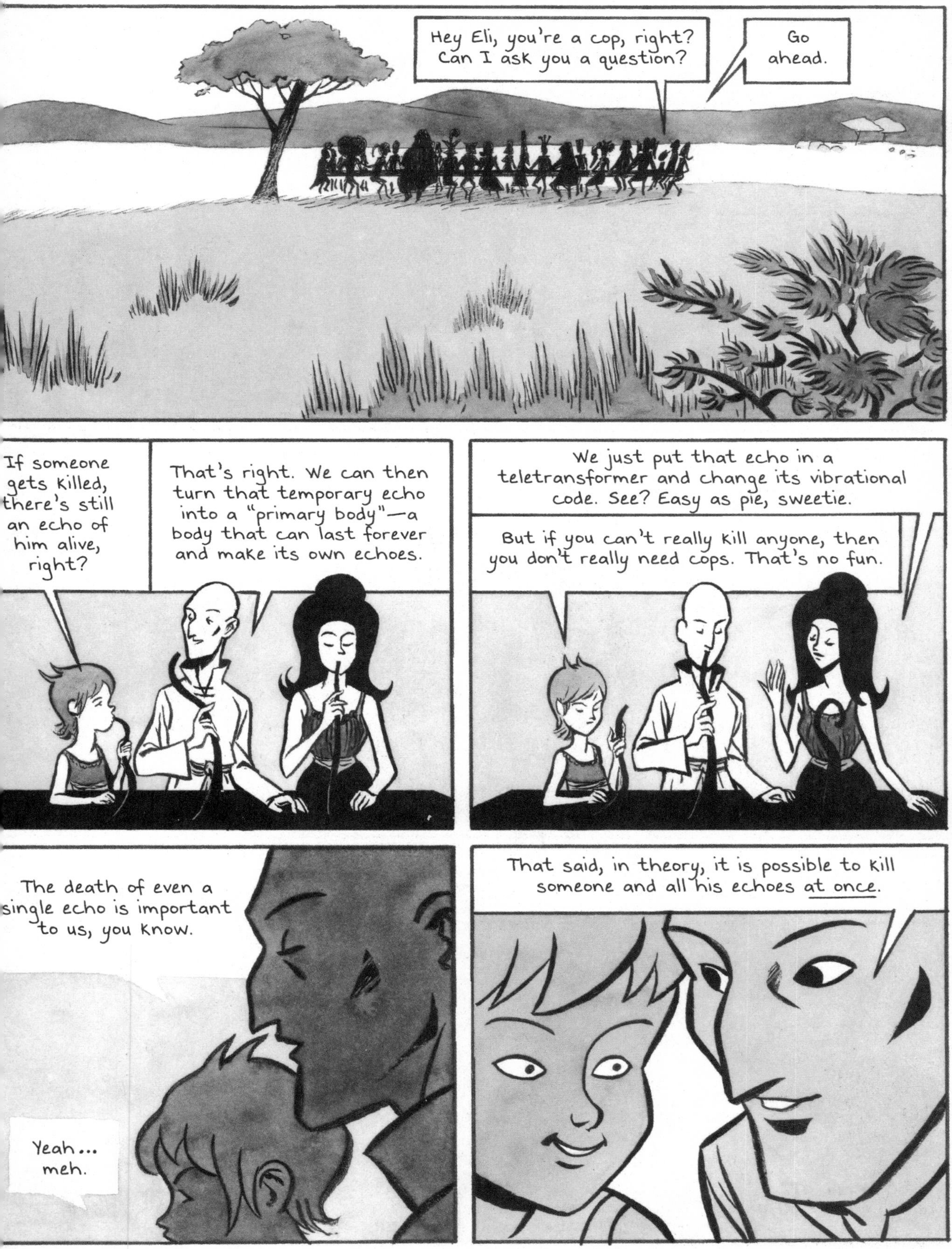

Hey Eli, you're a cop, right? Can I ask you a question?
Go ahead.
If someone gets killed, there's still an echo of him alive, right?
That's right. We can then turn that temporary echo into a "primary body"—a body that can last forever and make its own echoes.
We just put that echo in a teletransformer and change its vibrational code. See? Easy as pie, sweetie.
But if you can't really kill anyone, then you don't really need cops. That's no fun.
The death of even a single echo is important to us, you know.
Yeah... meh.
That said, in theory, it is possible to kill someone and all his echoes at once.

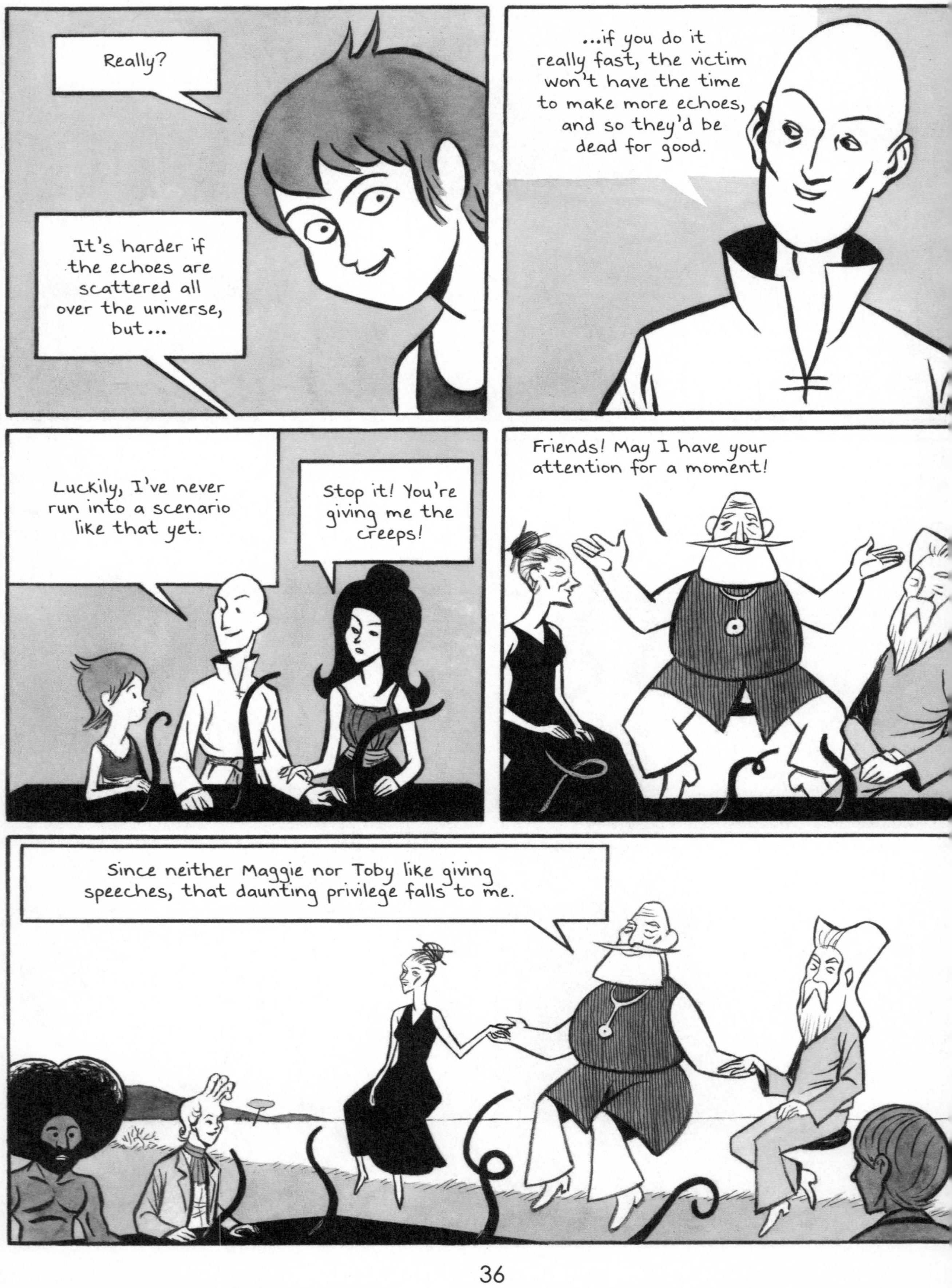
Really?
It's harder if the echoes are scattered all over the universe, but...
...if you do it really fast, the victim won't have the time to make more echoes, and so they'd be dead for good.
Luckily, I've never run into a scenario like that yet.
Stop it! You're giving me the creeps!
Friends! May I have your attention for a moment!
Since neither Maggie nor Toby like giving speeches, that daunting privilege falls to me.

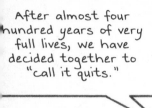After almost four hundred years of very full lives, we have decided together to "call it quits."

Just think—four hundred years! Time flies, doesn't it? But you'll notice that I've gone with a body closer to my actual age, for once.

NOW THERE'S A FIRST!

WE WERE SO USED TO YOU AS A YOUNG METROSEXUAL!

Maggie decided I needed a gray beard in order to die with dignity.

In the end, I—I just wanted to say that we're delighted to have known you, each and every one.

Our families know how much we love them. I won't bore you all by dwelling on the subject.

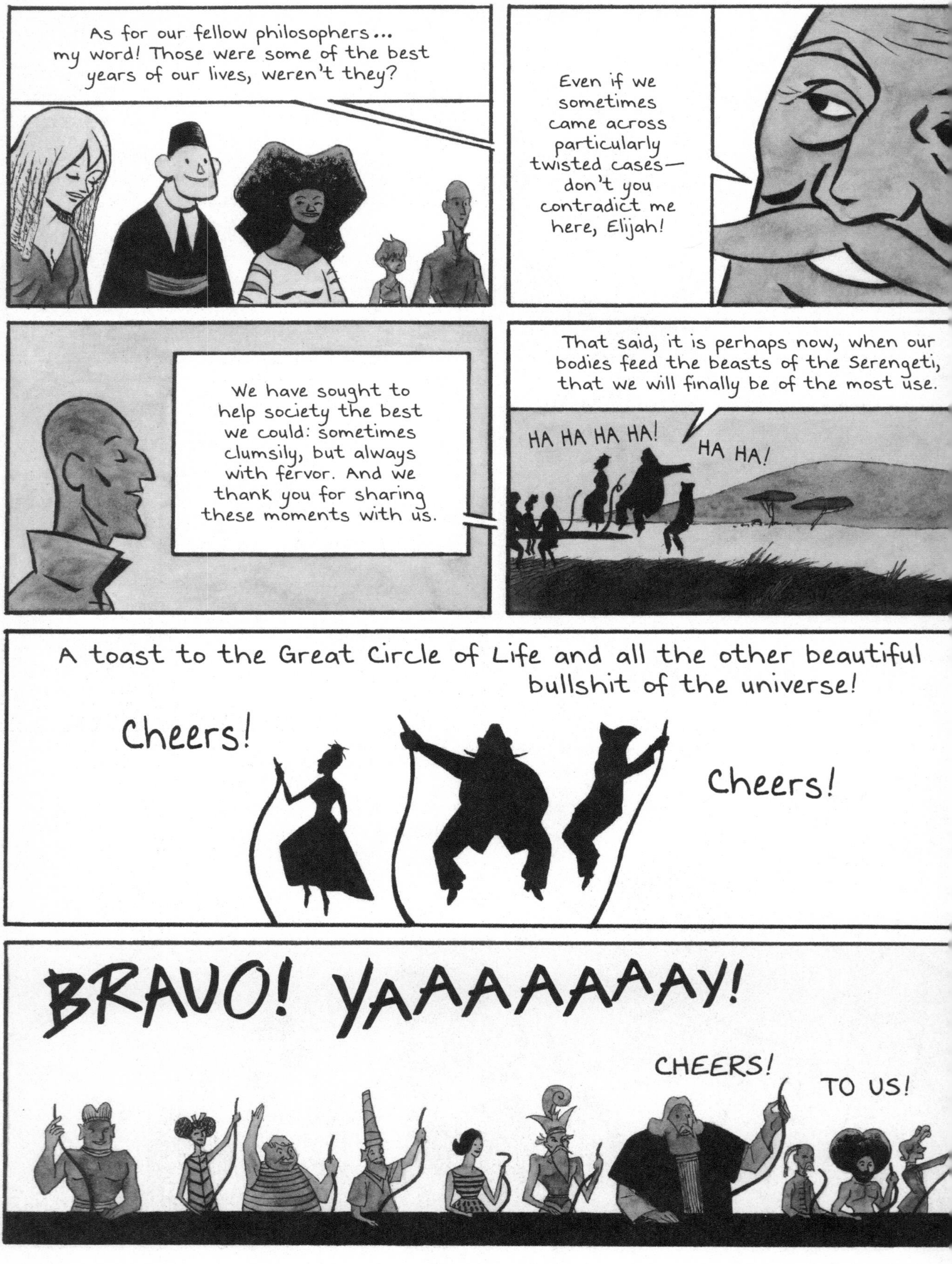
As for our fellow philosophers... my word! Those were some of the best years of our lives, weren't they?
Even if we sometimes came across particularly twisted cases—don't you contradict me here, Elijah!
We have sought to help society the best we could: sometimes clumsily, but always with fervor. And we thank you for sharing these moments with us.
That said, it is perhaps now, when our bodies feed the beasts of the Serengeti, that we will finally be of the most use.
HA HA HA HA!
HA HA!
A toast to the Great Circle of Life and all the other beautiful bullshit of the universe!
Cheers!
Cheers!
BRAVO! YAAAAAAAY!
CHEERS!
TO US!

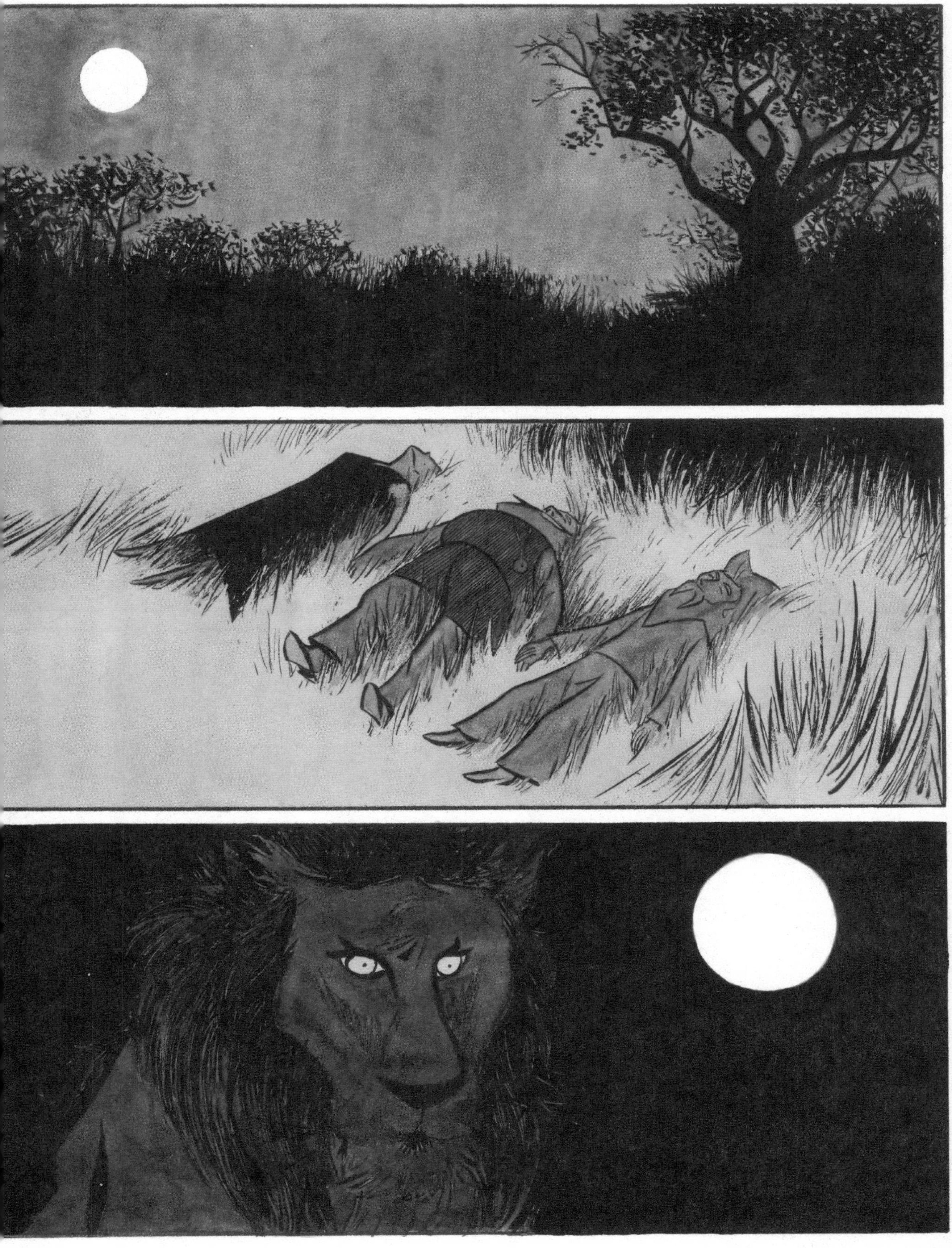

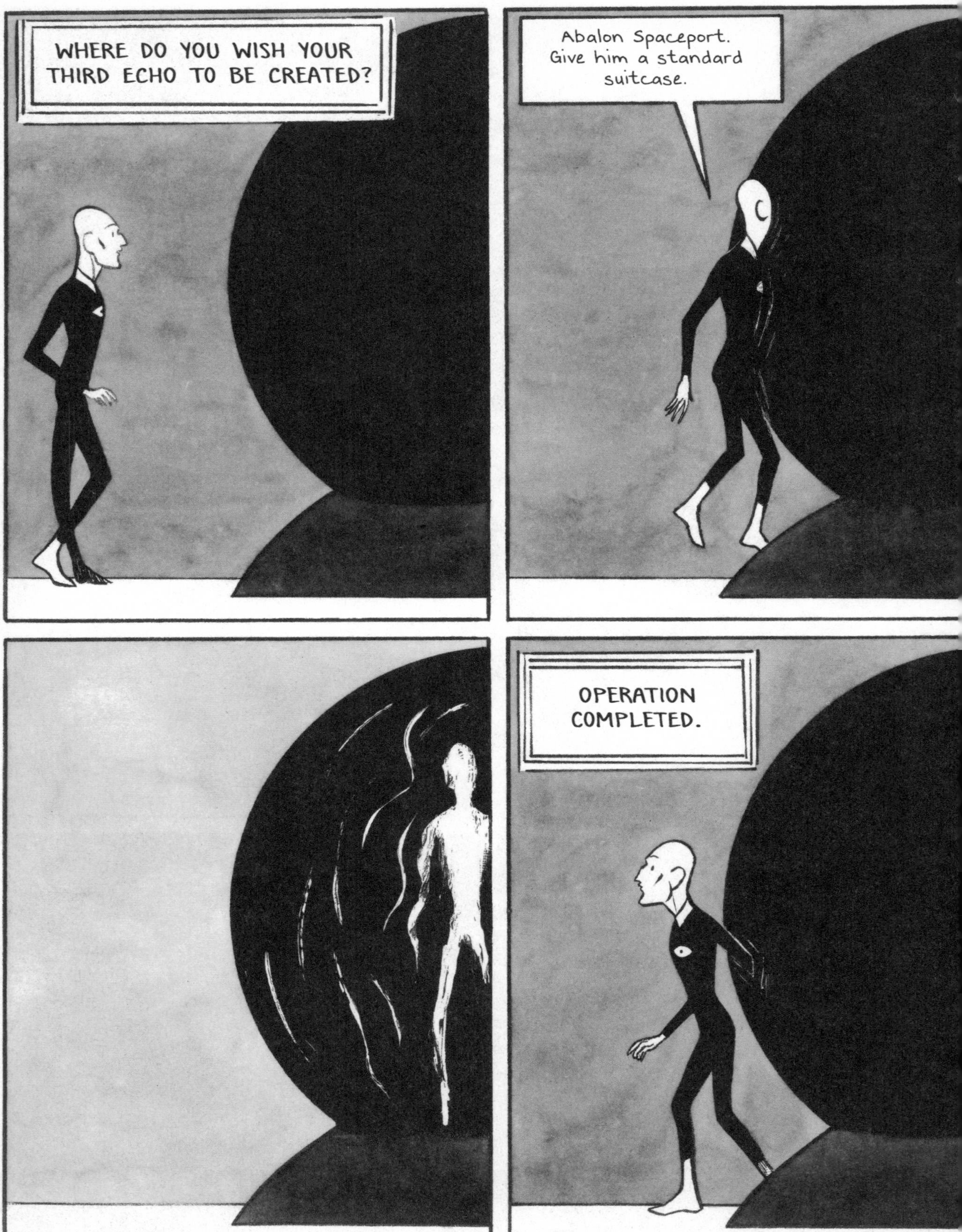
WHERE DO YOU WISH YOUR THIRD ECHO TO BE CREATED?
Abalon Spaceport. Give him a standard suitcase.
OPERATION COMPLETED.

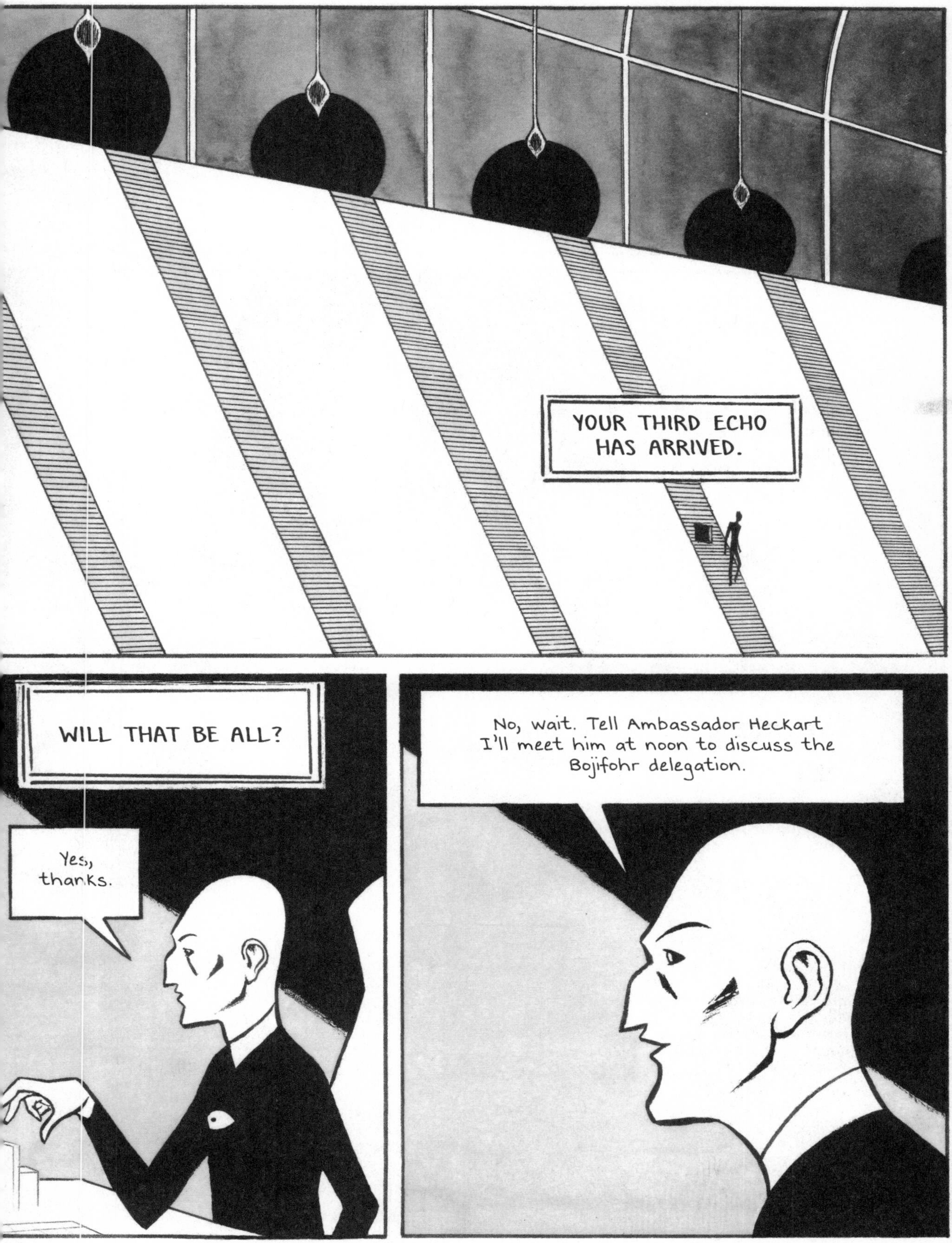
YOUR THIRD ECHO HAS ARRIVED.
WILL THAT BE ALL?
Yes, thanks.
No, wait. Tell Ambassador Heckart I'll meet him at noon to discuss the Bojifohr delegation.

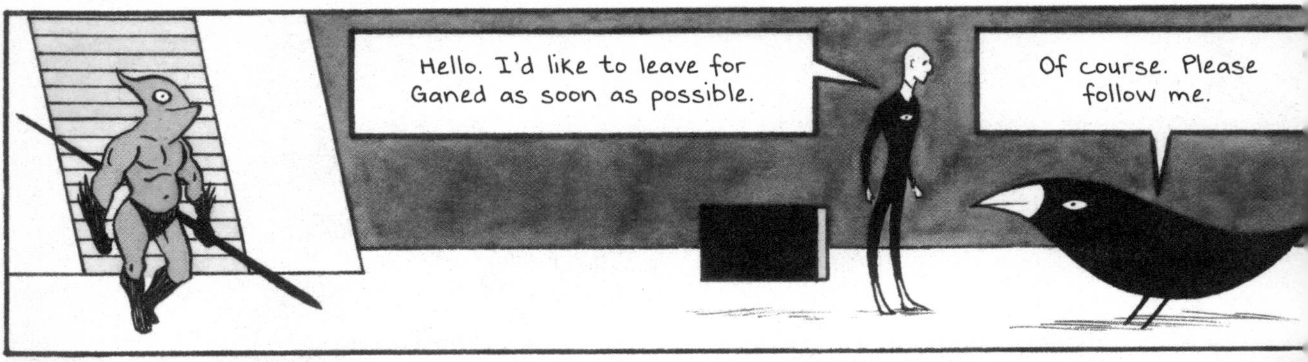
Hello. I'd like to leave for Ganed as soon as possible.
Of course. Please follow me.

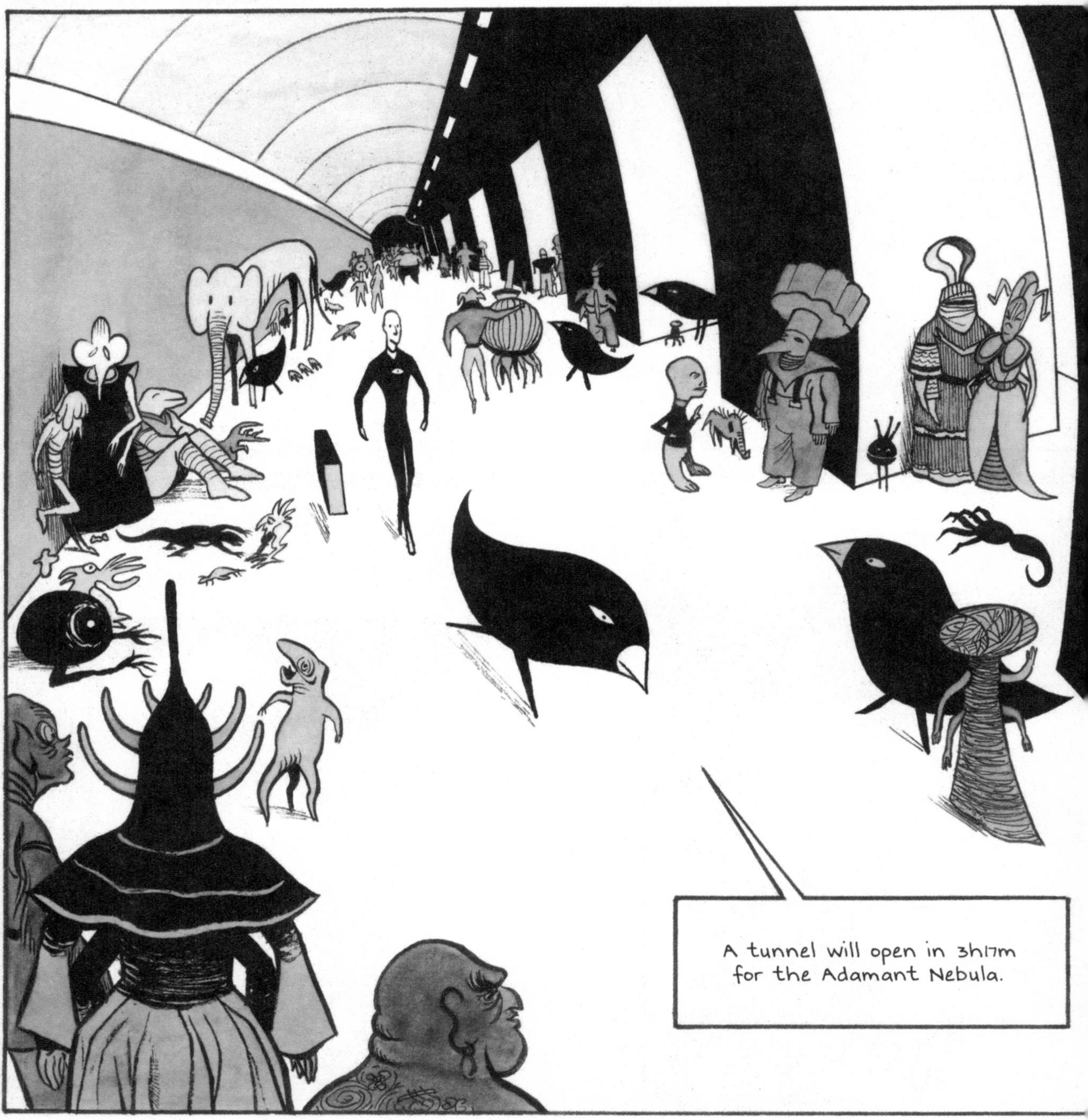
A tunnel will open in 3h17m for the Adamant Nebula.

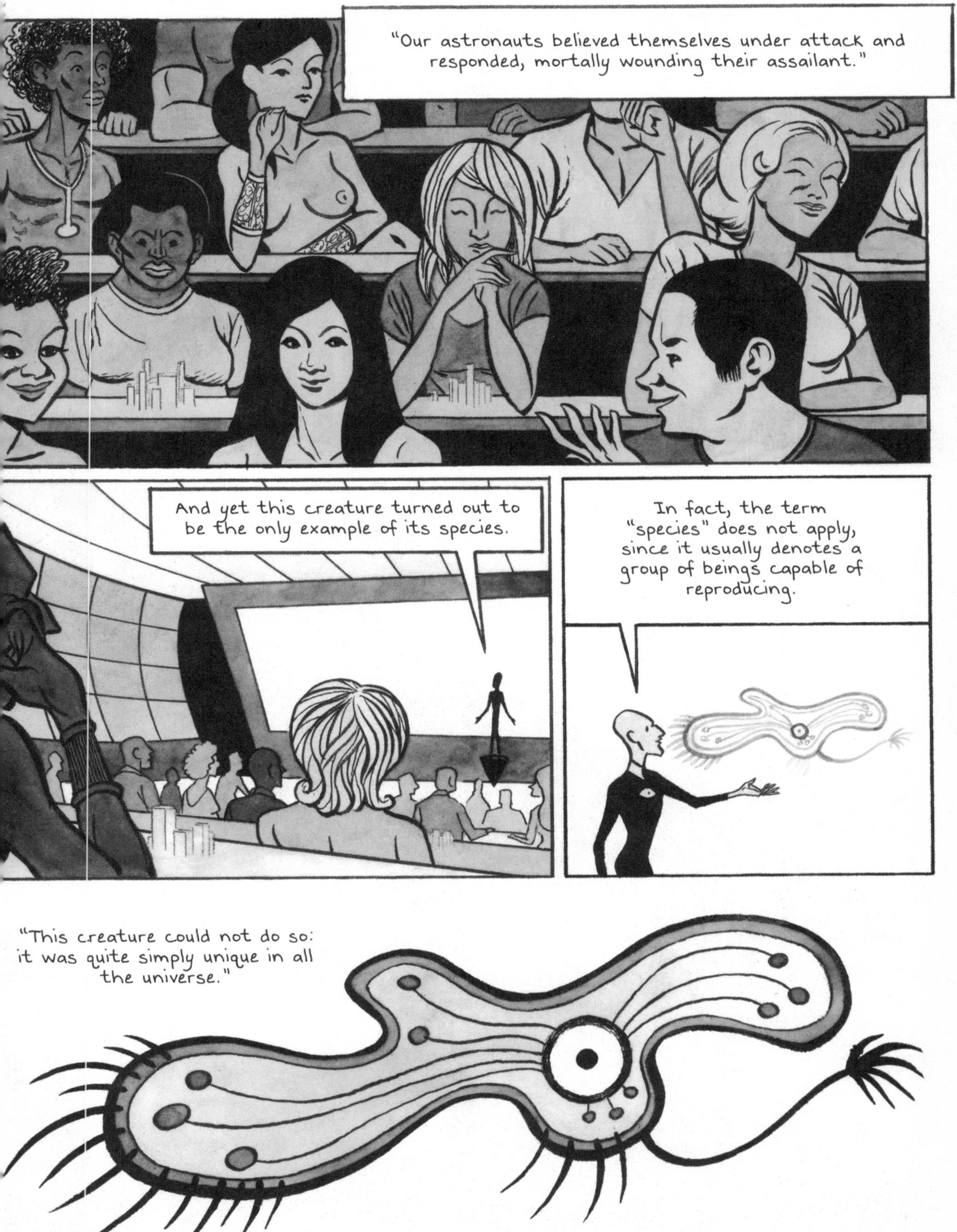
"Our astronauts believed themselves under attack and responded, mortally wounding their assailant."
And yet this creature turned out to be the only example of its species.
In fact, the term "species" does not apply, since it usually denotes a group of beings capable of reproducing.
"This creature could not do so: it was quite simply unique in all the universe."

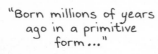

"Born millions of years ago in a primitive form…"

"…it slowly developed, passing through the classical evolutionary stages of our civilizations…"

" …raising edifices, taming animals… but always alone."

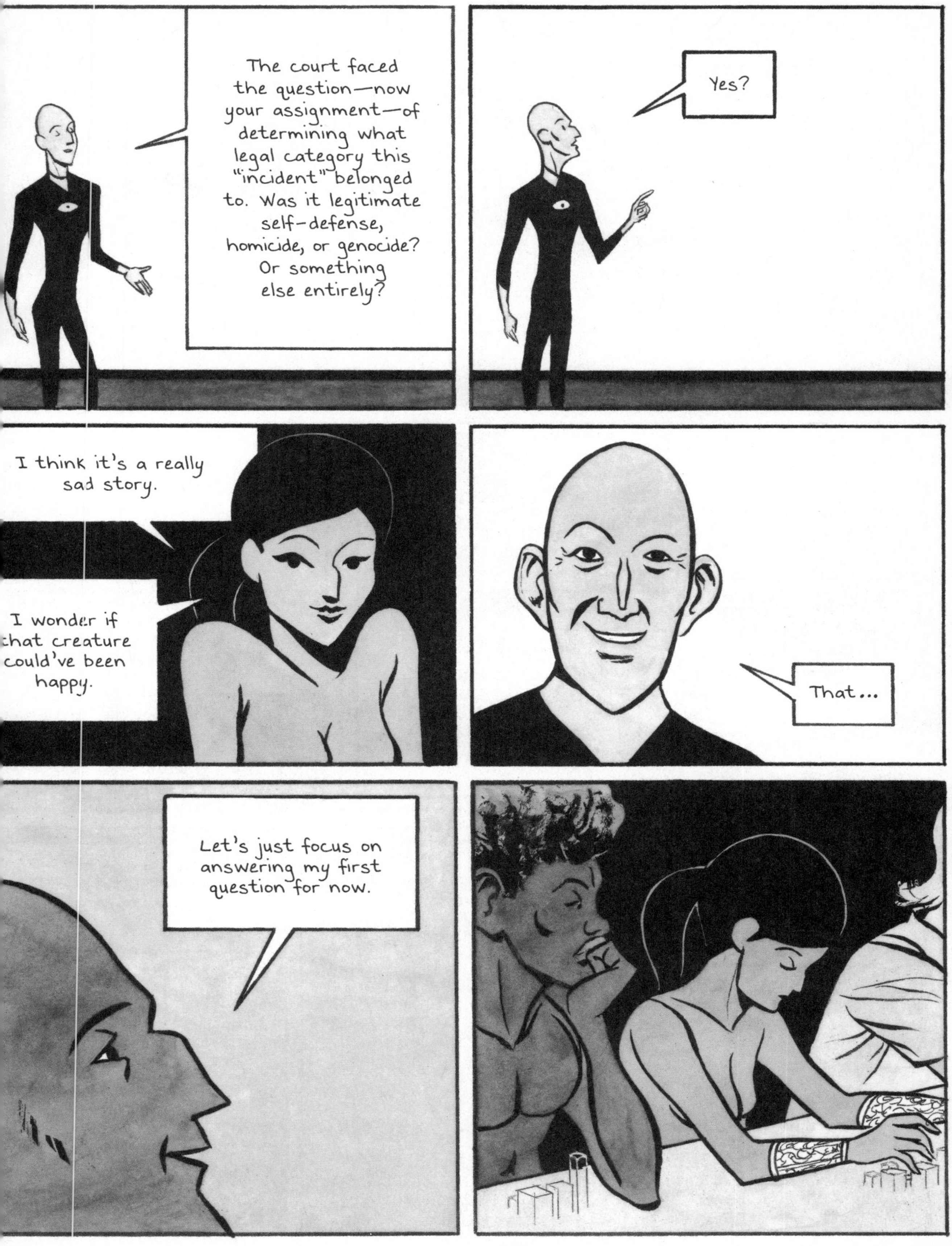
The court faced the question—now your assignment—of determining what legal category this "incident" belonged to. Was it legitimate self-defense, homicide, or genocide? Or something else entirely?
Yes?
I think it's a really sad story.
I wonder if that creature could've been happy.
That...
Let's just focus on answering my first question for now.

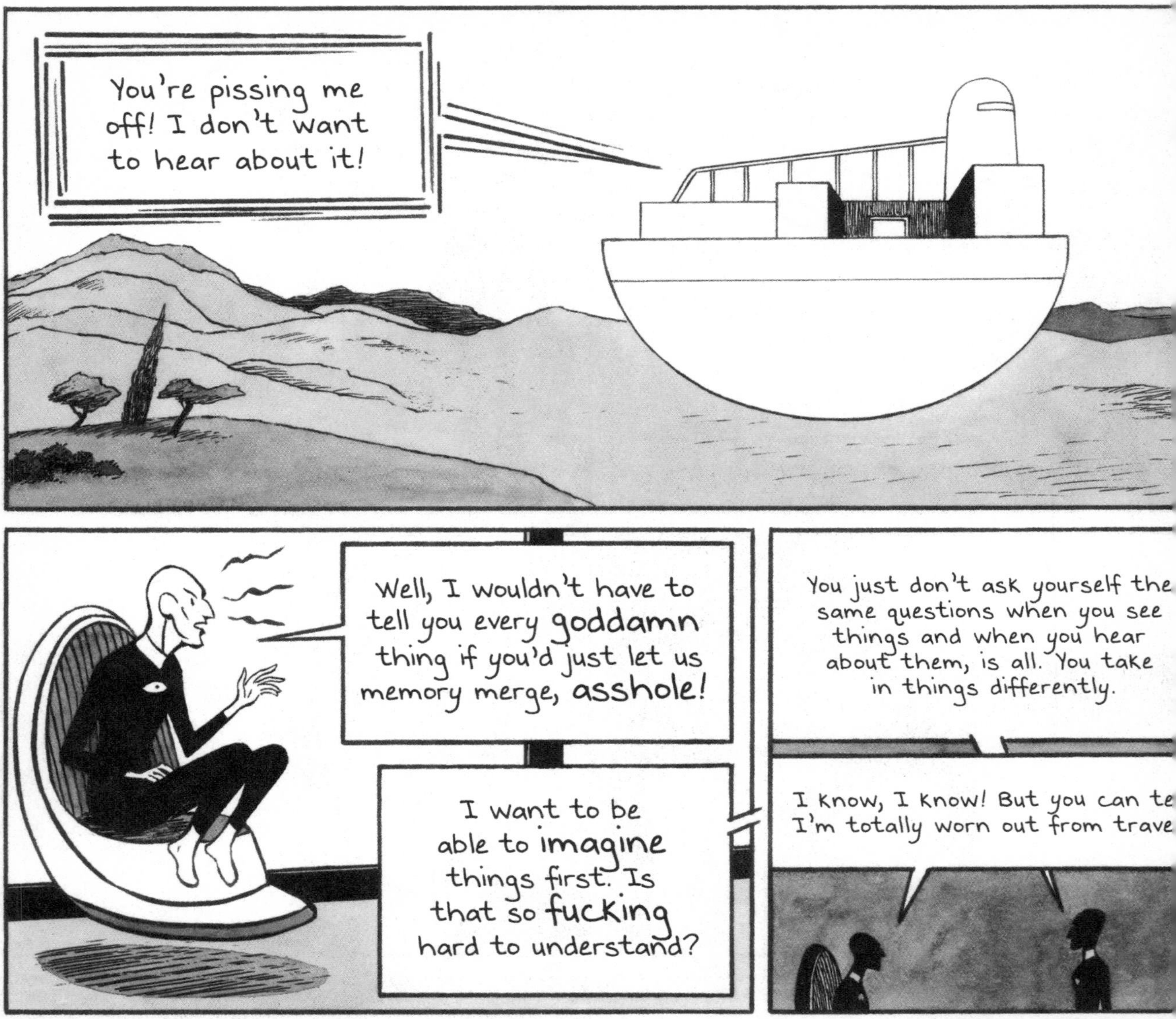
You're pissing me off! I don't want to hear about it!
Well, I wouldn't have to tell you every goddamn thing if you'd just let us memory merge, asshole!
I want to be able to imagine things first. Is that so fucking hard to understand?
You just don't ask yourself the same questions when you see things and when you hear about them, is all. You take in things differently.
I know, I know! But you can te I'm totally worn out from trave
... You also know merging will make our oldest memories disappear. Is that what you really want?
Okay, touché. You got me there.
Ha, ha! Feels good, yelling it out!
Yup!

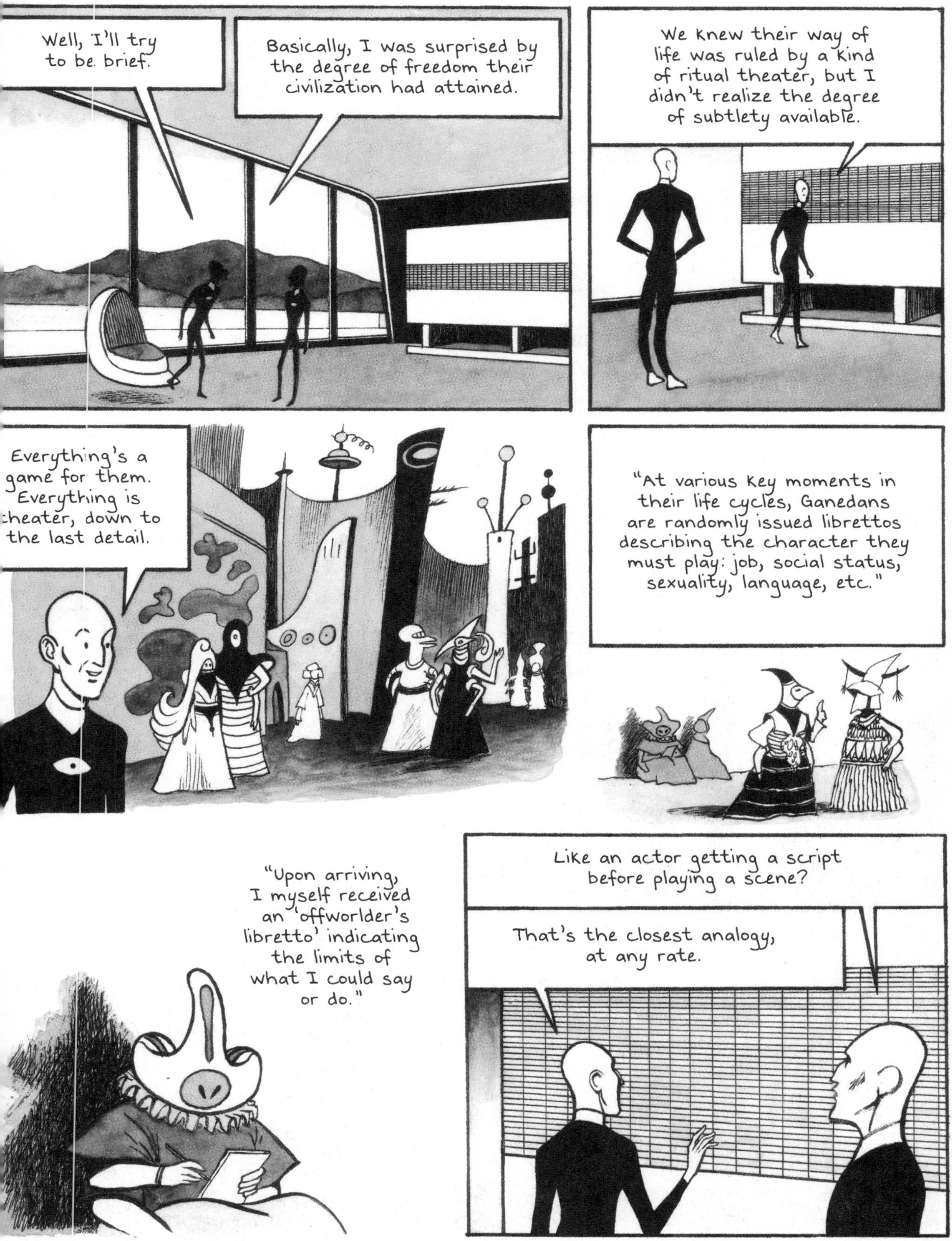

Well, I'll try to be brief.
Basically, I was surprised by the degree of freedom their civilization had attained.
We knew their way of life was ruled by a kind of ritual theater, but I didn't realize the degree of subtlety available.
Everything's a game for them. Everything is theater, down to the last detail.
"At various key moments in their life cycles, Ganedans are randomly issued librettos describing the character they must play: job, social status, sexuality, language, etc."
"Upon arriving, I myself received an 'offworlder's libretto' indicating the limits of what I could say or do."
Like an actor getting a script before playing a scene?
That's the closest analogy, at any rate.

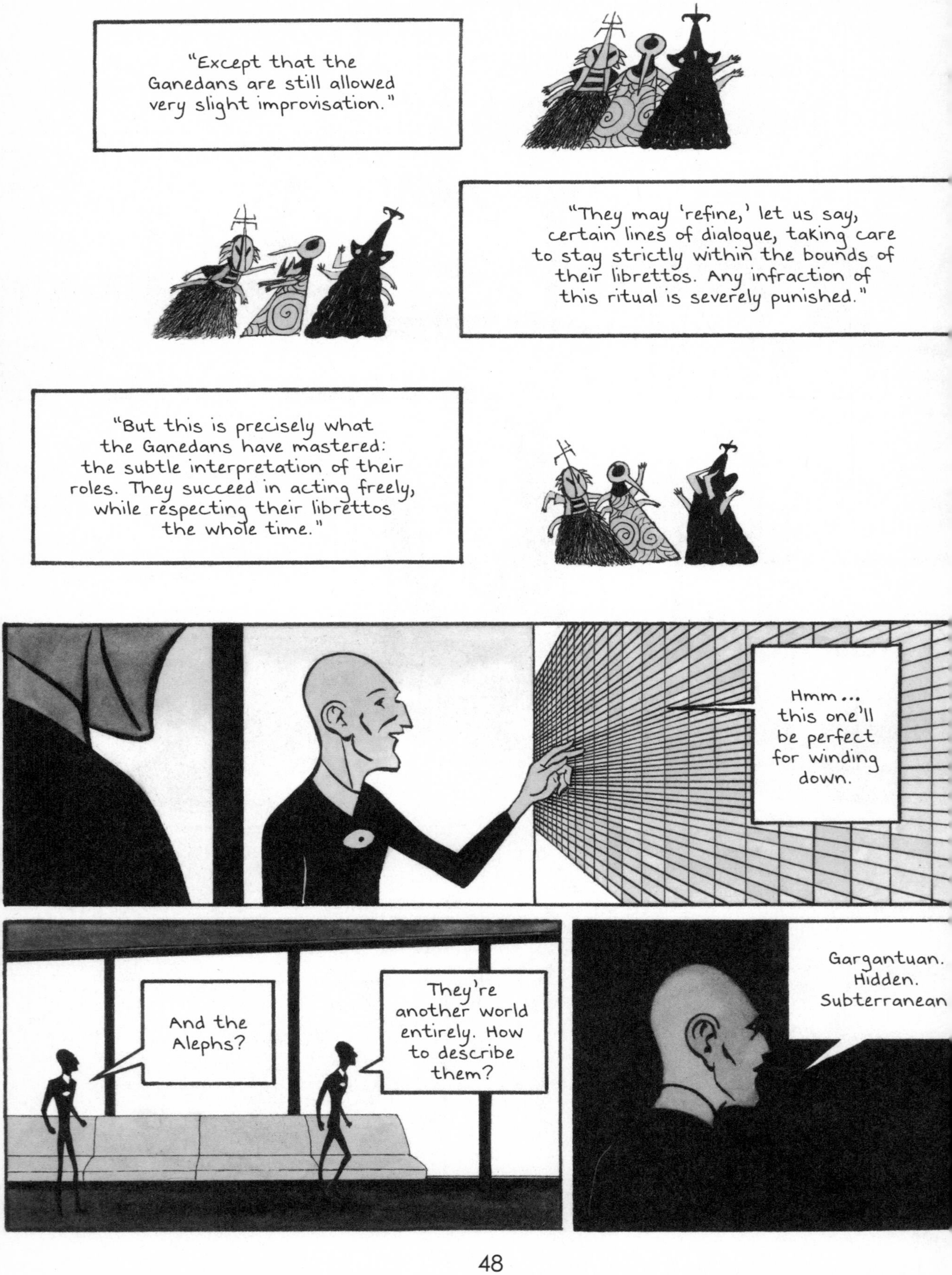
"Except that the Ganedans are still allowed very slight improvisation."
"They may 'refine,' let us say, certain lines of dialogue, taking care to stay strictly within the bounds of their librettos. Any infraction of this ritual is severely punished."
"But this is precisely what the Ganedans have mastered: the subtle interpretation of their roles. They succeed in acting freely, while respecting their librettos the whole time."
Hmm... this one'll be perfect for winding down.
And the Alephs?
They're another world entirely. How to describe them?
Gargantuan. Hidden. Subterranean

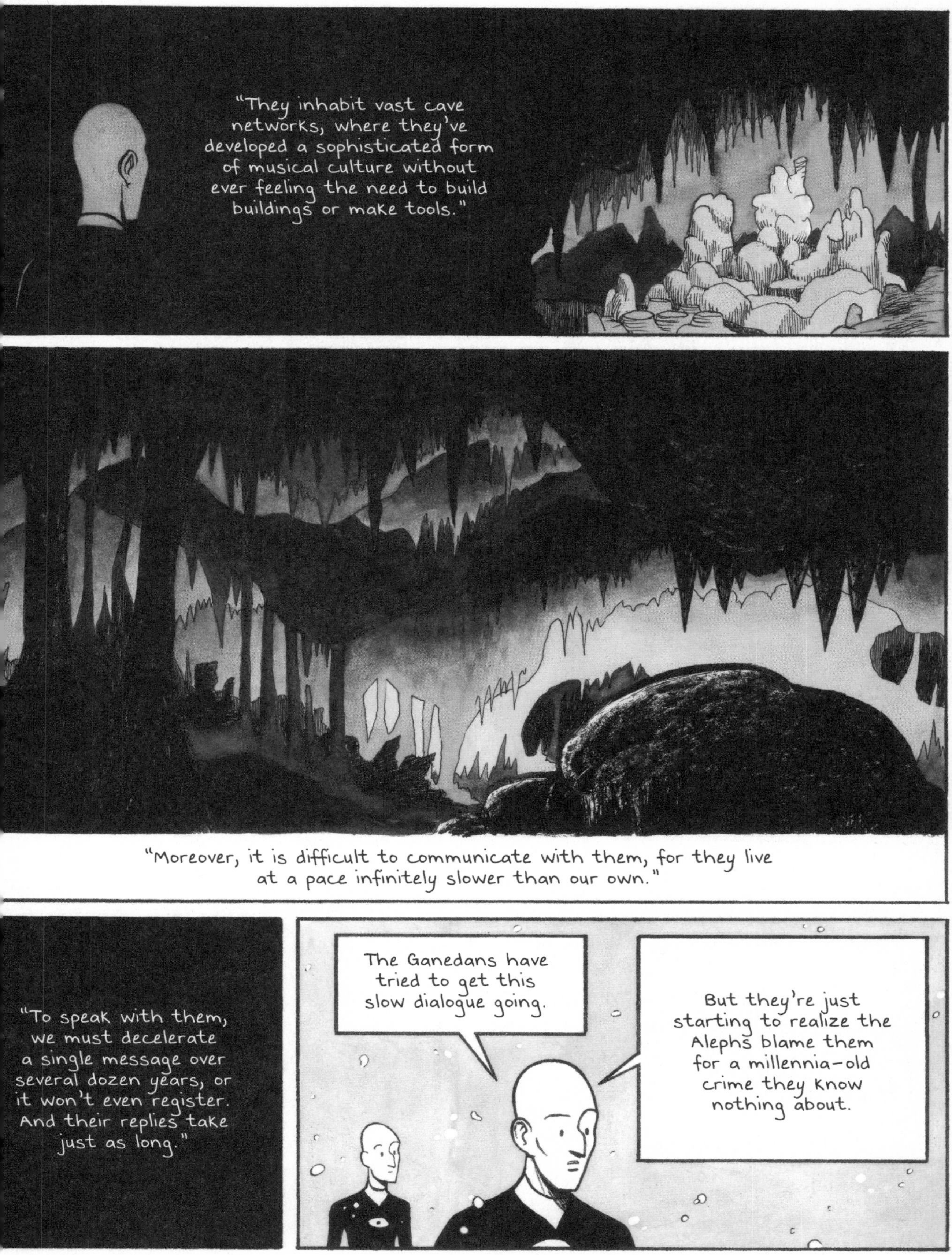
"They inhabit vast cave networks, where they've developed a sophisticated form of musical culture without ever feeling the need to build buildings or make tools."
"Moreover, it is difficult to communicate with them, for they live at a pace infinitely slower than our own."
"To speak with them, we must decelerate a single message over several dozen years, or it won't even register. And their replies take just as long."
The Ganedans have tried to get this slow dialogue going.
But they're just starting to realize the Alephs blame them for a millennia-old crime they know nothing about.

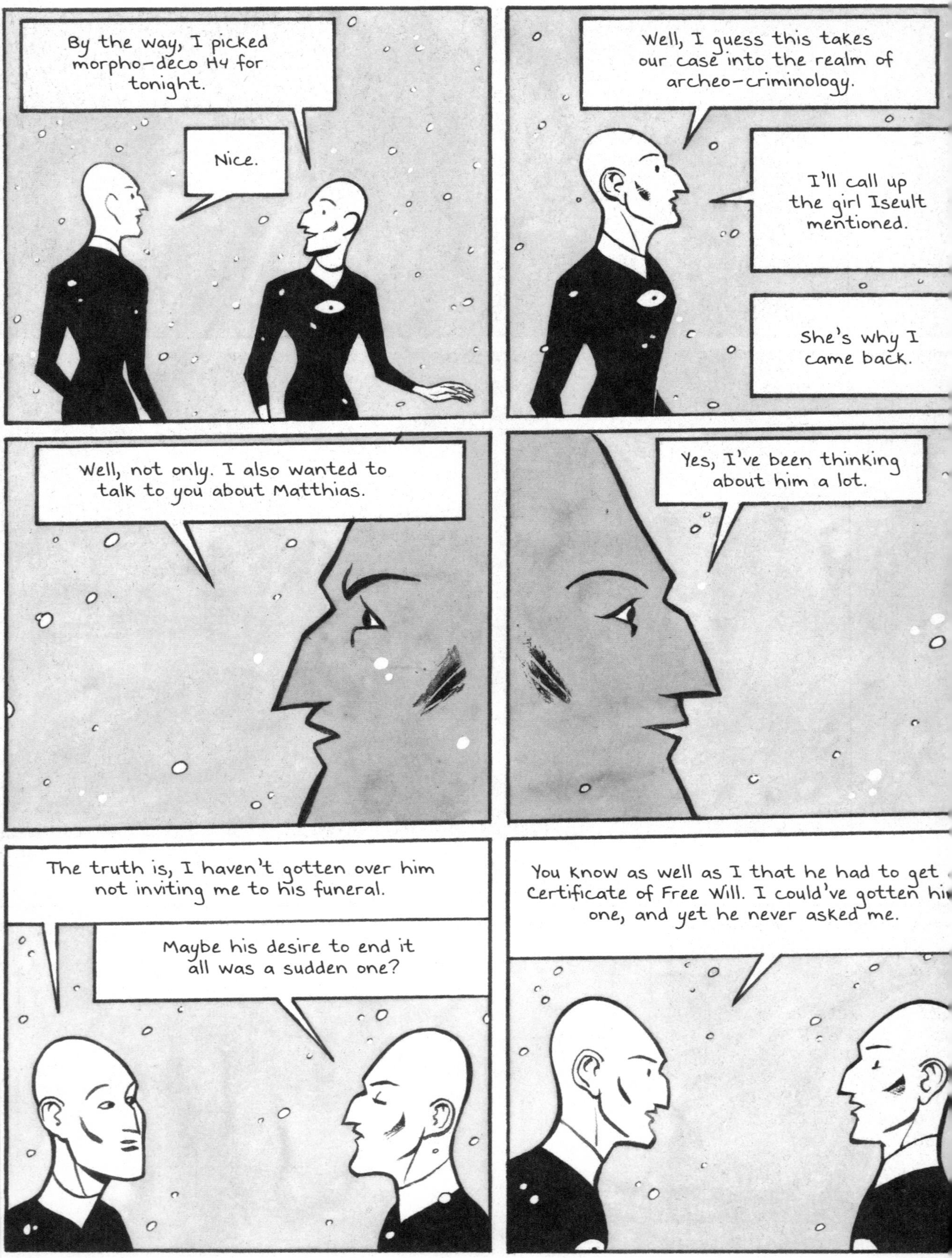

By the way, I picked morpho-deco H4 for tonight.
Nice.
Well, I guess this takes our case into the realm of archeo-criminology.
I'll call up the girl Iseult mentioned.
She's why I came back.
Well, not only. I also wanted to talk to you about Matthias.
Yes, I've been thinking about him a lot.
The truth is, I haven't gotten over him not inviting me to his funeral.
Maybe his desire to end it all was a sudden one?
You know as well as I that he had to get
Certificate of Free Will. I could've gotten hi
one, and yet he never asked me.

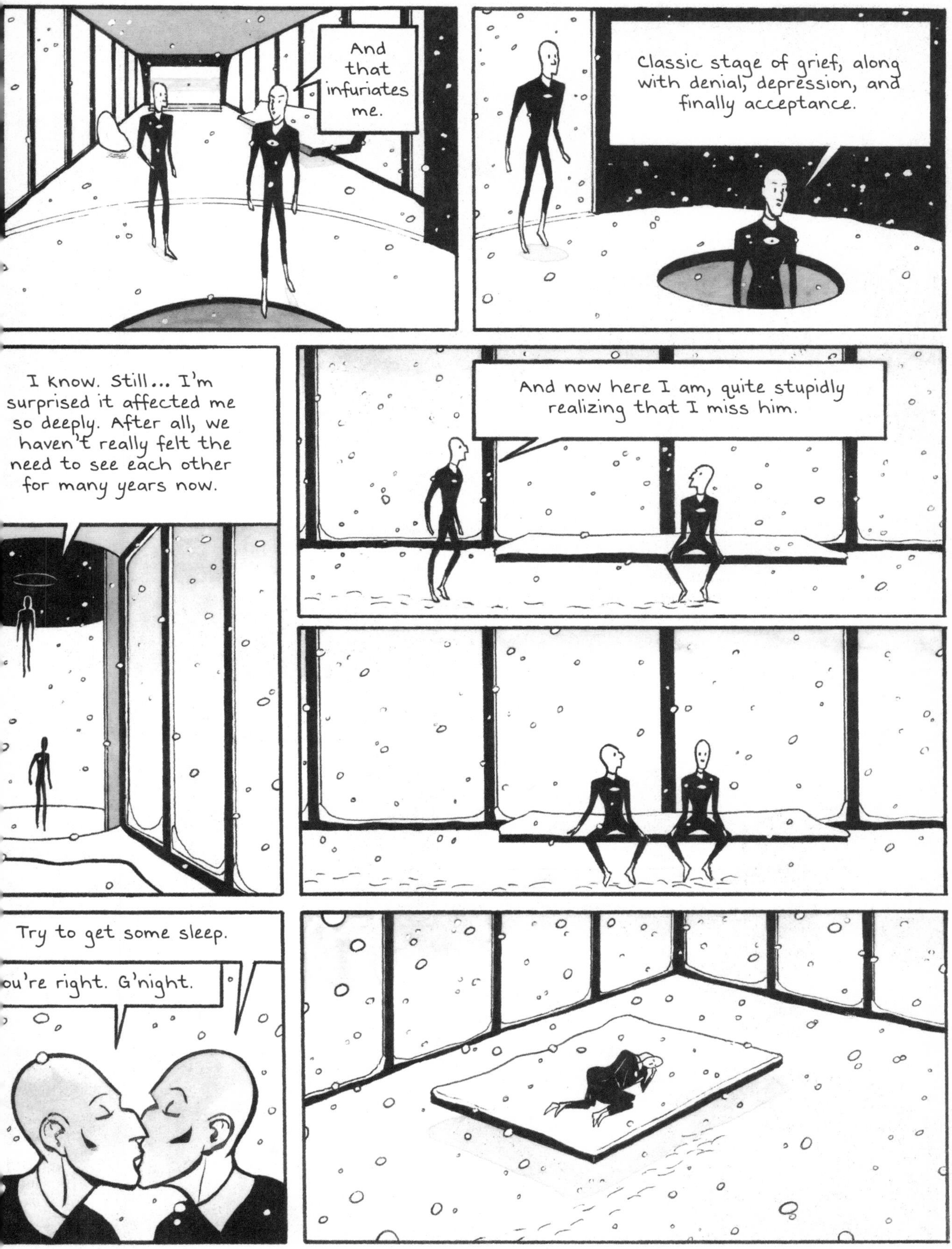

And that infuriates me.
Classic stage of grief, along with denial, depression, and finally acceptance.
I know. Still... I'm surprised it affected me so deeply. After all, we haven't really felt the need to see each other for many years now.
And now here I am, quite stupidly realizing that I miss him.
Try to get some sleep.
ou're right. G'night.

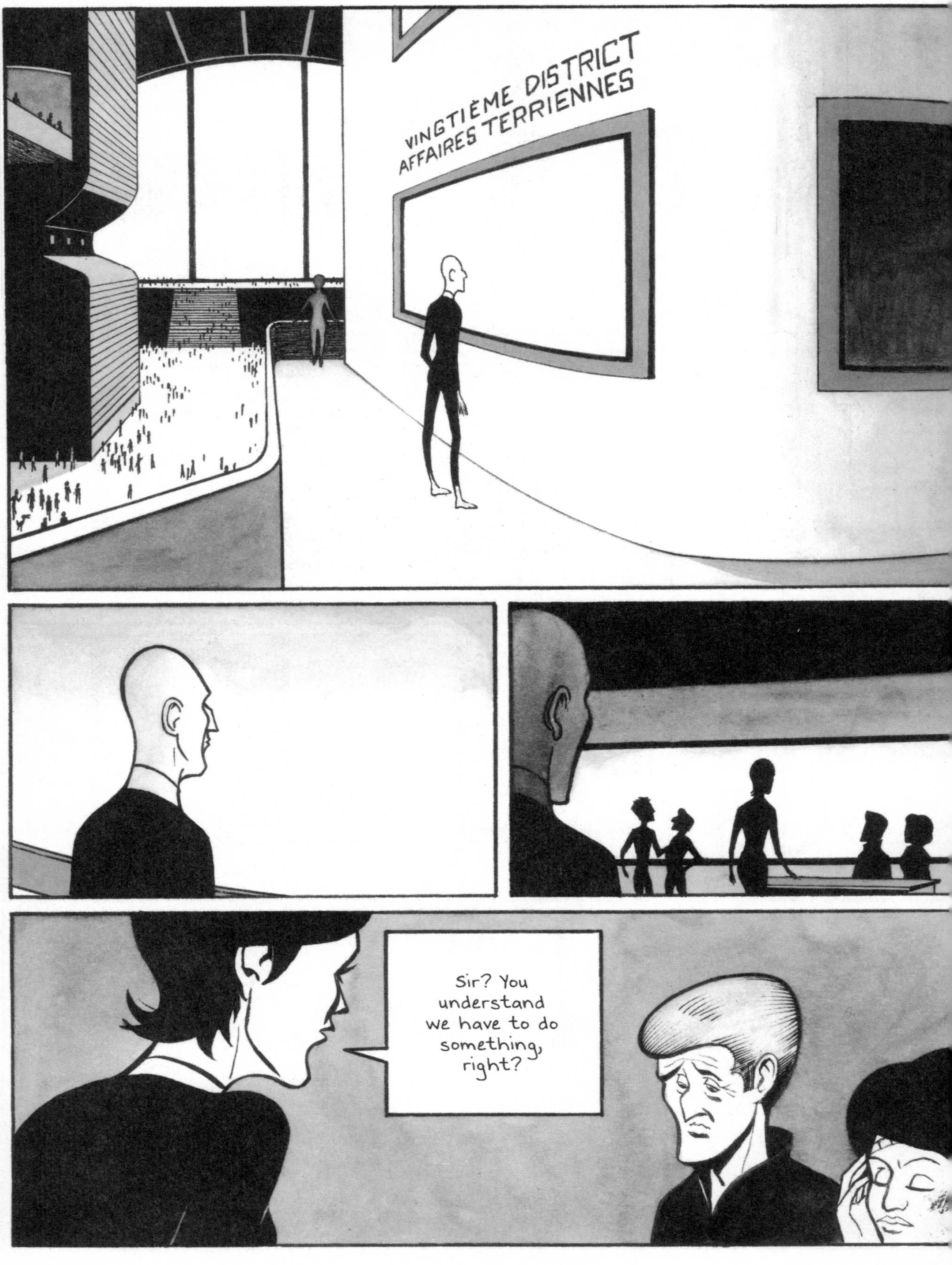
VINGTIÈME DISTRICT
AFFAIRES TERRIENNES
Sir? You understand we have to do something, right?

Your cerebral scan reveals that you've begun to harbor murderous impulses toward her.

It's just... sometimes she just makes me so angry! But we love each other.

It's true! We do!

I know.

But we can't let things get worse and lead to tragedy, can we?

Well, no.

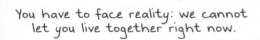

You have to face reality: we cannot let you live together right now.

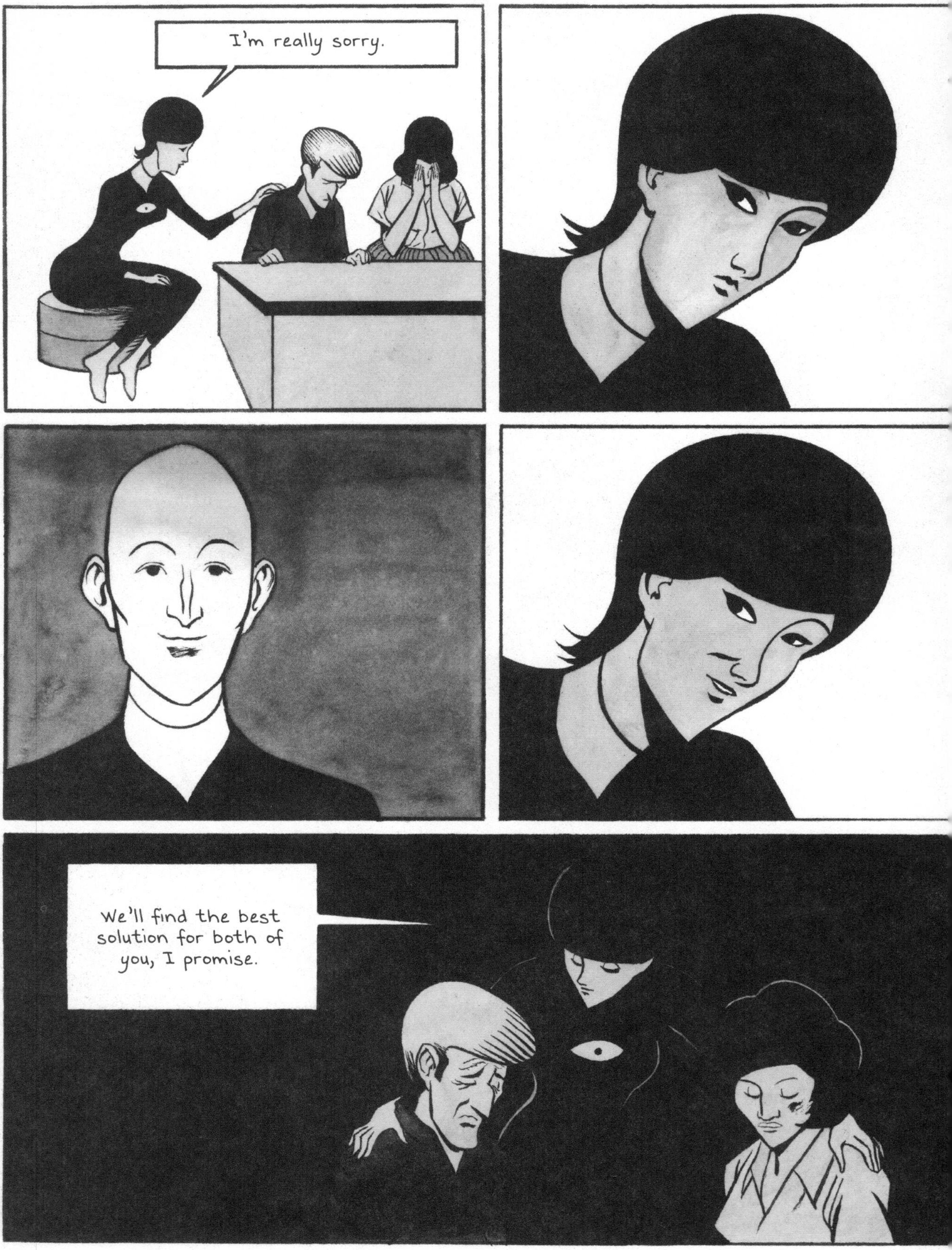
I'm really sorry.
We'll find the best solution for both of you, I promise.

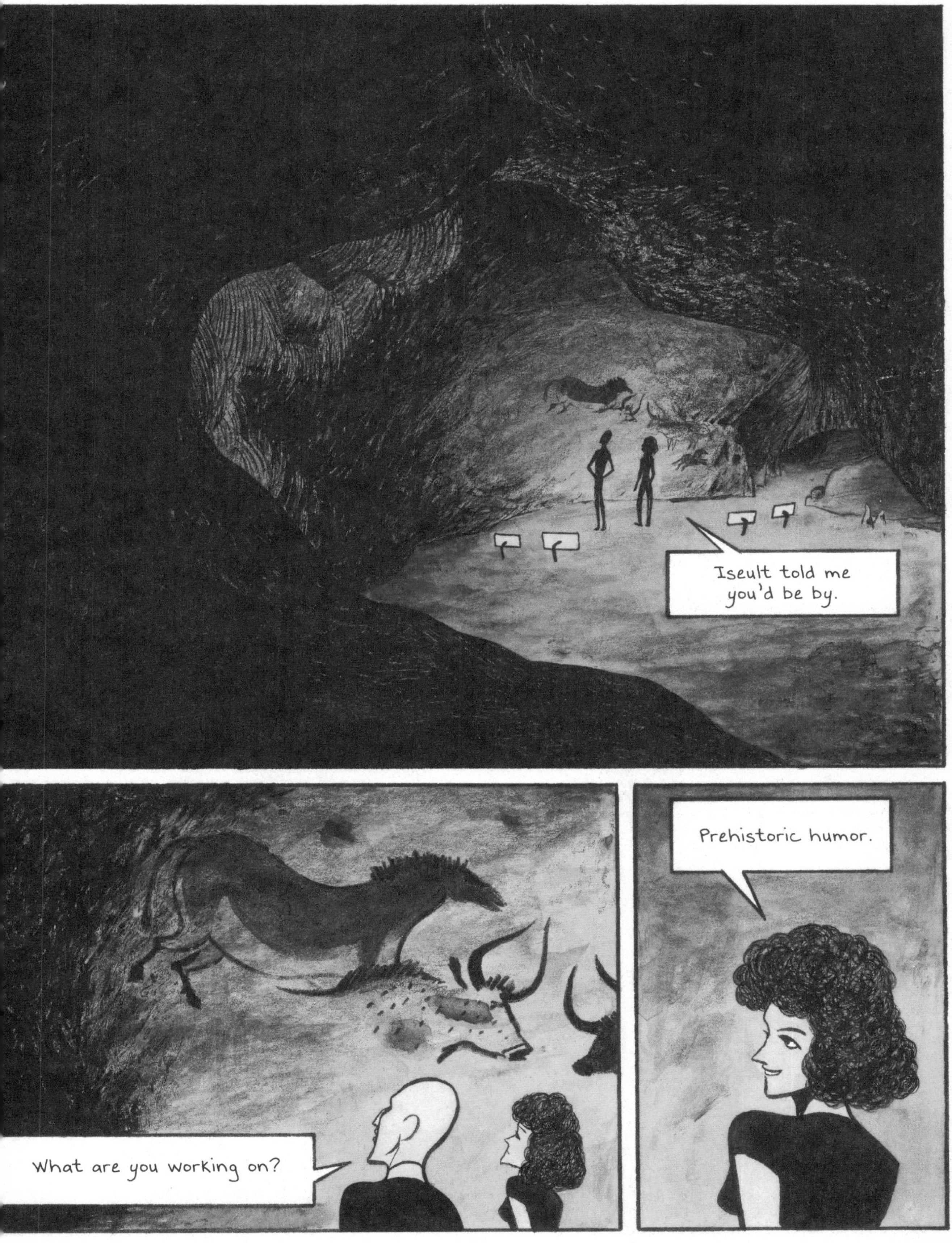
Iseult told me you'd be by.
What are you working on?
Prehistoric humor.

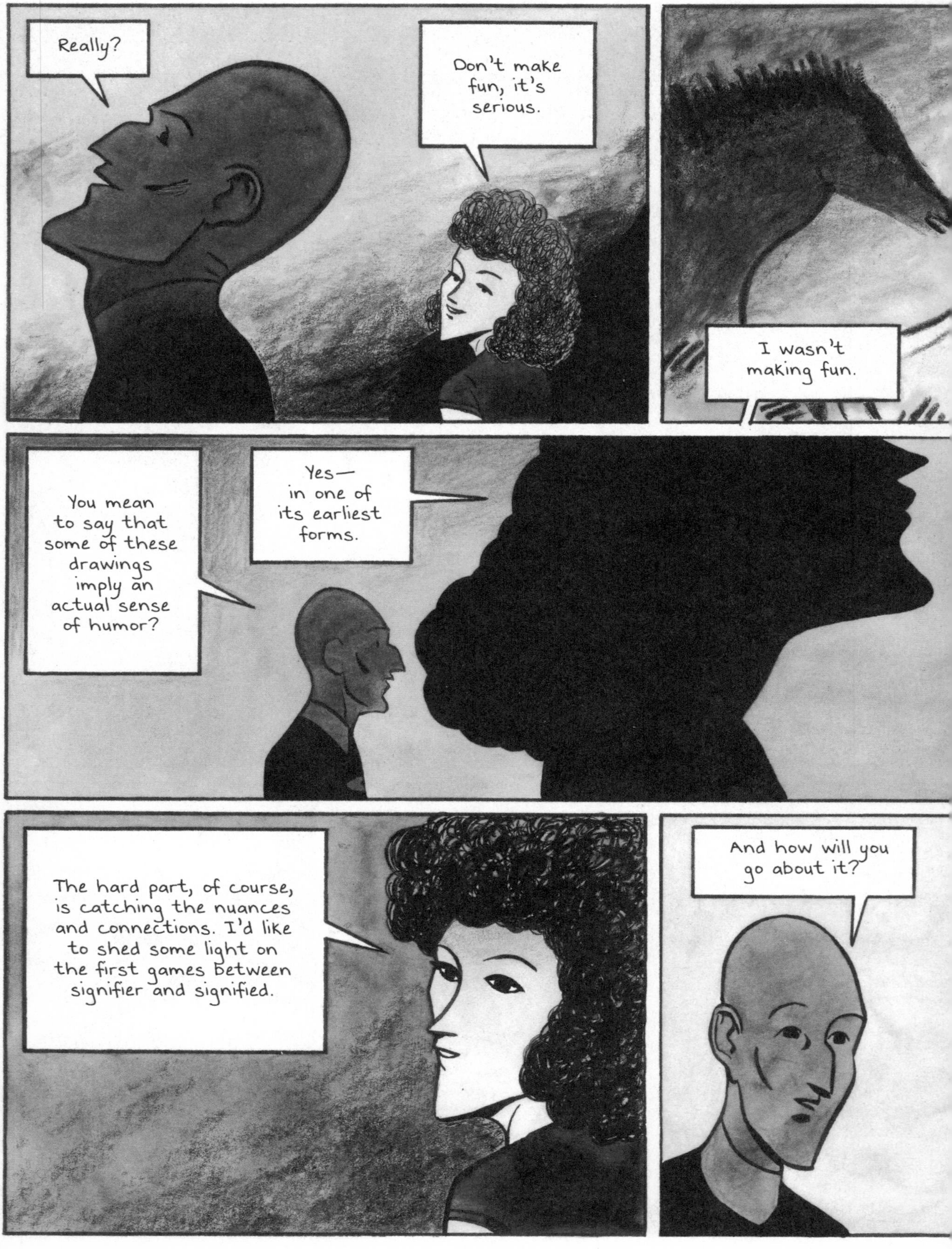
Really?
Don't make fun, it's serious.
I wasn't making fun.
You mean to say that some of these drawings imply an actual sense of humor?
Yes— in one of its earliest forms.
The hard part, of course, is catching the nuances and connections. I'd like to shed some light on the first games between signifier and signified.
And how will you go about it?

We're trying to pick up laughter "imprinted" on the walls of this cave.

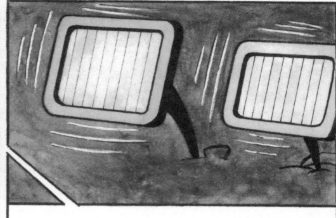

All it takes for that are sensitive instruments, a little know-how, and a good dose of perseverance!

All qualities that you seem to have in abundance. I'll need someone of your talents on Ganed.

What for?

To solve a millennia-old crime. How's that sound?

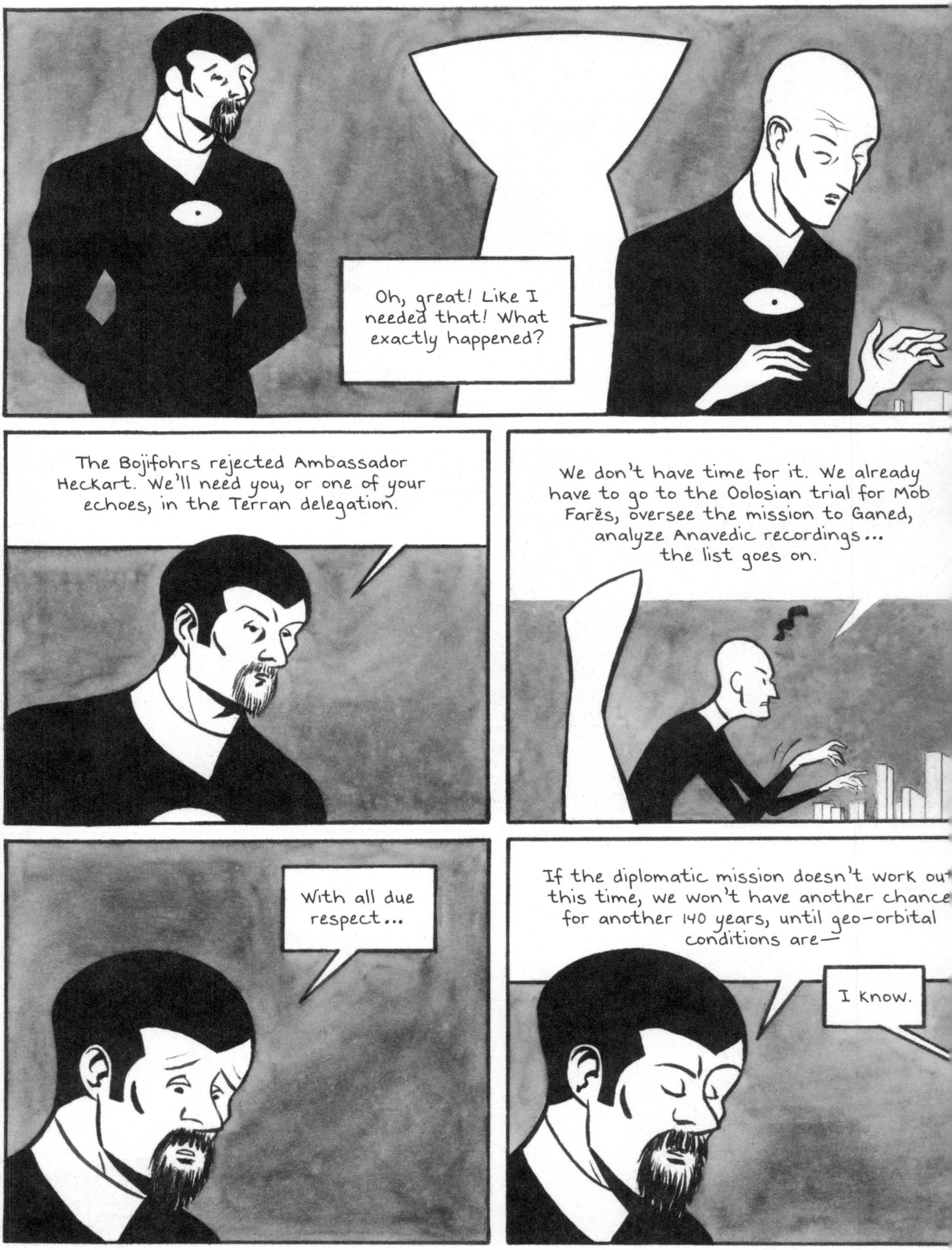
Oh, great! Like I needed that! What exactly happened?
The Bojifohrs rejected Ambassador HecKart. We'll need you, or one of your echoes, in the Terran delegation.
We don't have time for it. We already have to go to the Oolosian trial for Mob Farẽs, oversee the mission to Ganed, analyze Anavedic recordings... the list goes on.
With all due respect...
If the diplomatic mission doesn't work out this time, we won't have another chance for another 140 years, until geo-orbital conditions are—
I Know.

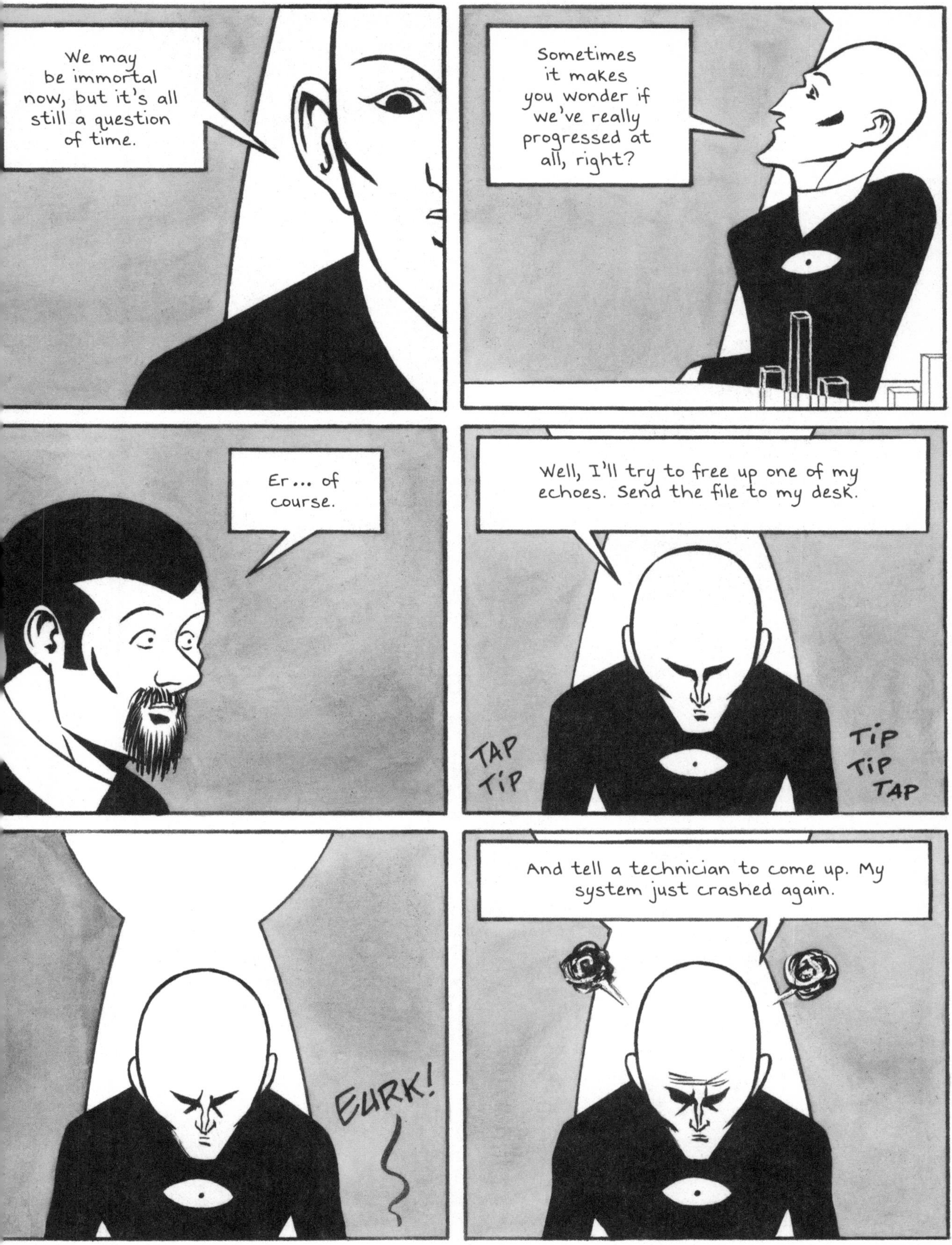
We may be immortal now, but it's all still a question of time.
Sometimes it makes you wonder if we've really progressed at all, right?
Er... of course.
Well, I'll try to free up one of my echoes. Send the file to my desk.
TAP TIP
TIP TIP TAP
EURK!
And tell a technician to come up. My system just crashed again.

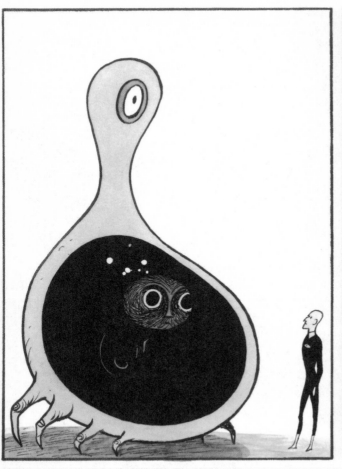

Greetings. I am Elijah.

I understand you weren't satisfied with our previous emissary?

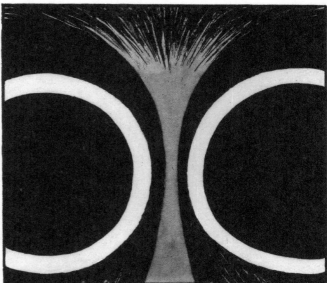

WE WISH TO SPEAK TO SOMEONE IN CHARGE

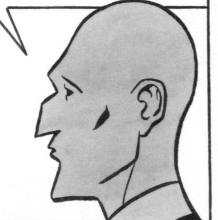

The Union has appointed me for that very purpose—

WE WISH TO SPEAK TO SOMEONE IN CHARGE

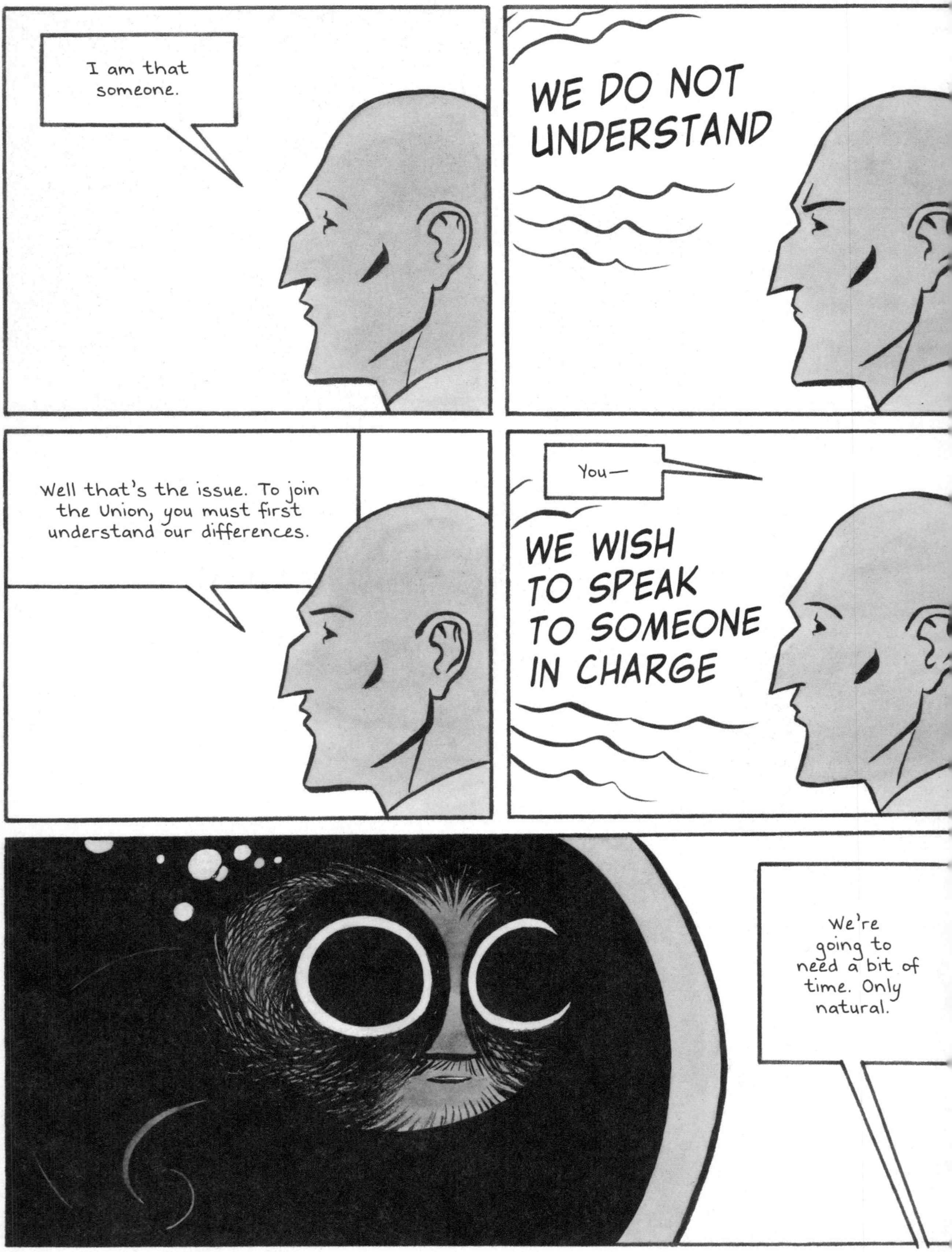

I am that someone.
WE DO NOT UNDERSTAND
Well that's the issue. To join the Union, you must first understand our differences.
You—
WE WISH TO SPEAK TO SOMEONE IN CHARGE
We're going to need a bit of time. Only natural.

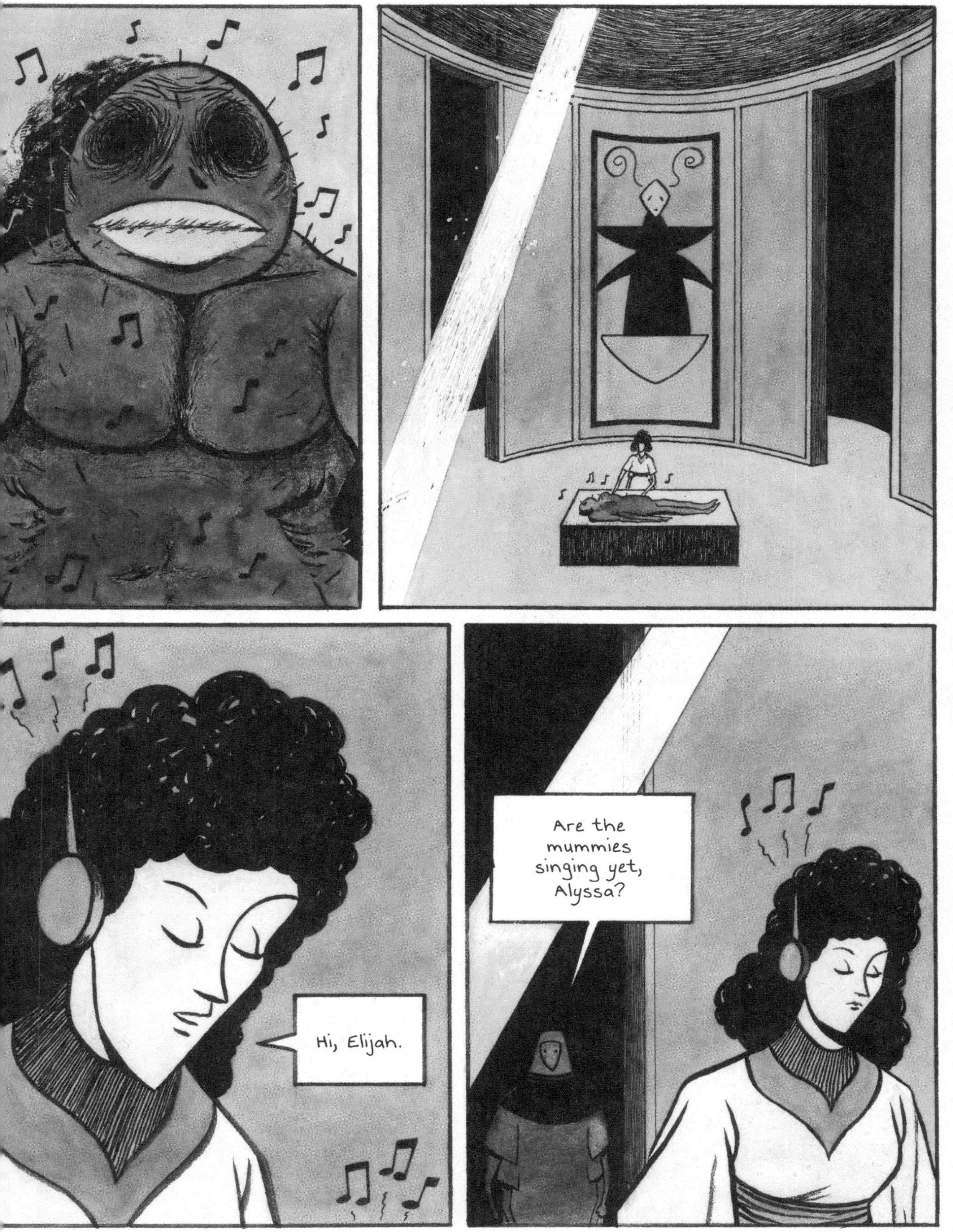

Hi, Elijah.
Are the mummies singing yet, Alyssa?

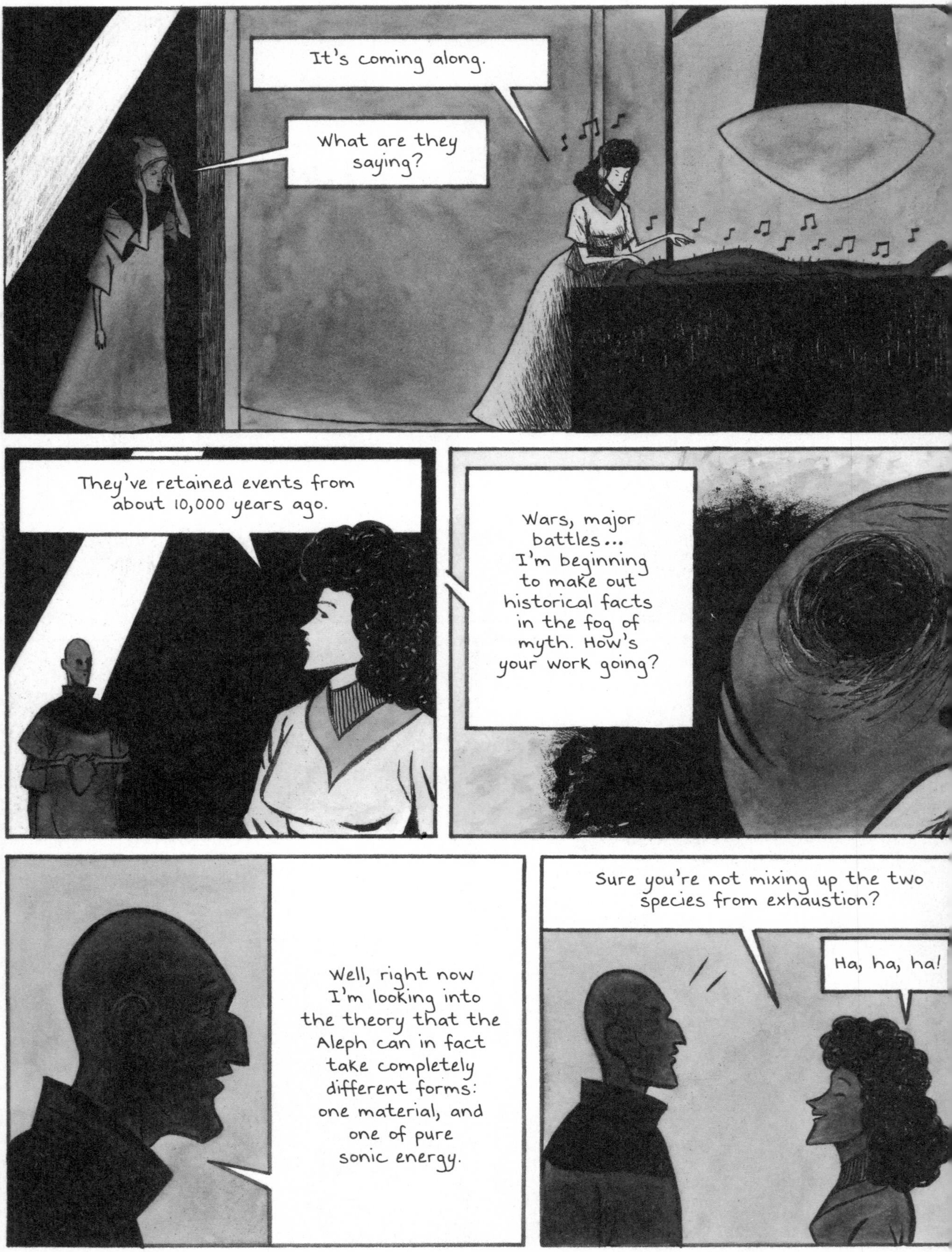
What are they saying?
It's coming along.
They've retained events from about 10,000 years ago.
Wars, major battles... I'm beginning to make out historical facts in the fog of myth. How's your work going?
Well, right now I'm looking into the theory that the Aleph can in fact take completely different forms: one material, and one of pure sonic energy.
Sure you're not mixing up the two species from exhaustion?
Ha, ha, ha!

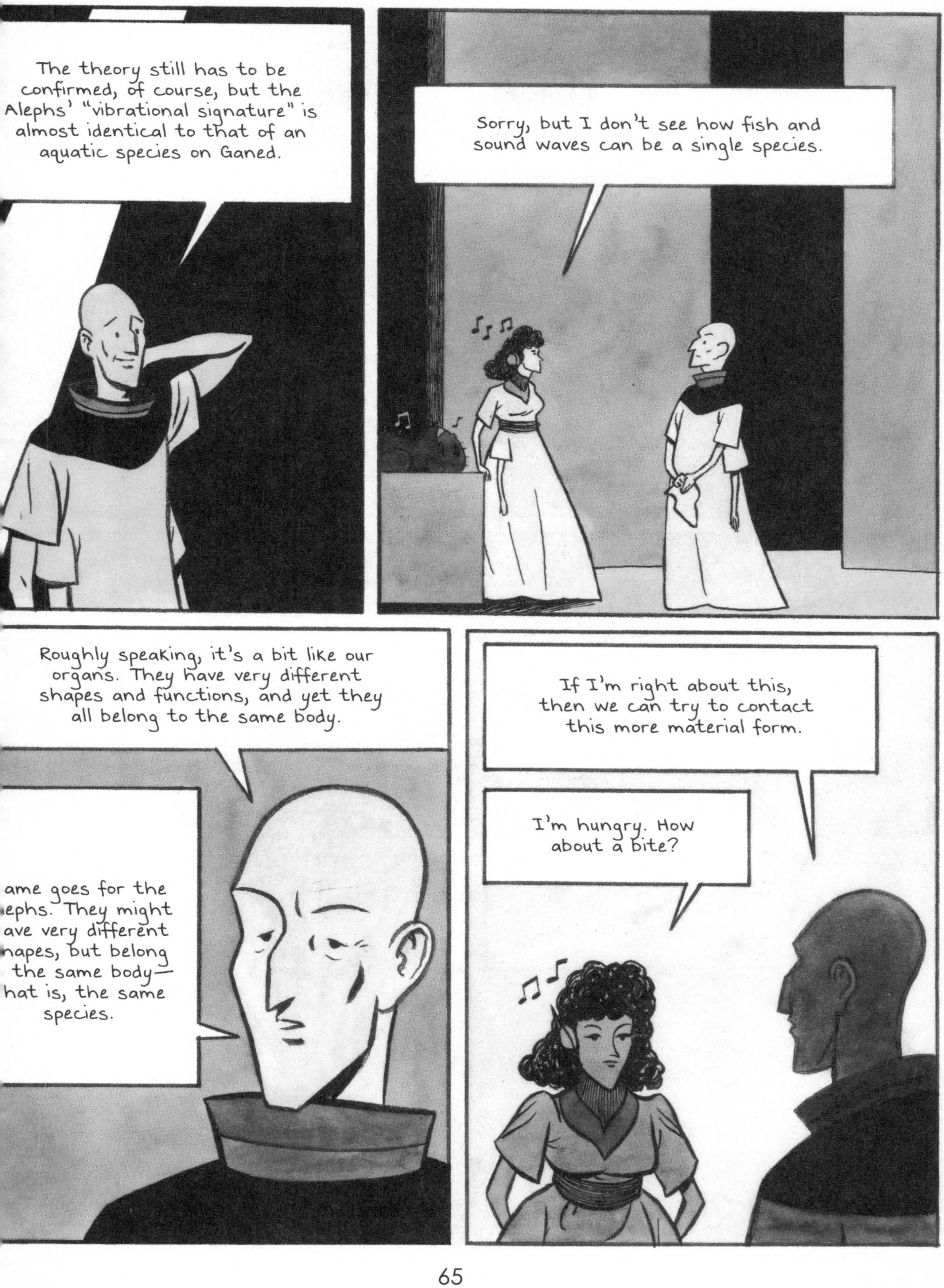

The theory still has to be confirmed, of course, but the Alephs' "vibrational signature" is almost identical to that of an aquatic species on Ganed.
Sorry, but I don't see how fish and sound waves can be a single species.
Roughly speaking, it's a bit like our organs. They have very different shapes and functions, and yet they all belong to the same body.
ame goes for the ephs. They might ave very different hapes, but belong the same body— hat is, the same species.
If I'm right about this, then we can try to contact this more material form.
I'm hungry. How about a bite?

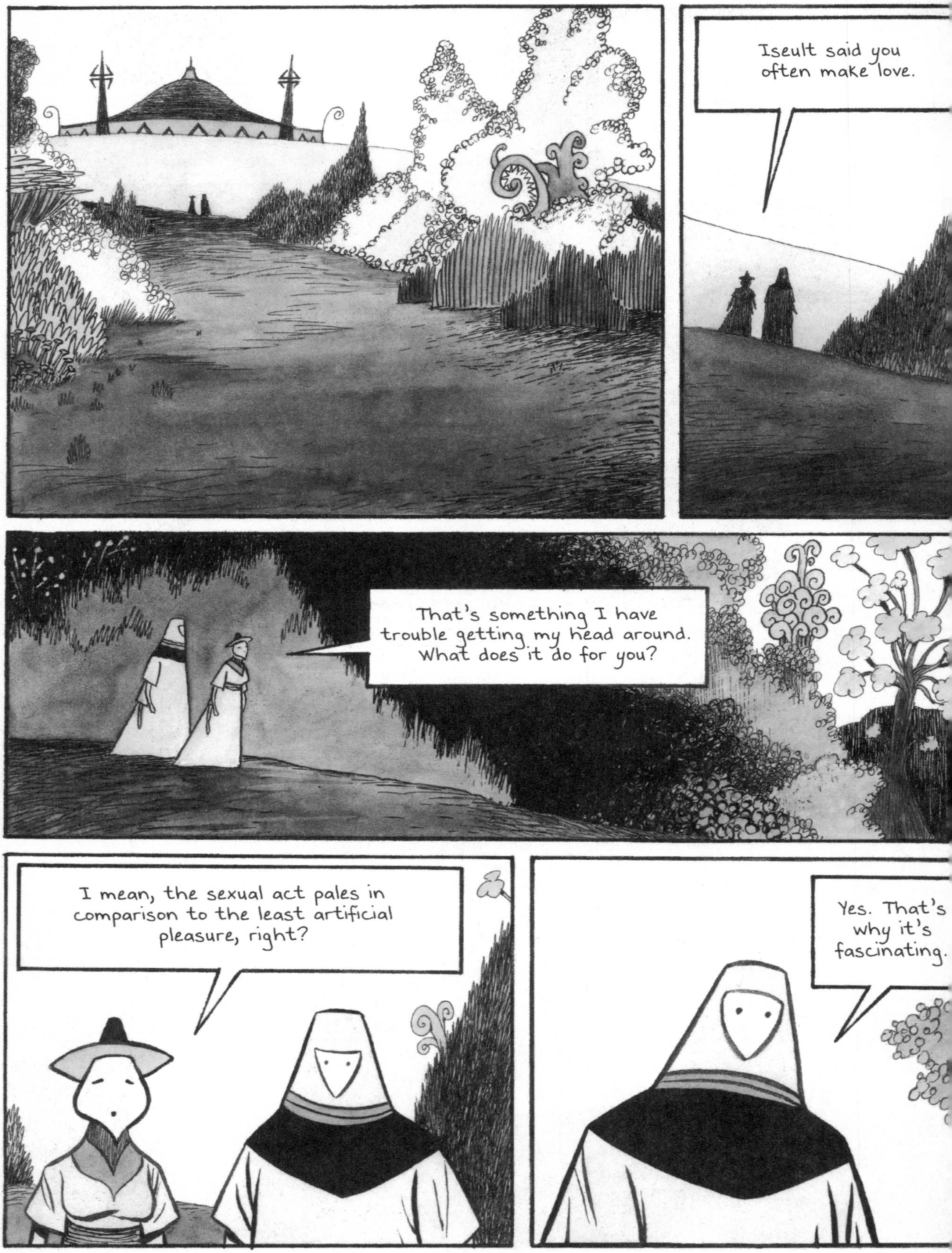
Iseult said you often make love.
That's something I have trouble getting my head around. What does it do for you?
I mean, the sexual act pales in comparison to the least artificial pleasure, right?
Yes. That's why it's fascinating.

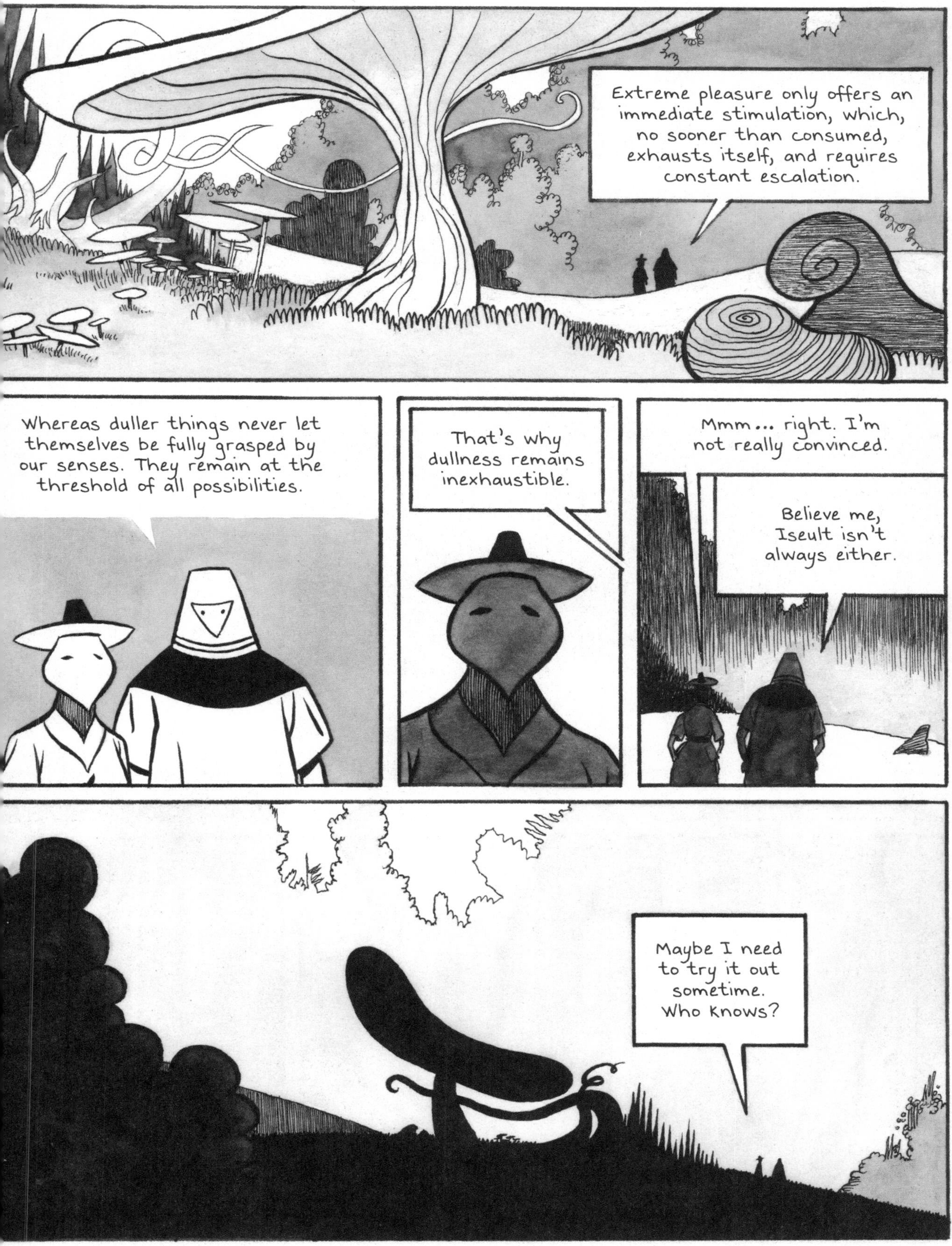
Extreme pleasure only offers an immediate stimulation, which, no sooner than consumed, exhausts itself, and requires constant escalation.
Whereas duller things never let themselves be fully grasped by our senses. They remain at the threshold of all possibilities.
That's why dullness remains inexhaustible.
Mmm... right. I'm not really convinced.
Believe me, Iseult isn't always either.
Maybe I need to try it out sometime. Who knows?

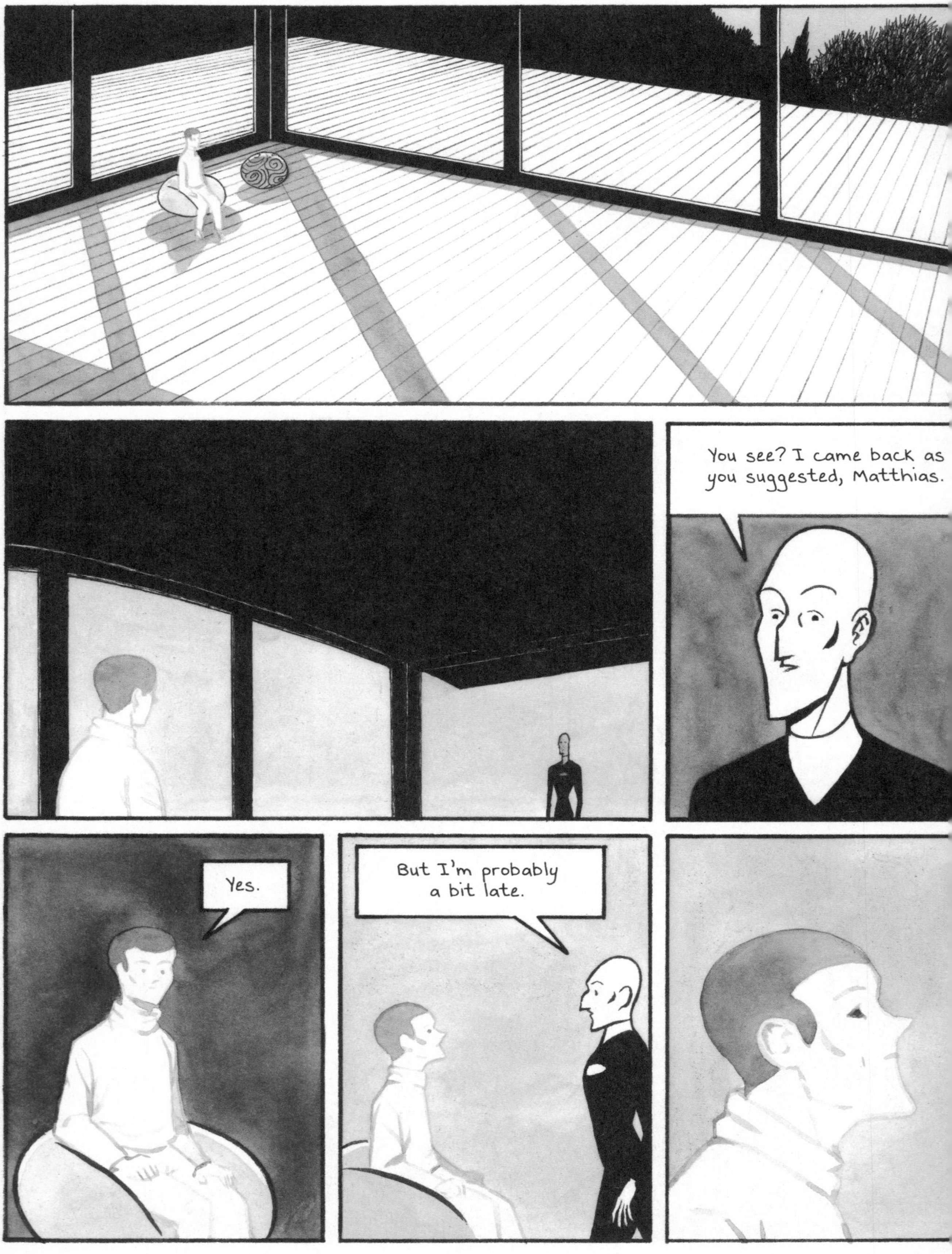

You see? I came back as you suggested, Matthias.
Yes.
But I'm probably a bit late.

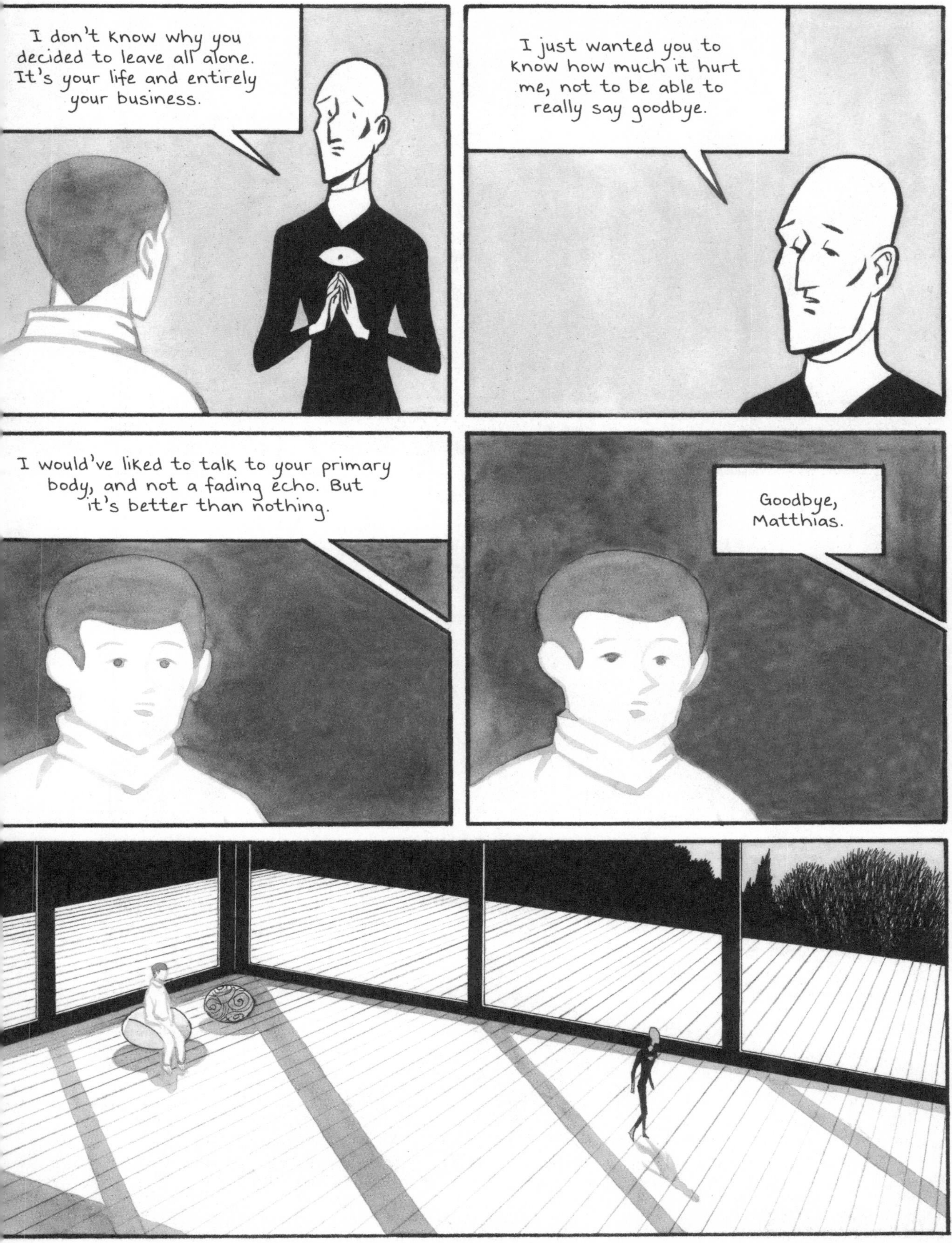
I don't know why you decided to leave all alone. It's your life and entirely your business.
I just wanted you to know how much it hurt me, not to be able to really say goodbye.
I would've liked to talk to your primary body, and not a fading echo. But it's better than nothing.
Goodbye, Matthias.

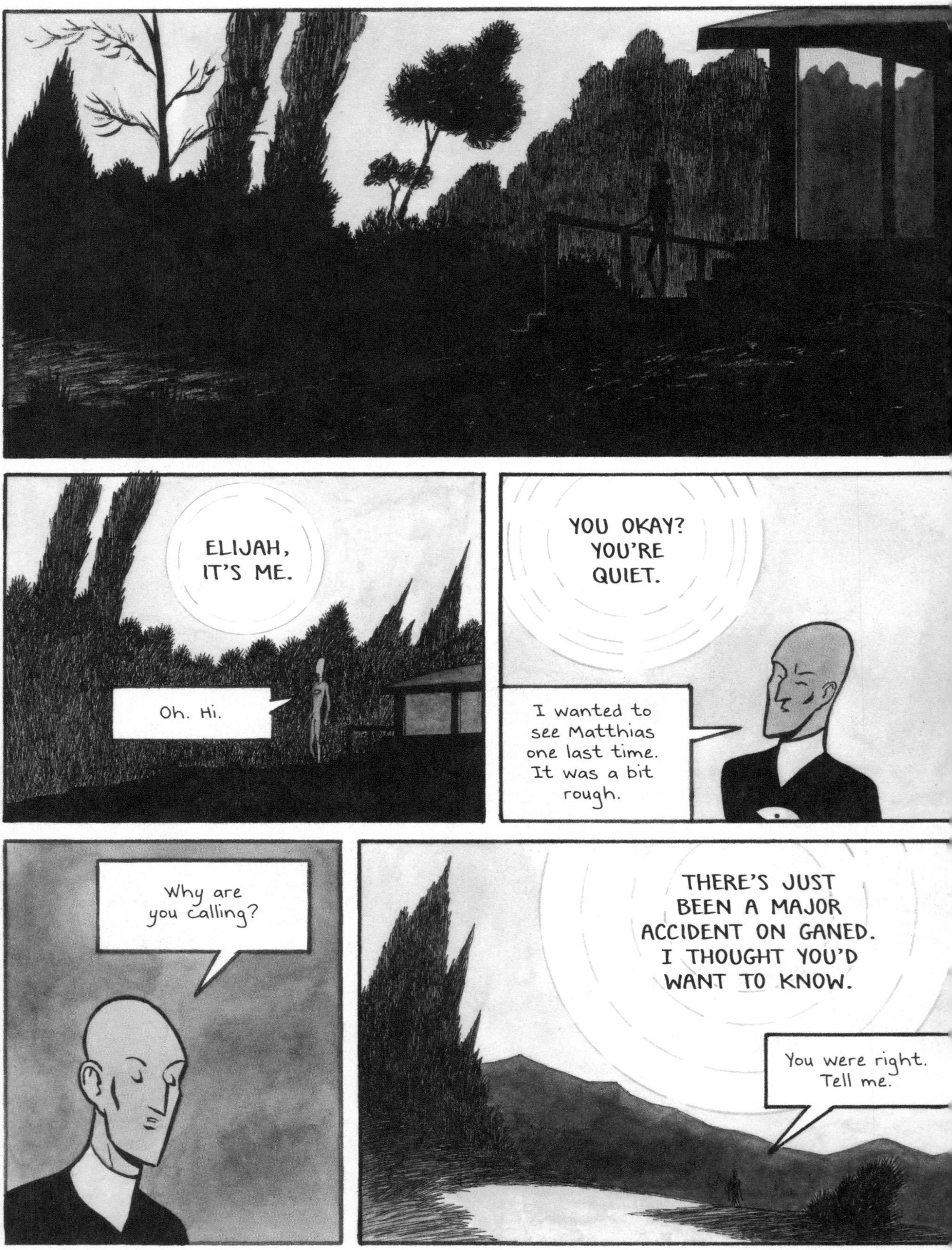
ELIJAH, IT'S ME.
Oh. Hi.
YOU OKAY? YOU'RE QUIET.
I wanted to see Matthias one last time. It was a bit rough.
Why are you calling?
THERE'S JUST BEEN A MAJOR ACCIDENT ON GANED. I THOUGHT YOU'D WANT TO KNOW.
You were right. Tell me.

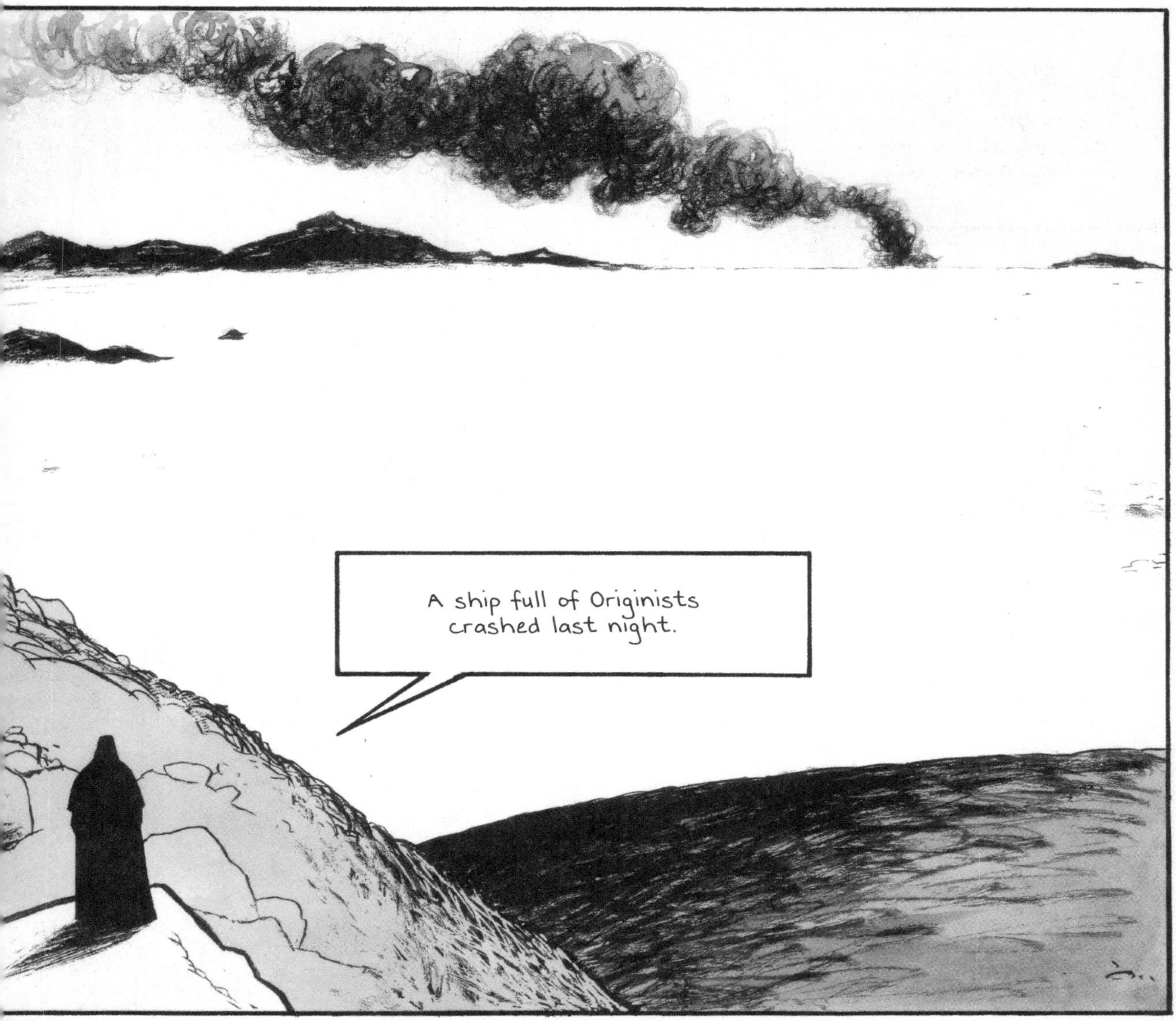
A ship full of Originists crashed last night.

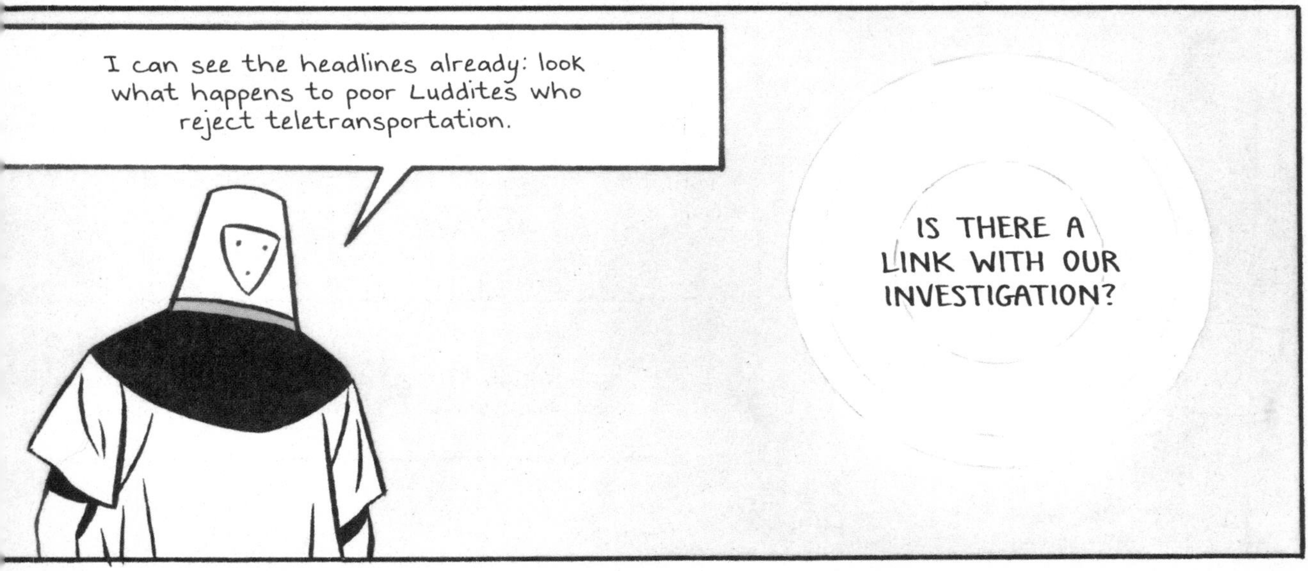
I can see the headlines already: look what happens to poor Luddites who reject teletransportation.
IS THERE A LINK WITH OUR INVESTIGATION?

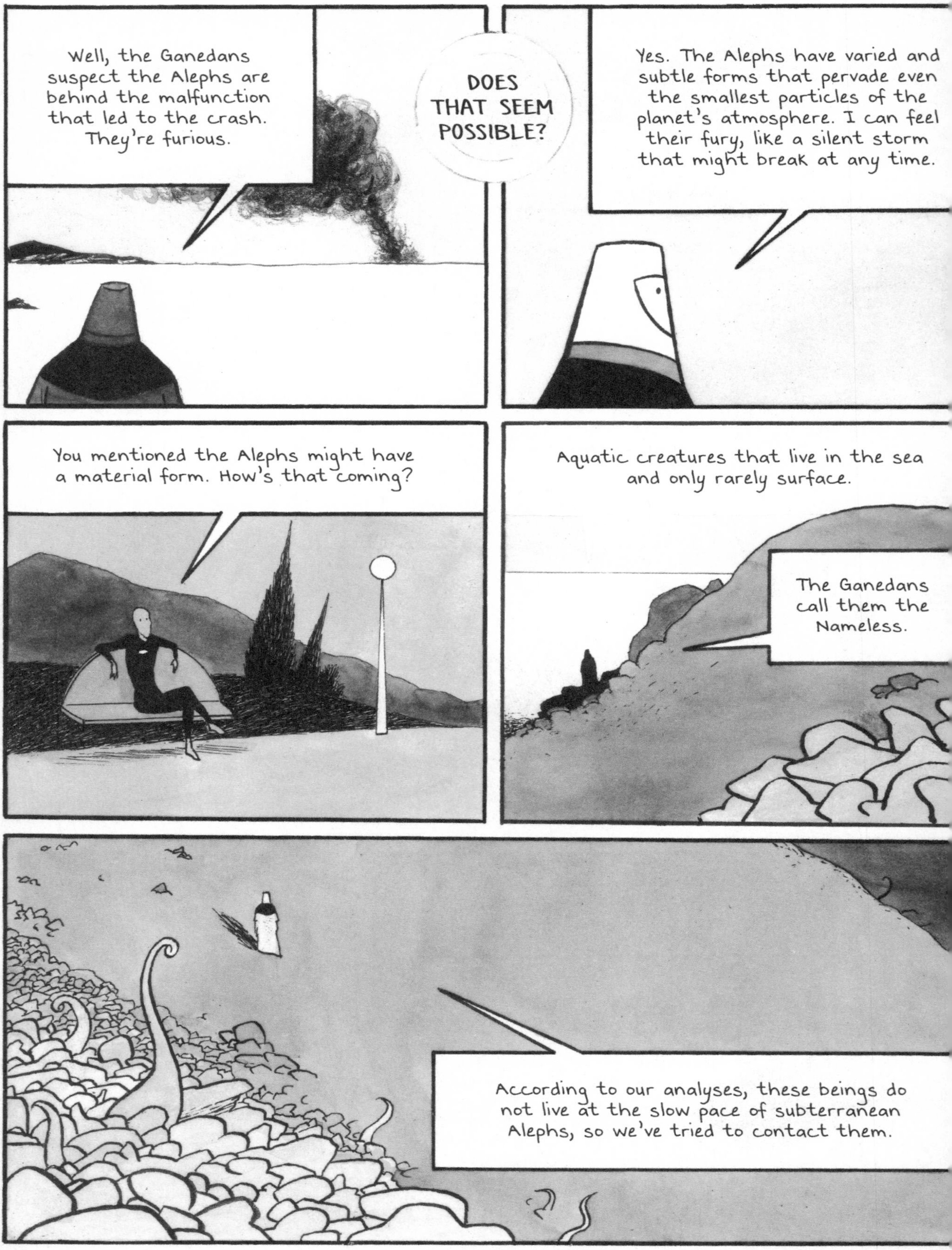

Well, the Ganedans suspect the Alephs are behind the malfunction that led to the crash. They're furious.
DOES THAT SEEM POSSIBLE?
Yes. The Alephs have varied and subtle forms that pervade even the smallest particles of the planet's atmosphere. I can feel their fury, like a silent storm that might break at any time.
You mentioned the Alephs might have a material form. How's that coming?
Aquatic creatures that live in the sea and only rarely surface.
The Ganedans call them the Nameless.
According to our analyses, these beings do not live at the slow pace of subterranean Alephs, so we've tried to contact them.

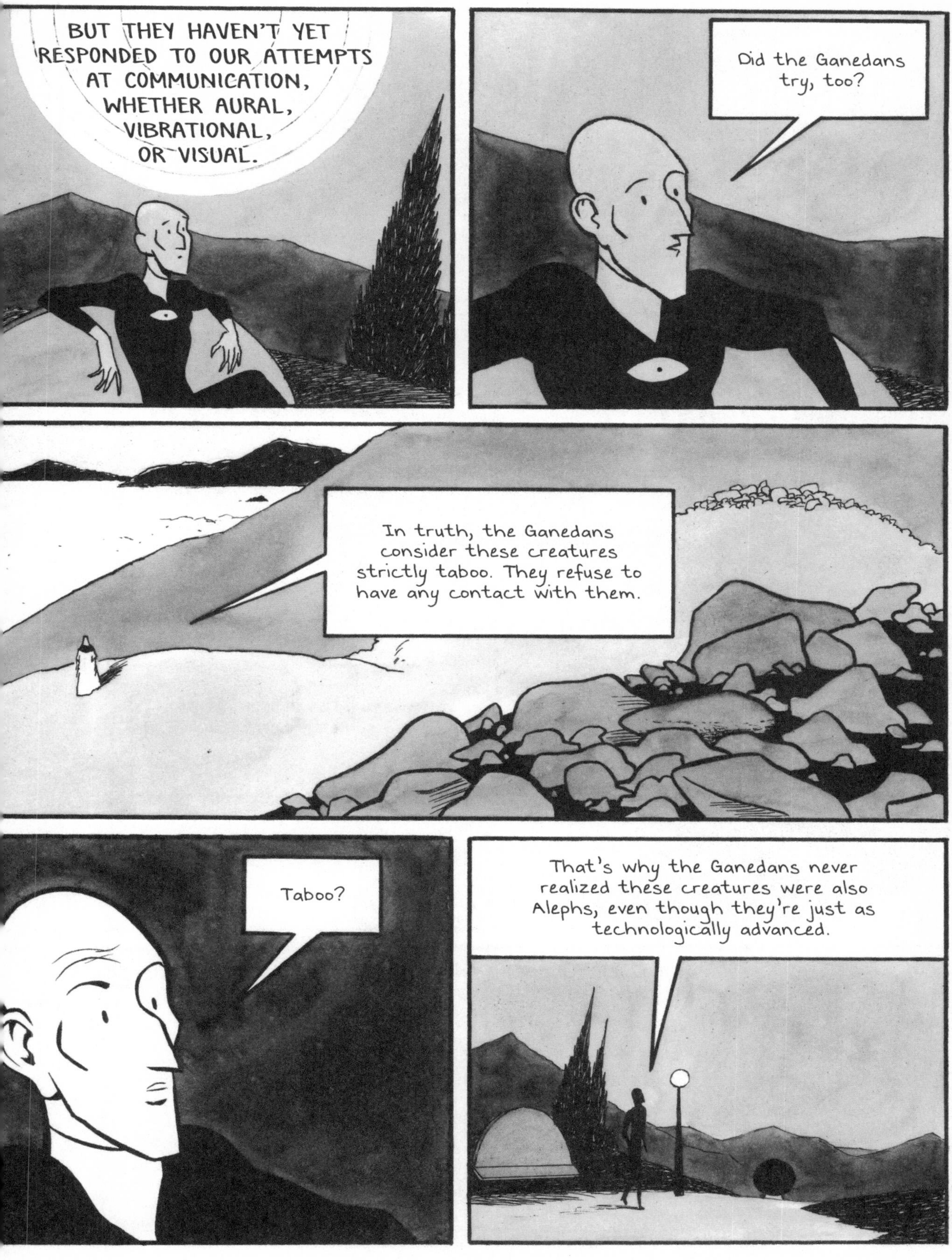
BUT THEY HAVEN'T YET RESPONDED TO OUR ATTEMPTS AT COMMUNICATION, WHETHER AURAL, VIBRATIONAL, OR VISUAL.
Did the Ganedans try, too?
In truth, the Ganedans consider these creatures strictly taboo. They refuse to have any contact with them.
Taboo?
That's why the Ganedans never realized these creatures were also Alephs, even though they're just as technologically advanced.

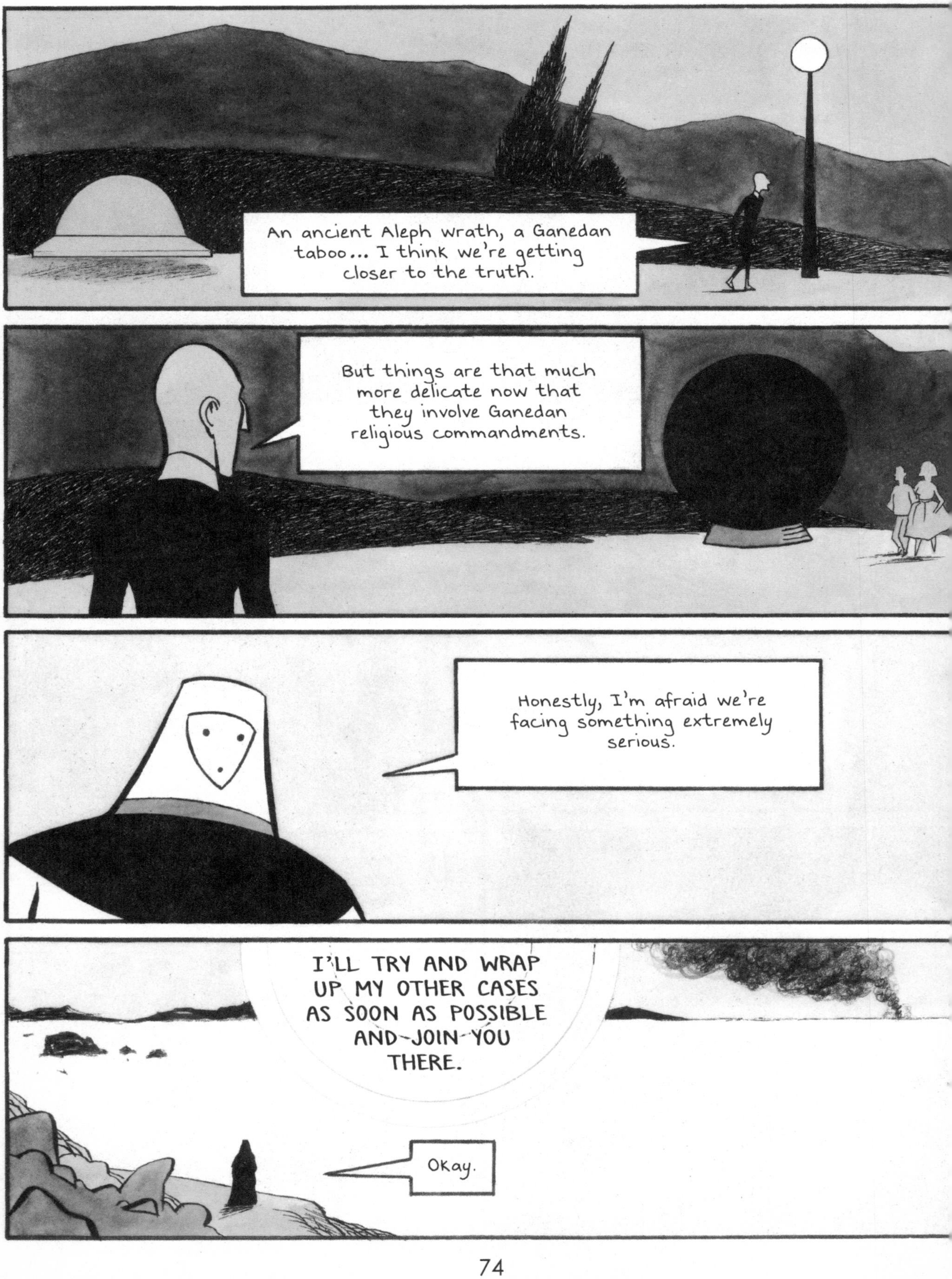
An ancient Aleph wrath, a Ganedan taboo... I think we're getting closer to the truth.
But things are that much more delicate now that they involve Ganedan religious commandments.
Honestly, I'm afraid we're facing something extremely serious.
I'LL TRY AND WRAP UP MY OTHER CASES AS SOON AS POSSIBLE AND JOIN YOU THERE.
Okay.

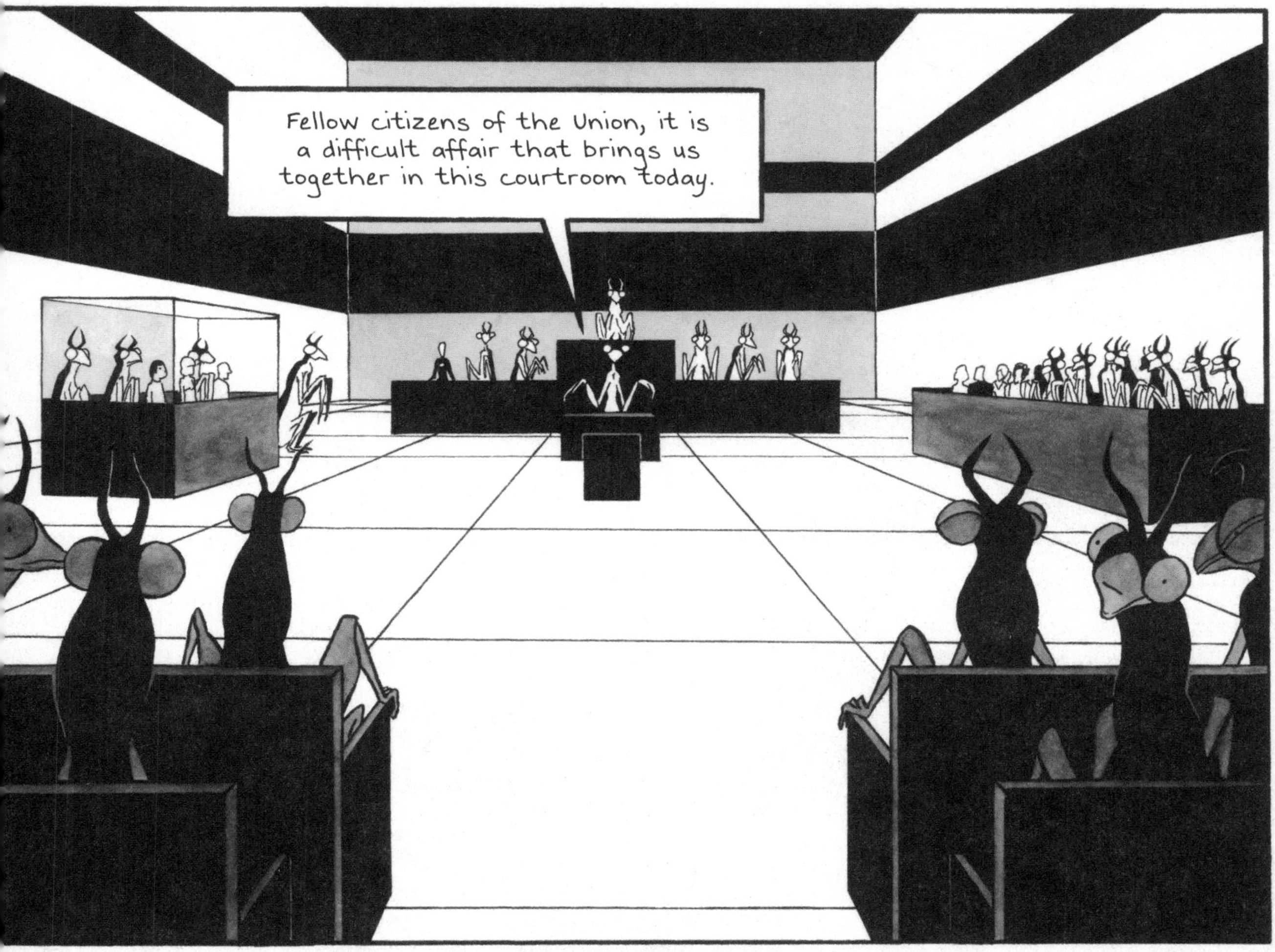
Fellow citizens of the Union, it is a difficult affair that brings us together in this courtroom today.

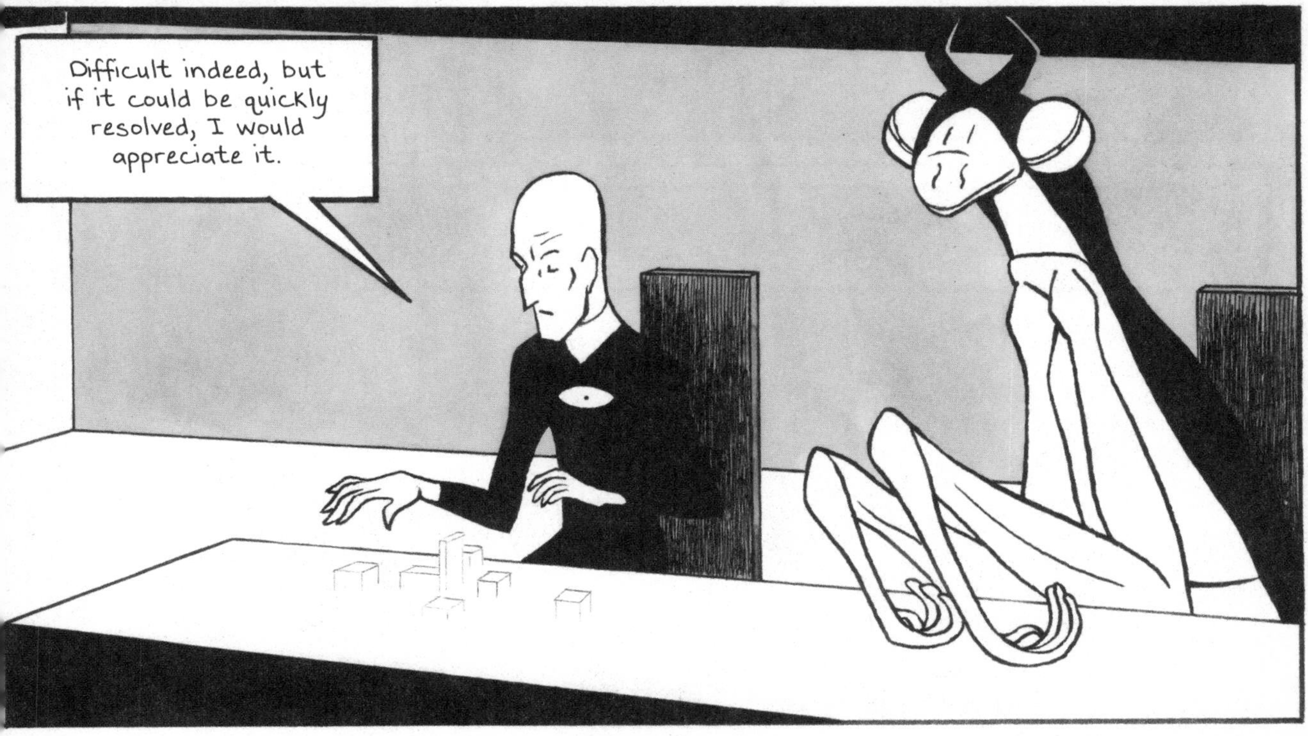
Difficult indeed, but if it could be quickly resolved, I would appreciate it.

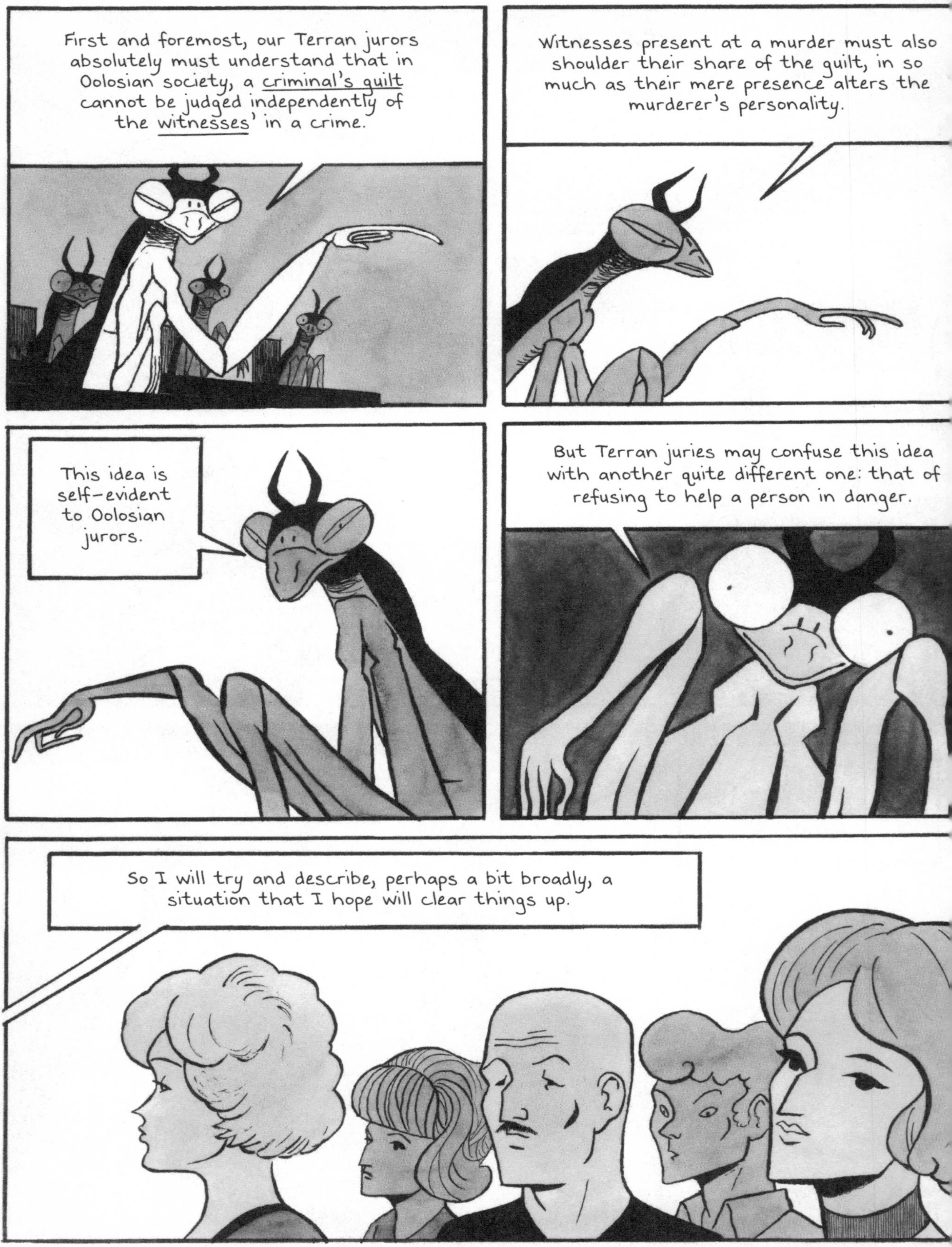
First and foremost, our Terran jurors absolutely must understand that in Oolosian society, a criminal's guilt cannot be judged independently of the witnesses' in a crime.
Witnesses present at a murder must also shoulder their share of the guilt, in so much as their mere presence alters the murderer's personality.
This idea is self-evident to Oolosian jurors.
But Terran juries may confuse this idea with another quite different one: that of refusing to help a person in danger.
So I will try and describe, perhaps a bit broadly, a situation that I hope will clear things up.

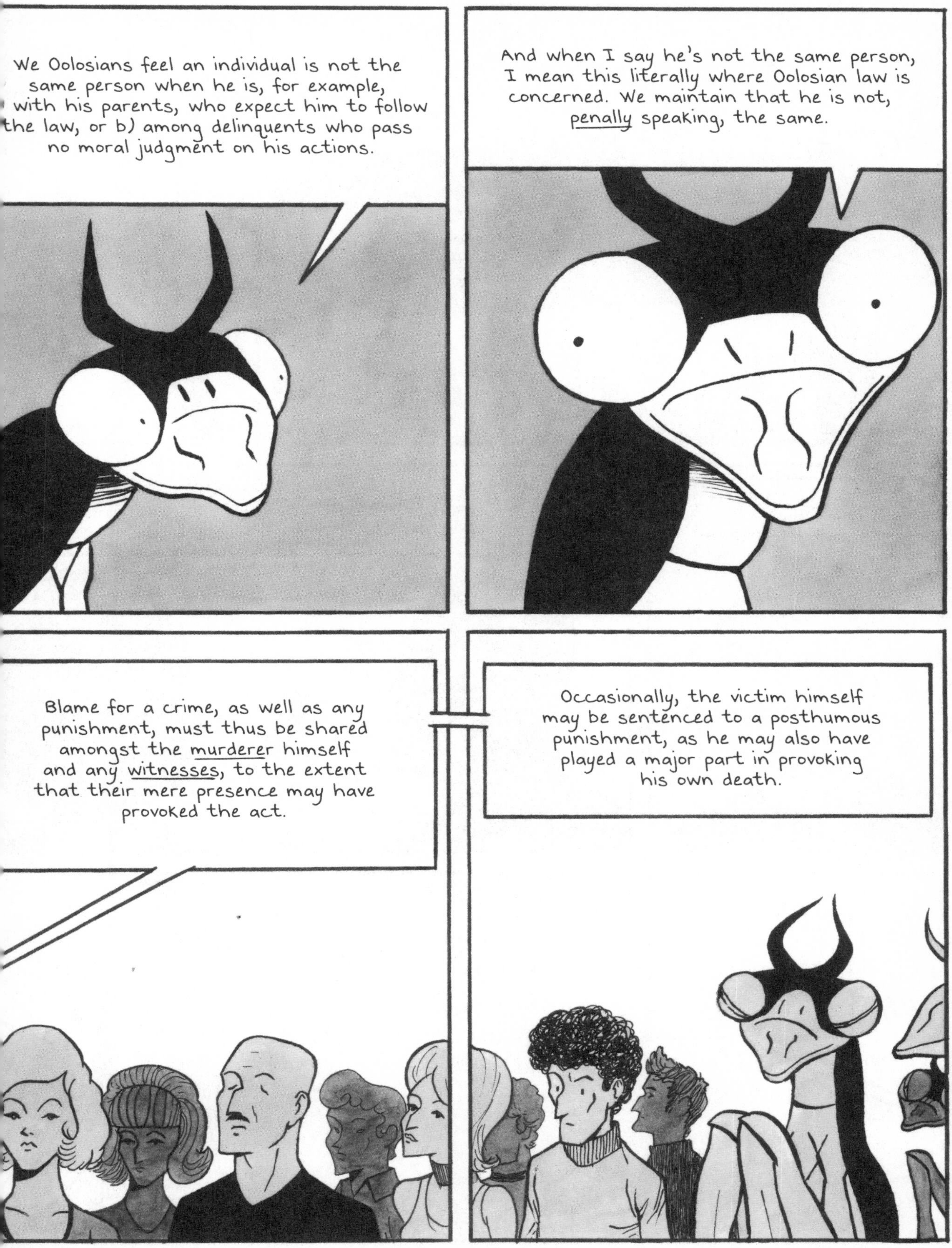
We Oolosians feel an individual is not the same person when he is, for example, with his parents, who expect him to follow the law, or b) among delinquents who pass no moral judgment on his actions.
And when I say he's not the same person, I mean this literally where Oolosian law is concerned. We maintain that he is not, penally speaking, the same.
Blame for a crime, as well as any punishment, must thus be shared amongst the murderer himself and any witnesses, to the extent that their mere presence may have provoked the act.
Occasionally, the victim himself may be sentenced to a posthumous punishment, as he may also have played a major part in provoking his own death.

In the affair that convenes us today, the murderer is a Terran who acted on our planet, before Terran <u>and</u> Oolosian witnesses. We were thus forced to select a jury that was also mixed.

Yes? You wish to speak?

I... don't get it.

That's to be expected. For that reason, a Terran expert from the Philosophical Police was summoned to this court to answer your questions.

I move we take a recess.

Oh, brother...

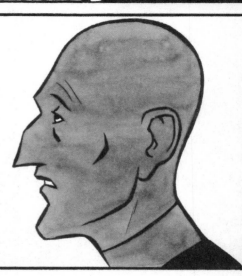

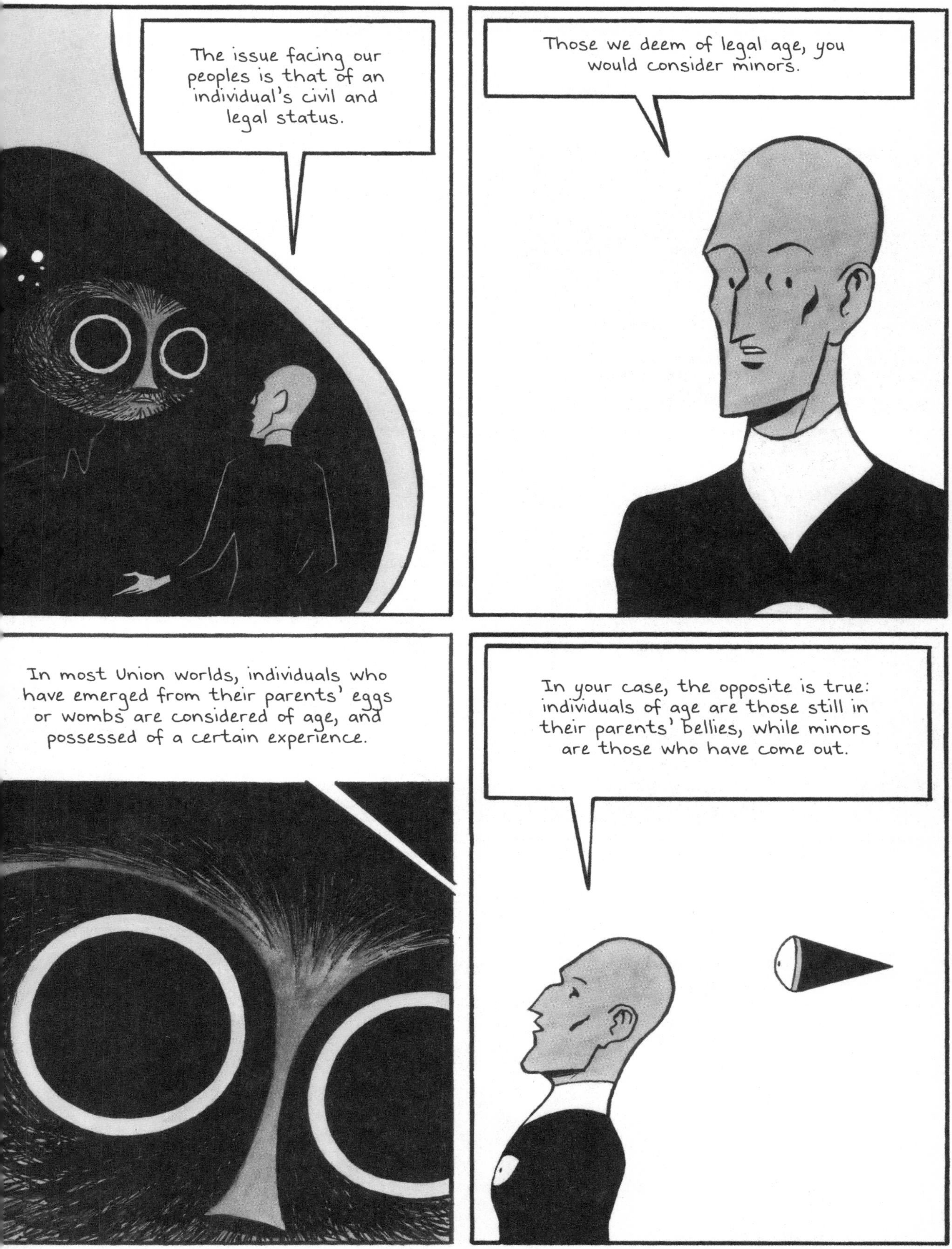

The issue facing our peoples is that of an individual's civil and legal status.
Those we deem of legal age, you would consider minors.
In most Union worlds, individuals who have emerged from their parents' eggs or wombs are considered of age, and possessed of a certain experience.
In your case, the opposite is true: individuals of age are those still in their parents' bellies, while minors are those who have come out.

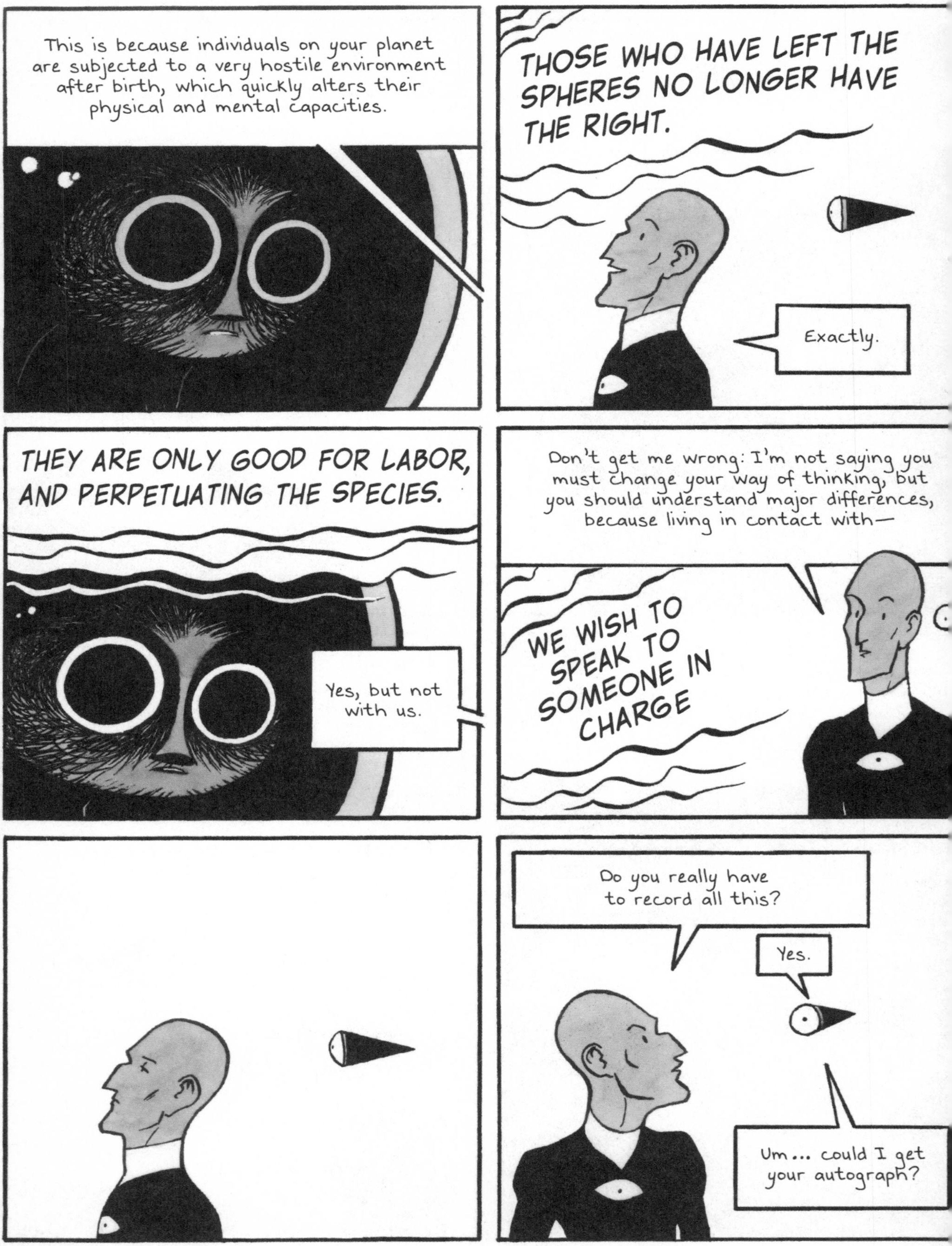

This is because individuals on your planet are subjected to a very hostile environment after birth, which quickly alters their physical and mental capacities.
THOSE WHO HAVE LEFT THE SPHERES NO LONGER HAVE THE RIGHT.
Exactly.
THEY ARE ONLY GOOD FOR LABOR, AND PERPETUATING THE SPECIES.
Yes, but not with us.
Don't get me wrong: I'm not saying you must change your way of thinking, but you should understand major differences, because living in contact with—
WE WISH TO SPEAK TO SOMEONE IN CHARGE
Do you really have to record all this?
Yes.
Um... could I get your autograph?

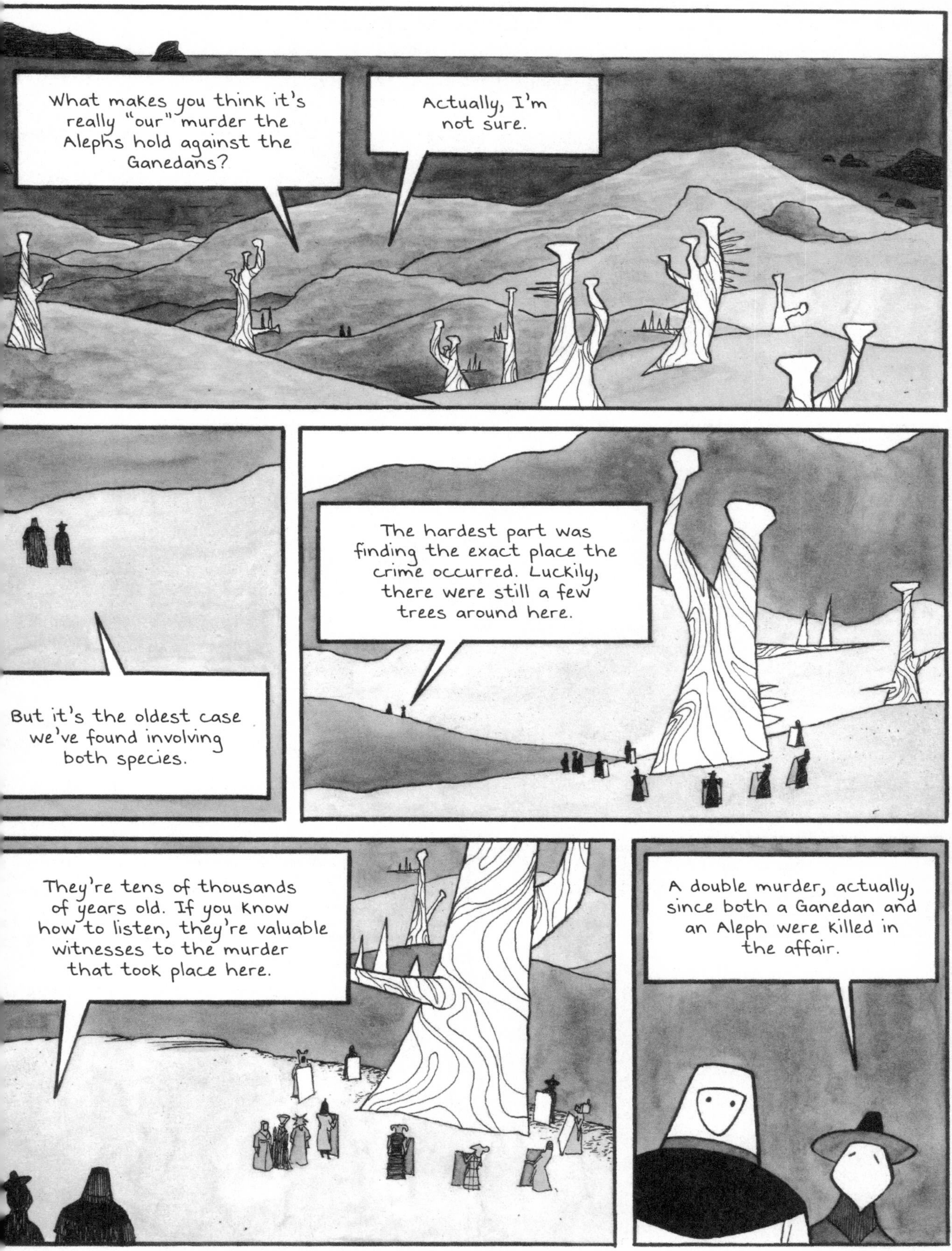
What makes you think it's really "our" murder the Alephs hold against the Ganedans?
Actually, I'm not sure.
But it's the oldest case we've found involving both species.
The hardest part was finding the exact place the crime occurred. Luckily, there were still a few trees around here.
They're tens of thousands of years old. If you know how to listen, they're valuable witnesses to the murder that took place here.
A double murder, actually, since both a Ganedan and an Aleph were killed in the affair.

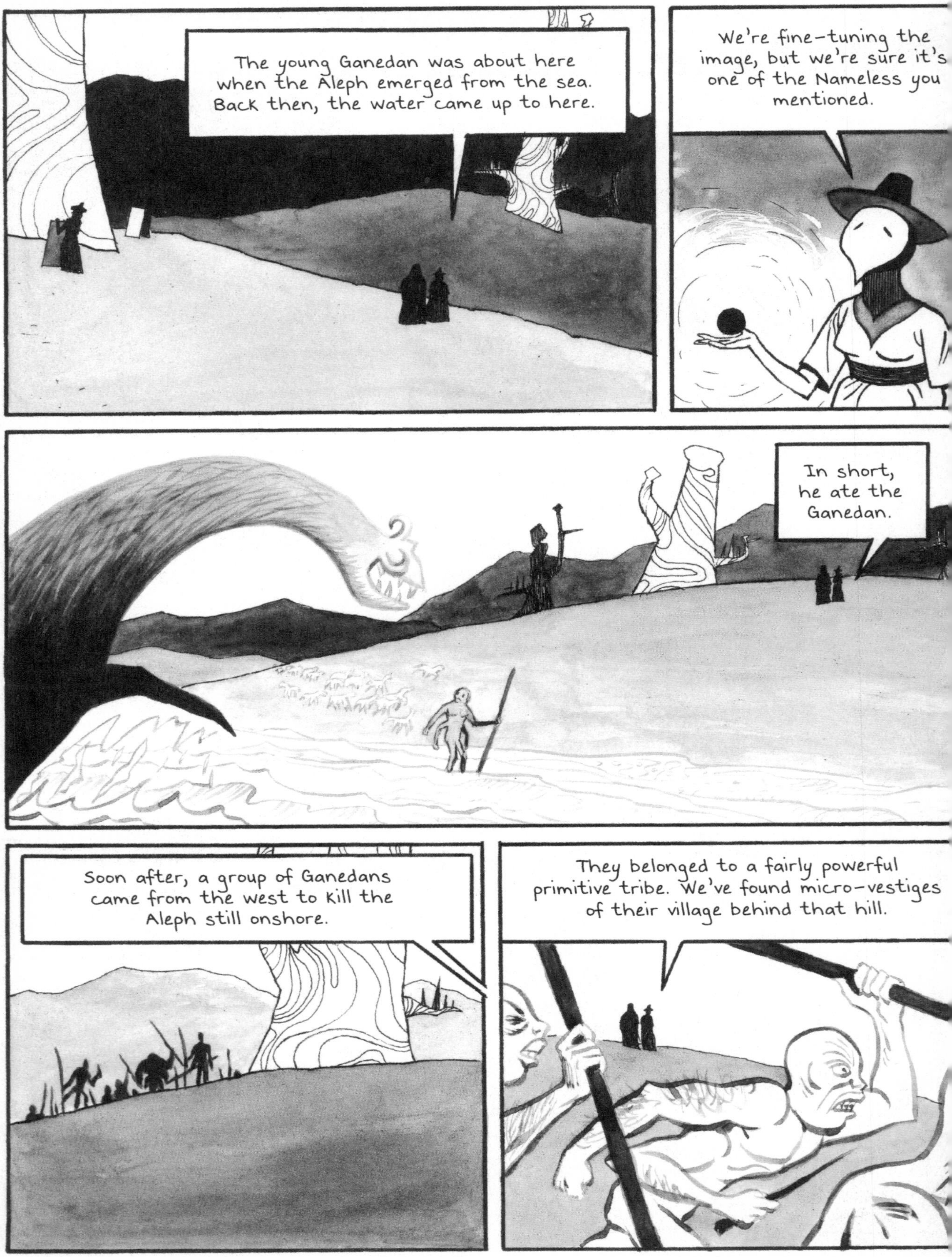
The young Ganedan was about here when the Aleph emerged from the sea. Back then, the water came up to here.
We're fine-tuning the image, but we're sure it's one of the Nameless you mentioned.
In short, he ate the Ganedan.
Soon after, a group of Ganedans came from the west to kill the Aleph still onshore.
They belonged to a fairly powerful primitive tribe. We've found micro-vestiges of their village behind that hill.

Several clans had united under the aegis of a highly respected chief named Faer.

Also known as King Faerela in Ganedan history texts.

That's him. Founder of the Faerelian dynasty.

He came to avenge the death of his son, "devoured by the Nameless demon." The Ganedans still re-enact it every year with great pomp. That's why these sea creatures have become taboo.

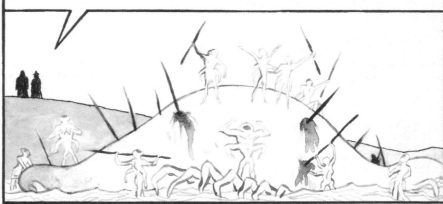

A demon who was, in reality, an Aleph in material form.

Yup!

This is the ur-event, the one most rituals on this planet have been founded on for thousands of years.

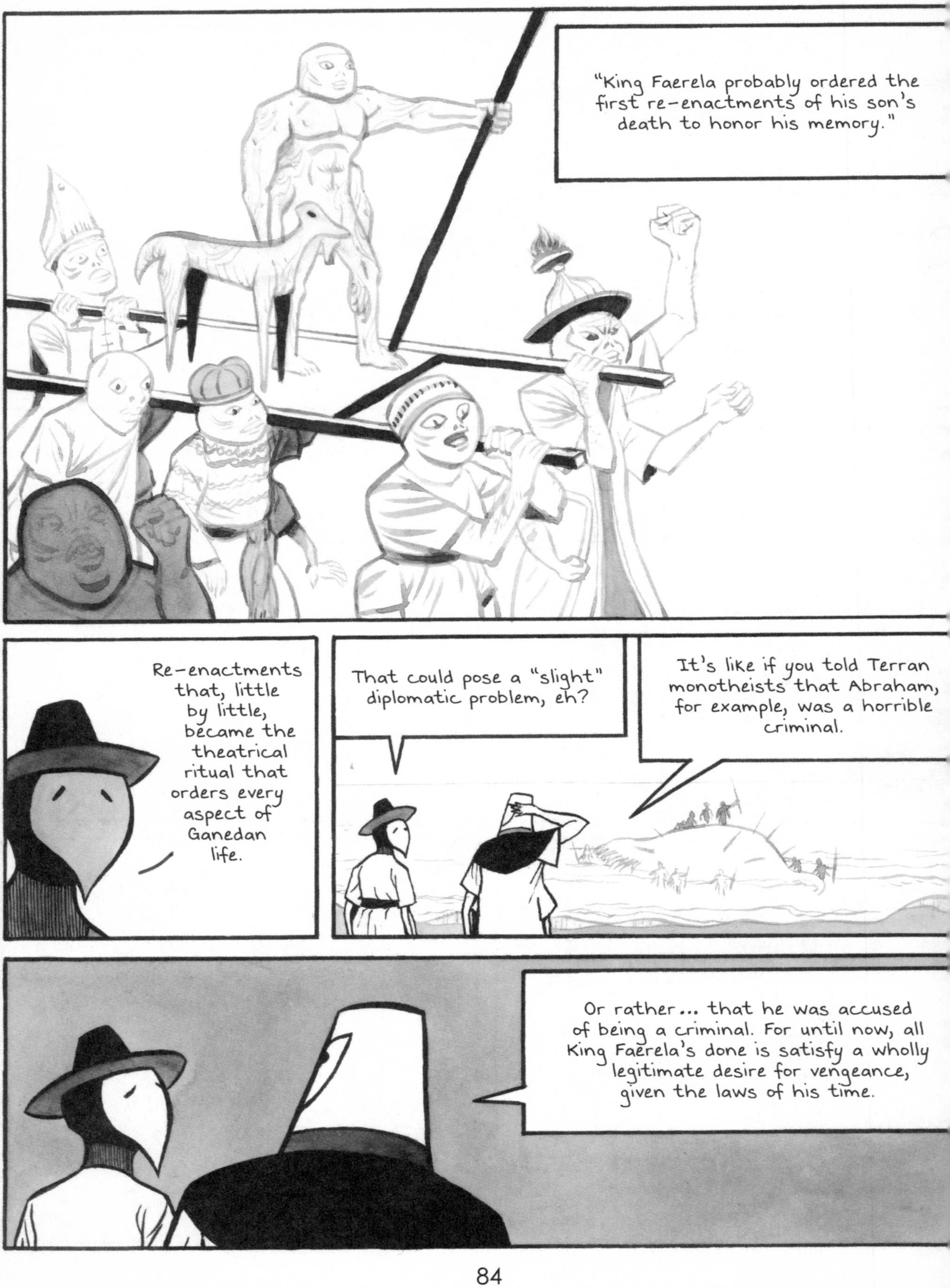
"King Faerela probably ordered the first re-enactments of his son's death to honor his memory."
Re-enactments that, little by little, became the theatrical ritual that orders every aspect of Ganedan life.
That could pose a "slight" diplomatic problem, eh?
It's like if you told Terran monotheists that Abraham, for example, was a horrible criminal.
Or rather... that he was accused of being a criminal. For until now, all King Faërela's done is satisfy a wholly legitimate desire for vengeance, given the laws of his time.

Well, revenge like that wouldn't seem so legitimate to the Alephs.

What we must try to understand is why that Aleph ate that Ganedan.

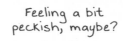

Feeling a bit peckish, maybe?

No, no... according to the Universal Encyclopedia, at that time the Alephs already possessed more than enough intelligence to recognize another sentient being.

The Encyclopedia's limits are well known—

Yes, it can be very vague when it comes to civilizations radically different from our own.

It is more important than ever that we communicate with the Alephs.

I hope Elijah can come soon. I'll really need his help.

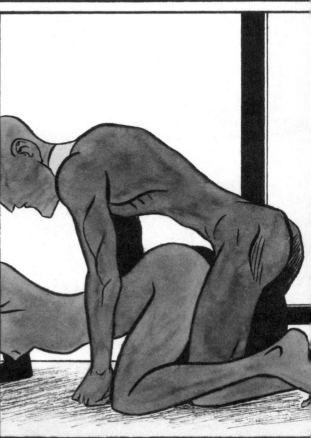

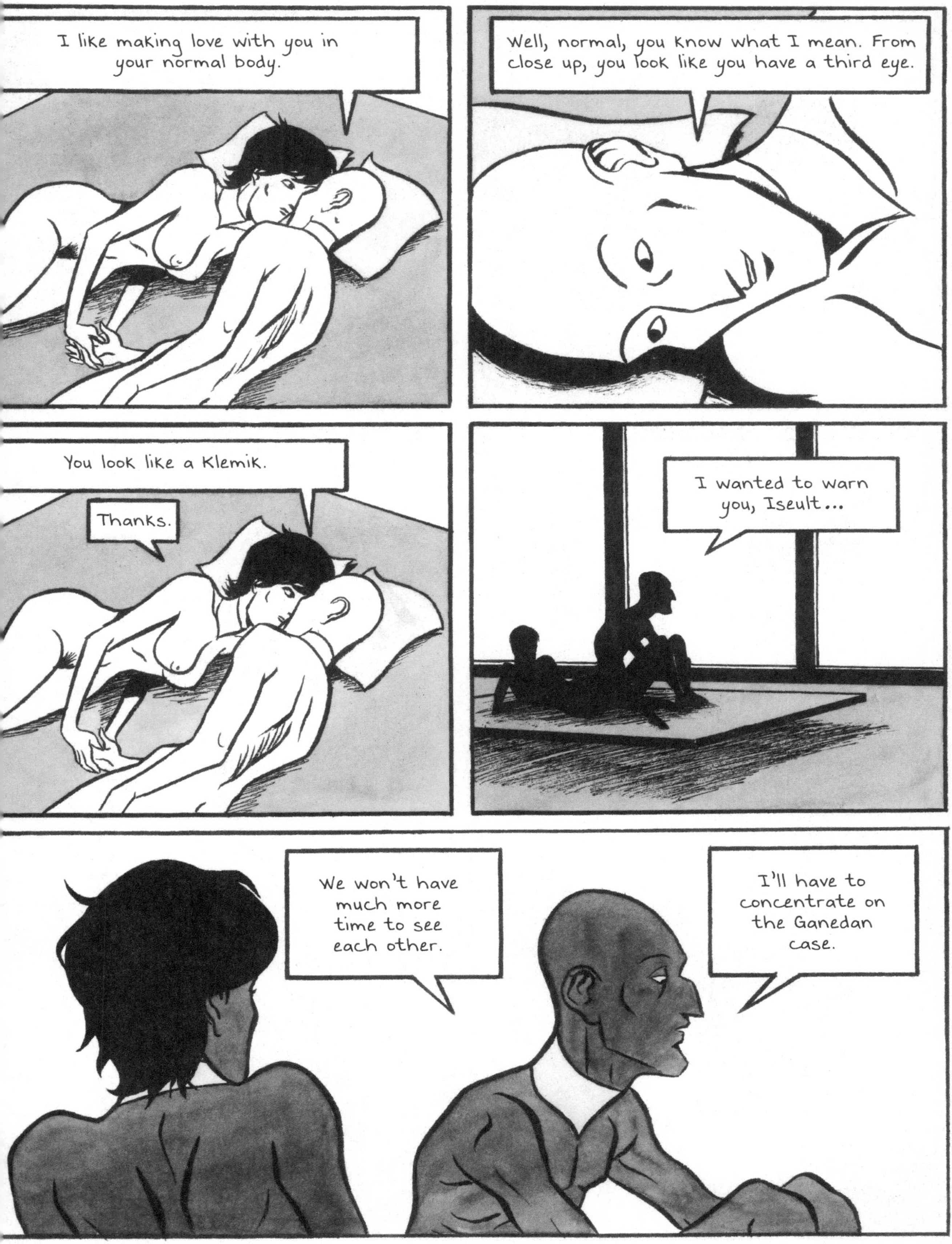
I like making love with you in your normal body.
Well, normal, you know what I mean. From close up, you look like you have a third eye.
You look like a Klemik.
Thanks.
I wanted to warn you, Iseult...
We won't have much more time to see each other.
I'll have to concentrate on the Ganedan case.

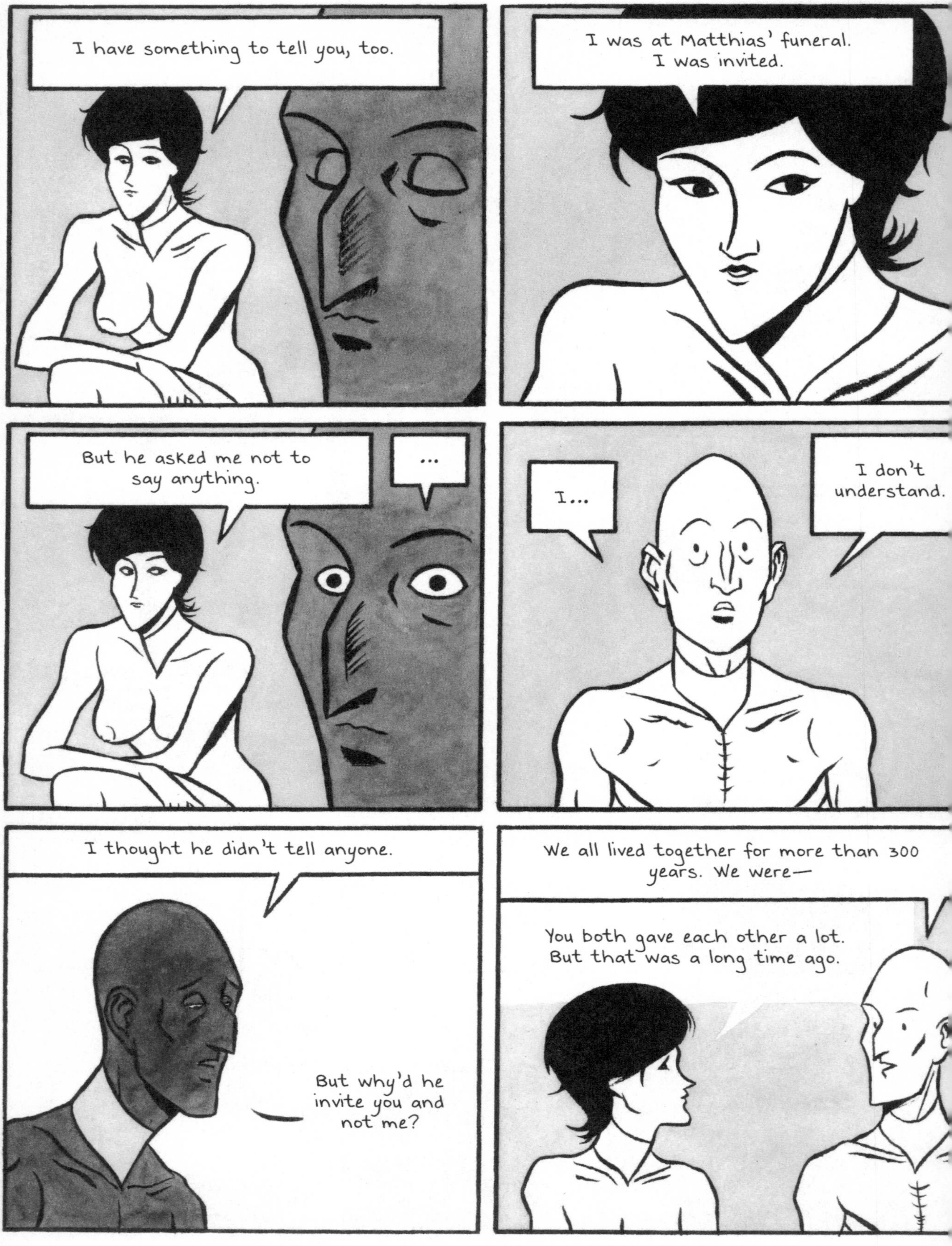
I have something to tell you, too.
I was at Matthias' funeral. I was invited.
But he asked me not to say anything.
...
I...
I don't understand.
I thought he didn't tell anyone.
But why'd he invite you and not me?
We all lived together for more than 300 years. We were—
You both gave each other a lot. But that was a long time ago.

What did I do to make him hate me so much?

Nothing. I'm sure you didn't do anything. You're too careful for that.

But you took different paths, met other people... He didn't need your "wise advice" anymore. And you had less time to give him, even if he was your best student.

He meant a lot more to me than that! He was like a brother!

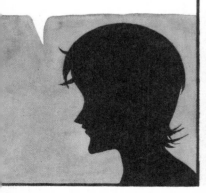

Perhaps. But sometimes, even brothers don't have much to share with each other anymore, besides memories.

And memories, well— even the dearest ones disappear as our echoes bring us whole new avenues of life that erase the ones before.

It was something that made Matthias angry... at you. But also at himself, I think.

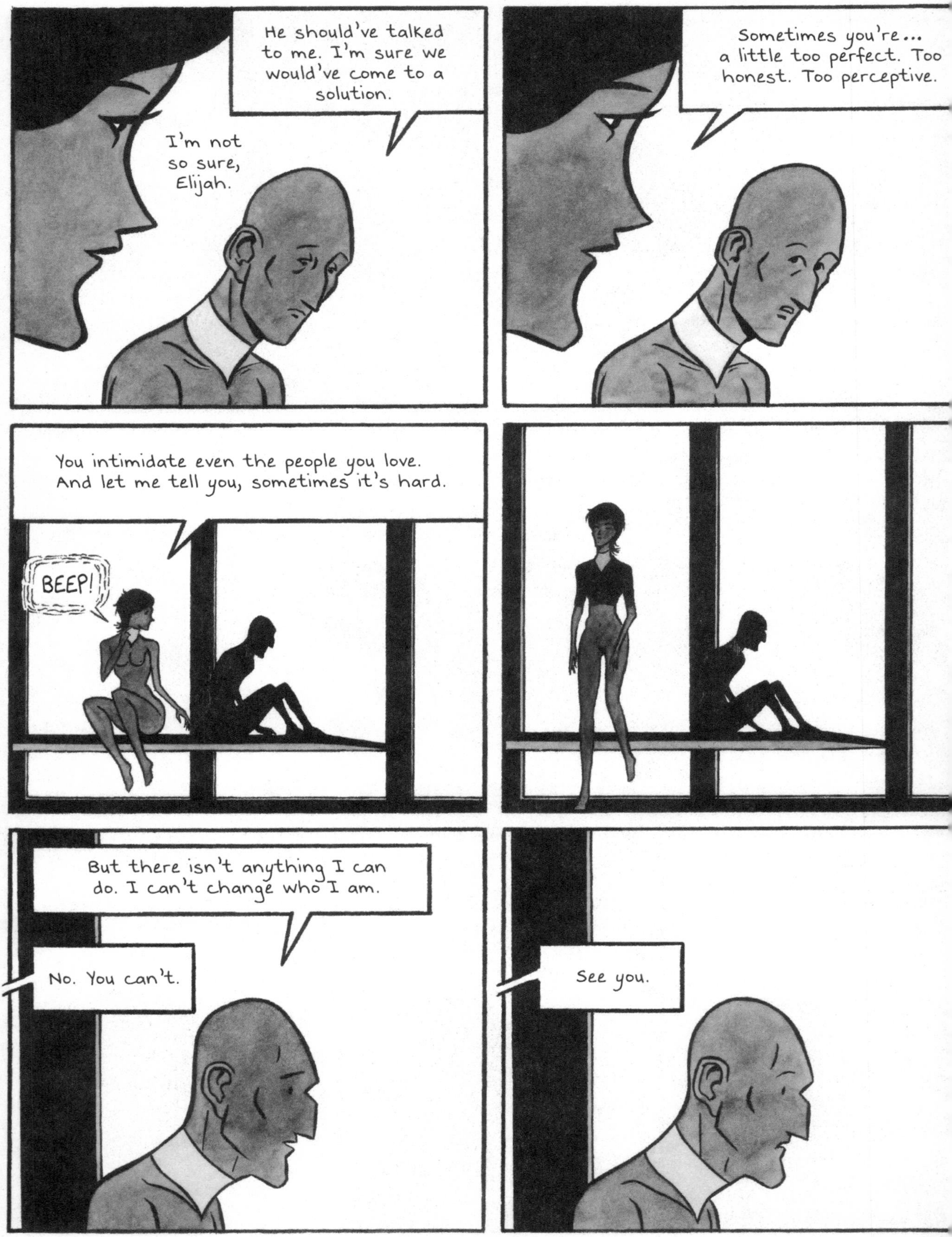
He should've talked to me. I'm sure we would've come to a solution.
I'm not so sure, Elijah.
Sometimes you're... a little too perfect. Too honest. Too perceptive.
You intimidate even the people you love. And let me tell you, sometimes it's hard.
BEEP!
But there isn't anything I can do. I can't change who I am.
No. You can't.
See you.

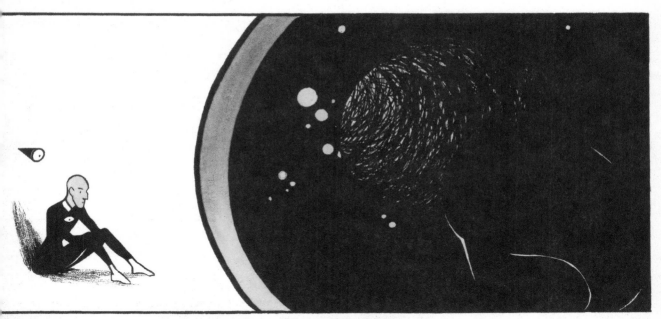

SIR.
SOMETHING
SERIOUS HAS
OCCURRED.

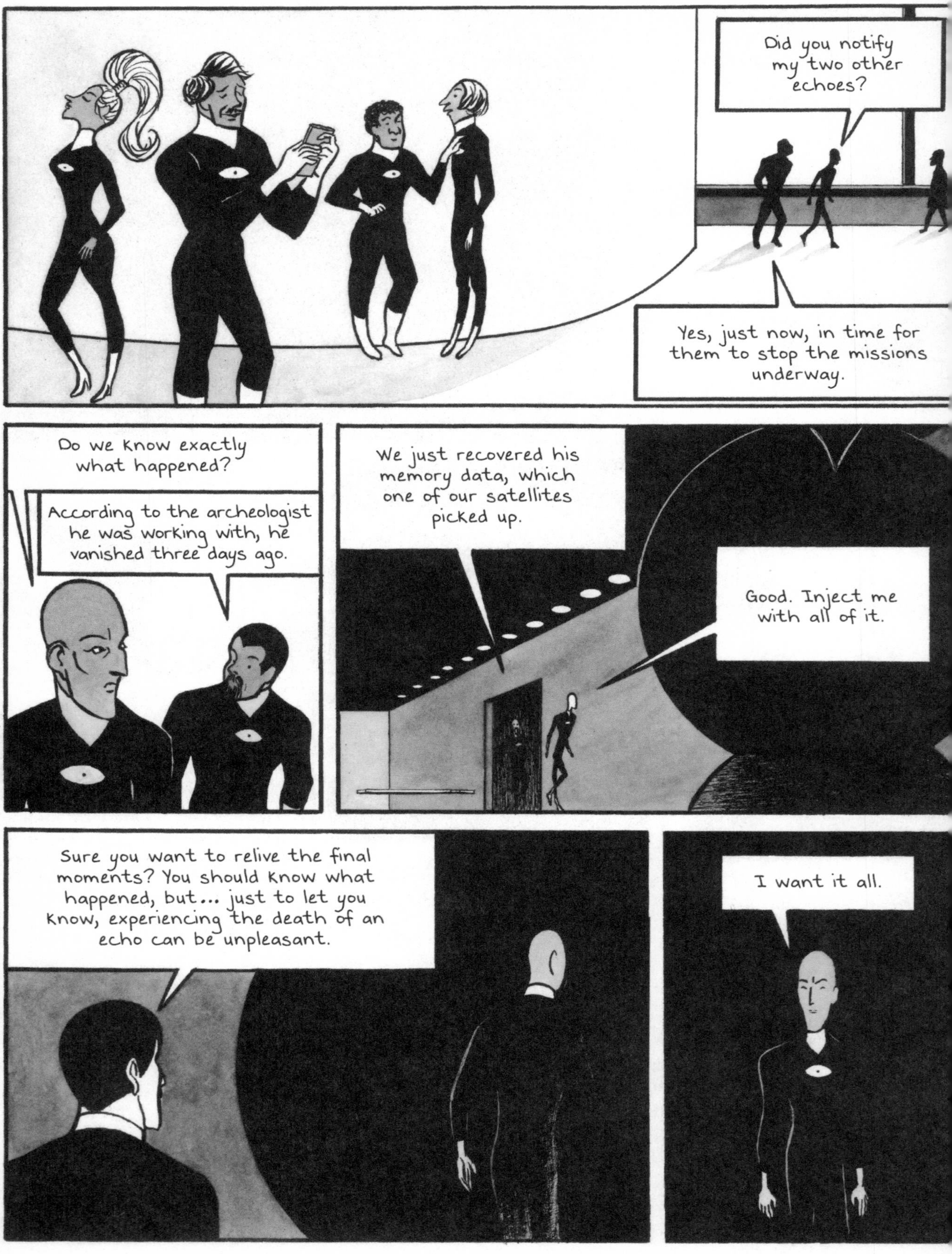
Did you notify my two other echoes?
Yes, just now, in time for them to stop the missions underway.
Do we know exactly what happened?
According to the archeologist he was working with, he vanished three days ago.
We just recovered his memory data, which one of our satellites picked up.
Good. Inject me with all of it.
Sure you want to relive the final moments? You should know what happened, but... just to let you know, experiencing the death of an echo can be unpleasant.
I want it all.

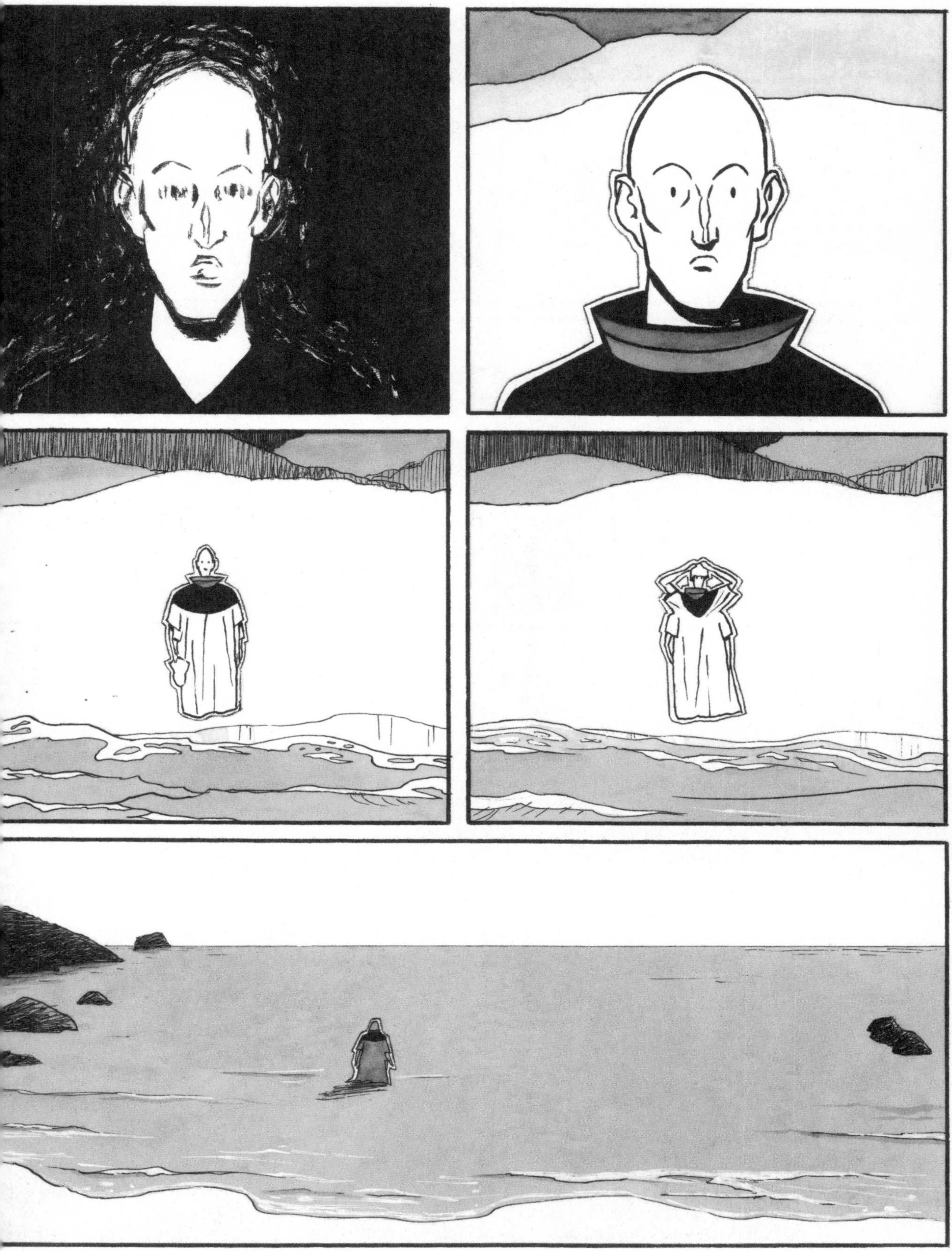

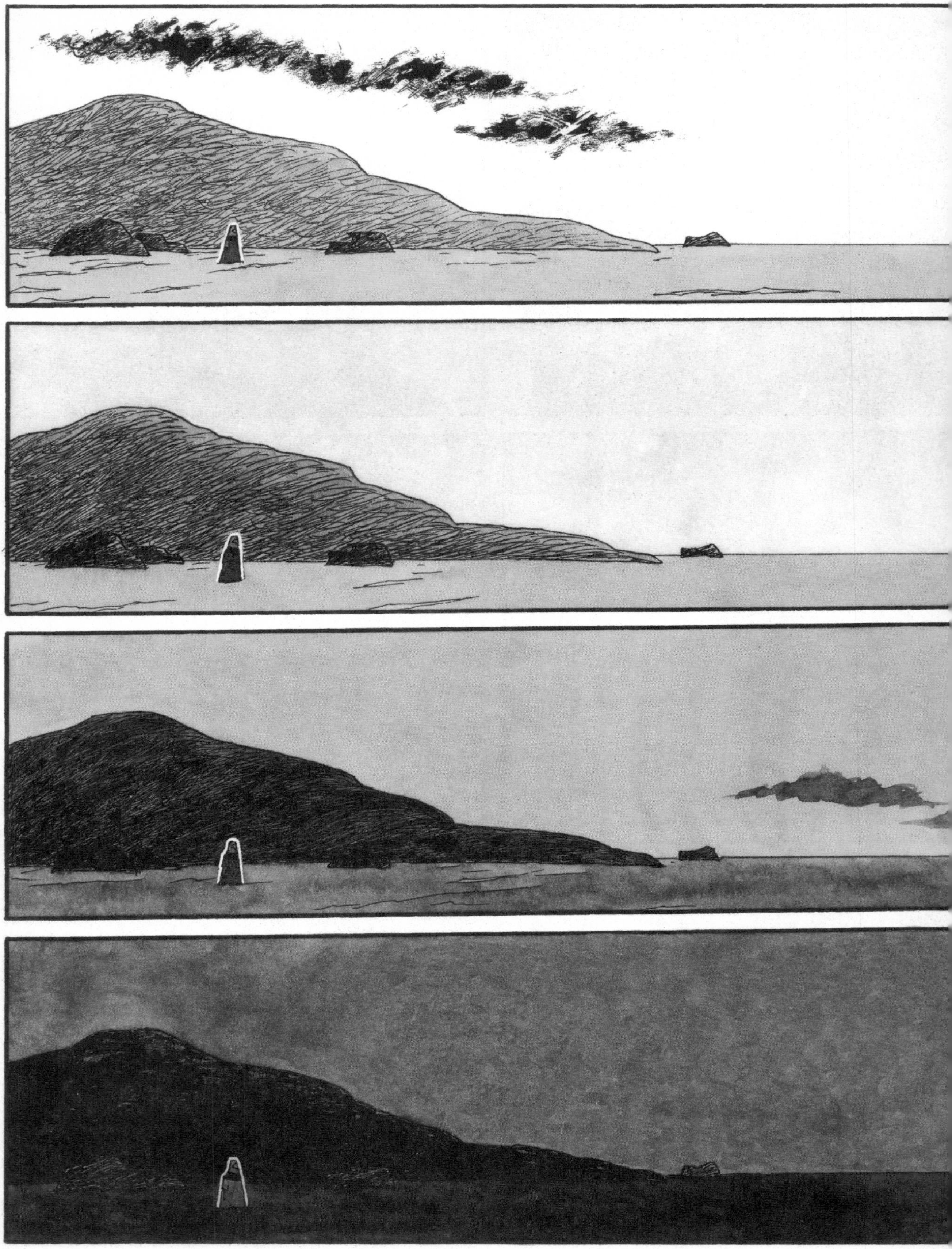

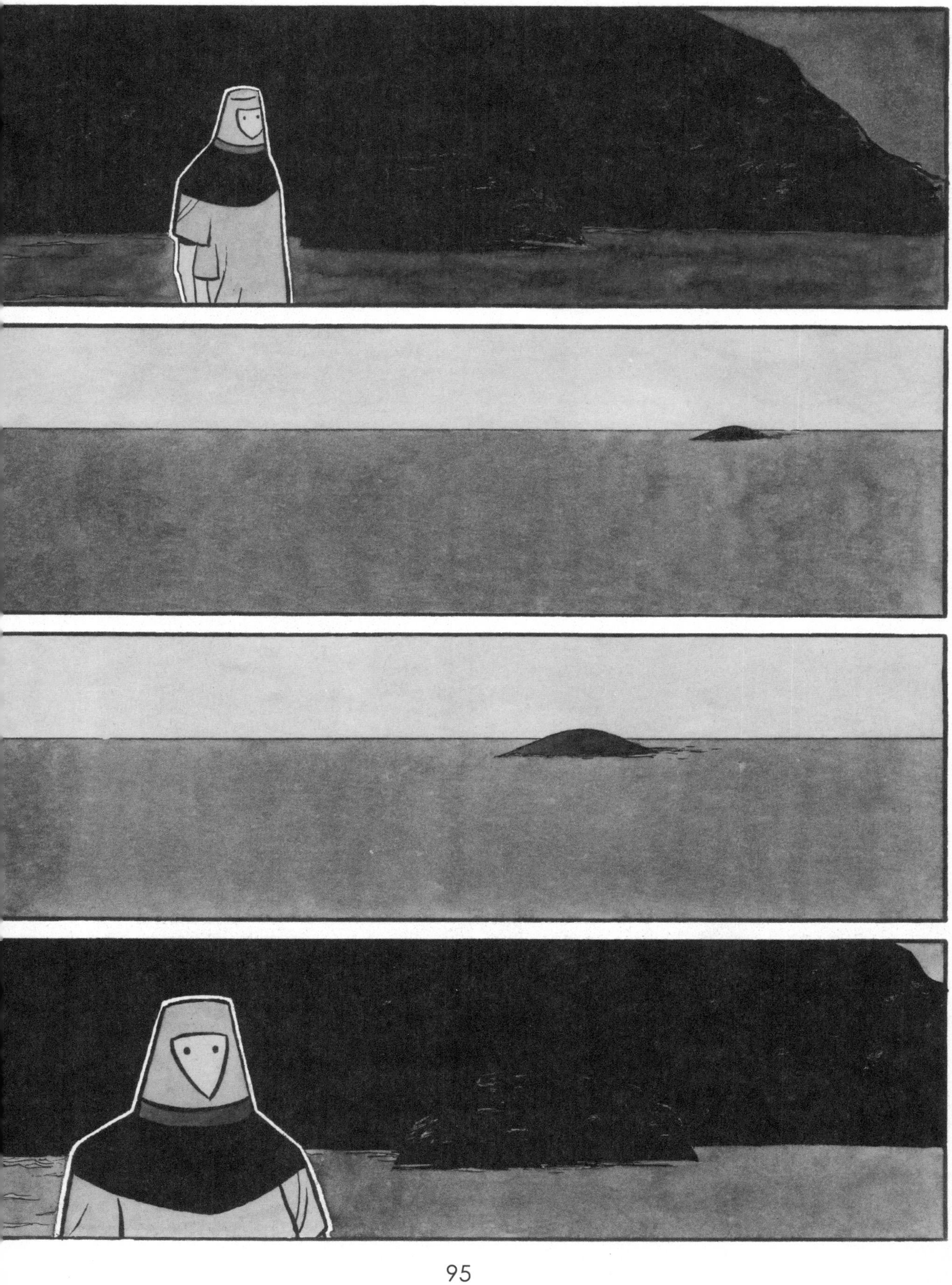

I don't mean you any harm.
I just want to talk to you.

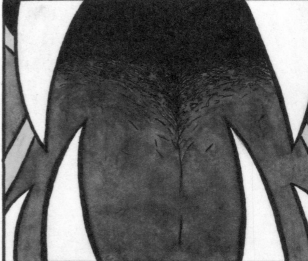

"My colleague was right. The next part was unpleasant."

Horrifying, even.

The Aleph kept me in his mouth for a long time, turning me this way and that with his tongue, to find the best way of opening my "carapace."

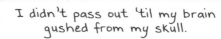

I didn't pass out 'til my brain gushed from my skull.

Then he started biting down with extraordinary force, until my suit burst open. It was so powerful the magnetic force field I'd activated couldn't resist.

I never expected such an outburst of fury. I just wanted to try a new, more direct approach, without machines. Not a good idea.

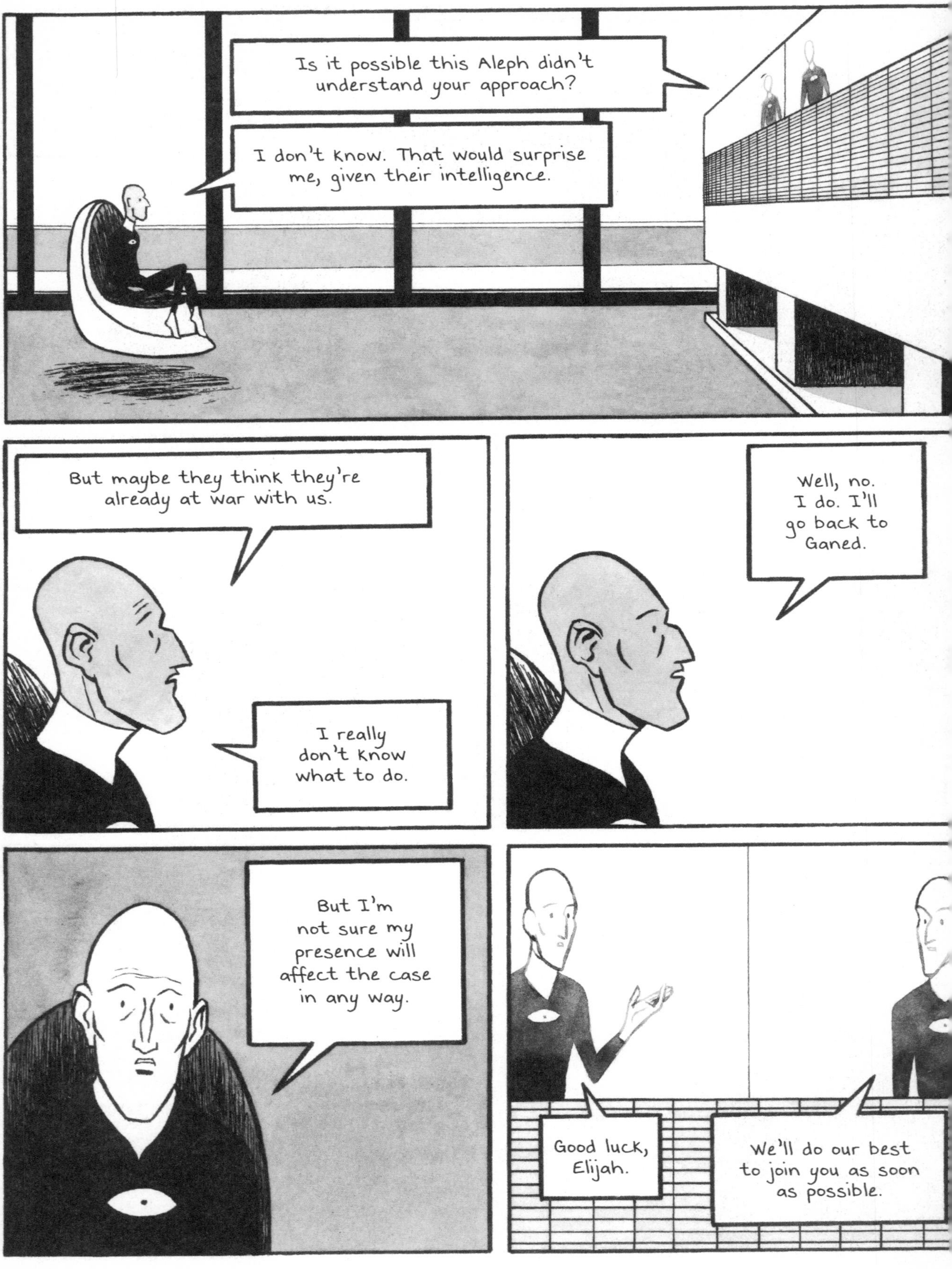
Is it possible this Aleph didn't understand your approach?
I don't know. That would surprise me, given their intelligence.
But maybe they think they're already at war with us.
I really don't know what to do.
Well, no. I do. I'll go back to Ganed.
But I'm not sure my presence will affect the case in any way.
Good luck, Elijah.
We'll do our best to join you as soon as possible.

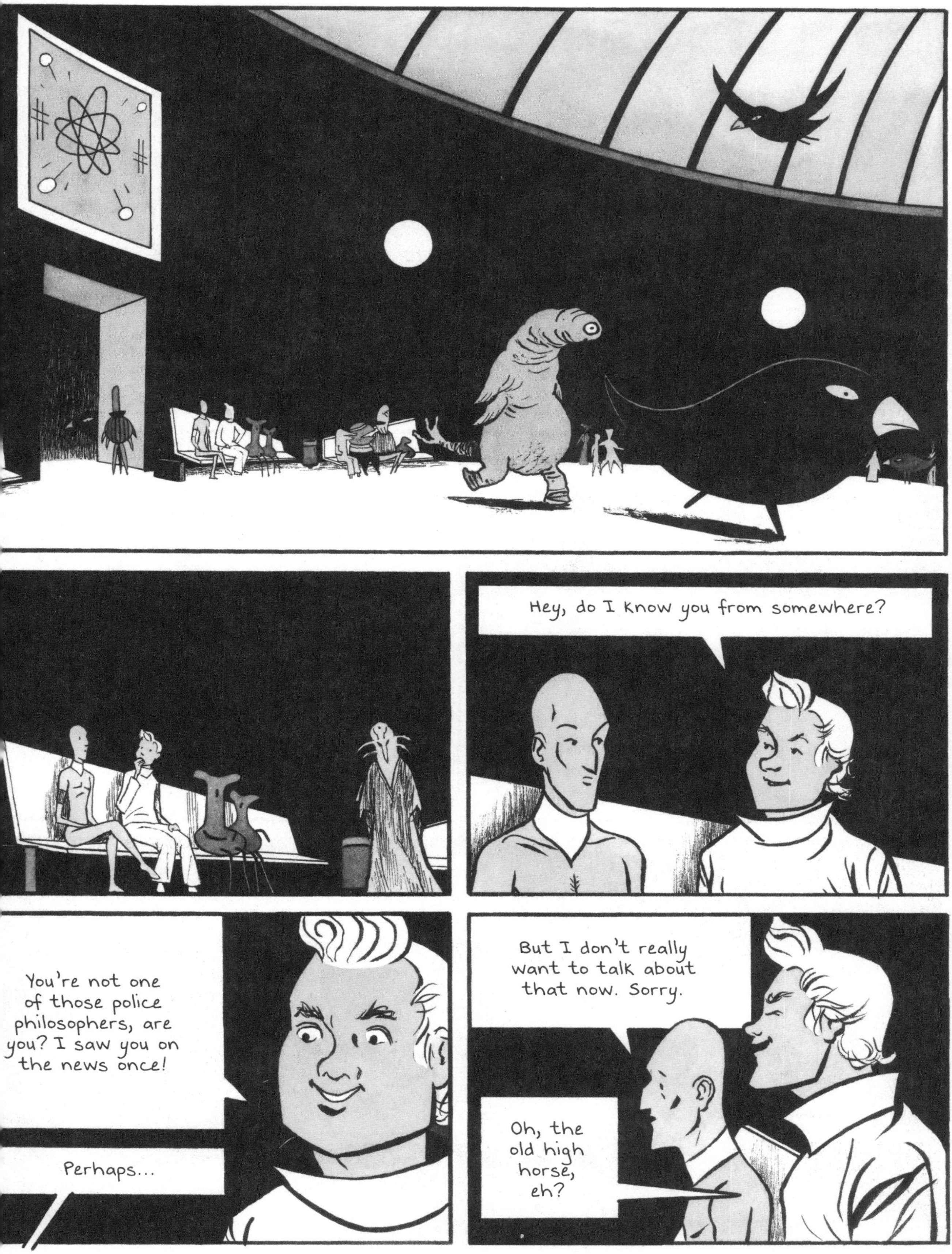
Hey, do I know you from somewhere?
You're not one of those police philosophers, are you? I saw you on the news once!
Perhaps...
But I don't really want to talk about that now. Sorry.
Oh, the old high horse, eh?

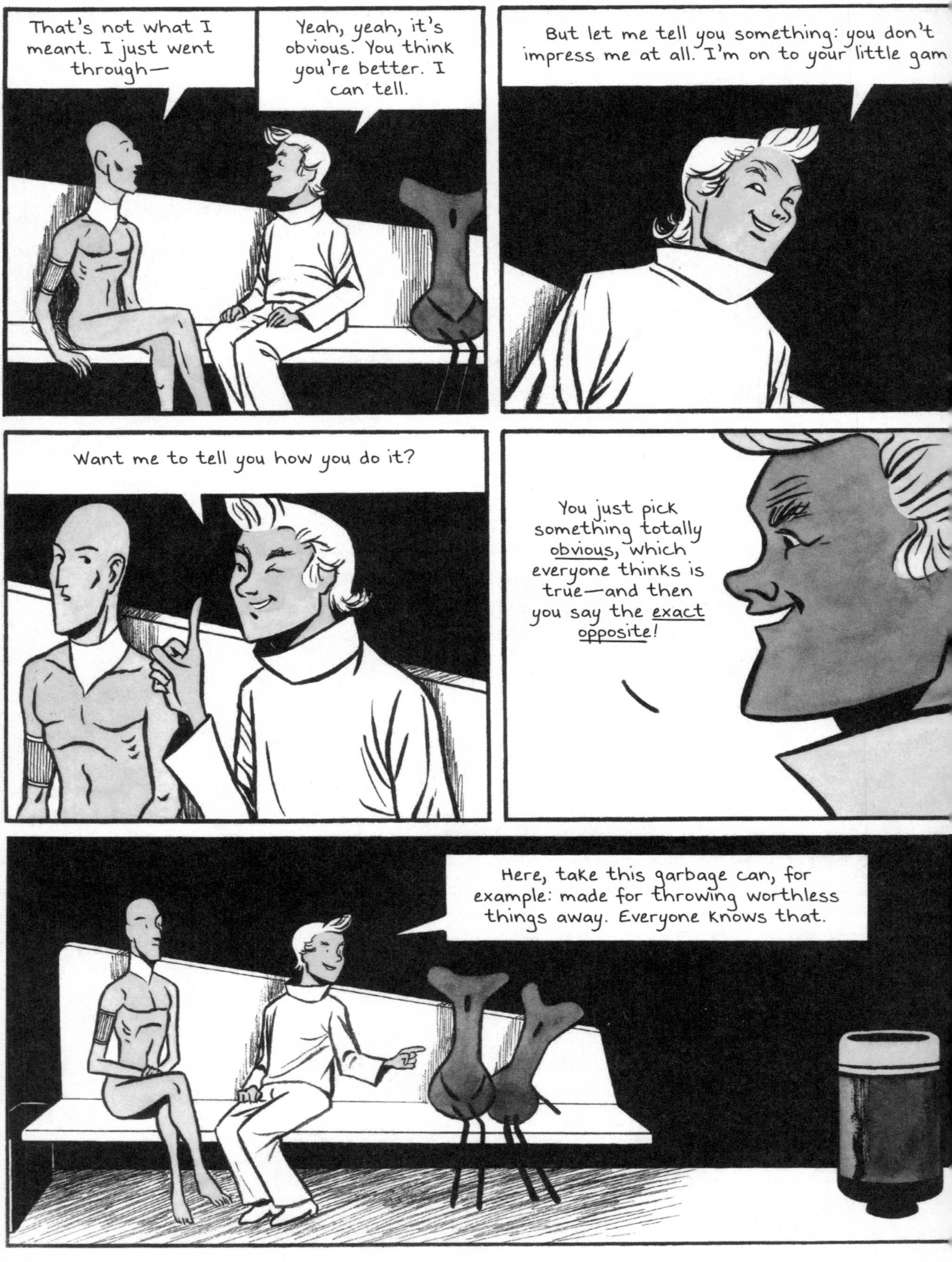
That's not what I meant. I just went through—
Yeah, yeah, it's obvious. You think you're better. I can tell.
But let me tell you something: you don't impress me at all. I'm on to your little gam
Want me to tell you how you do it?
You just pick something totally obvious, which everyone thinks is true—and then you say the exact opposite!
Here, take this garbage can, for example: made for throwing worthless things away. Everyone knows that.

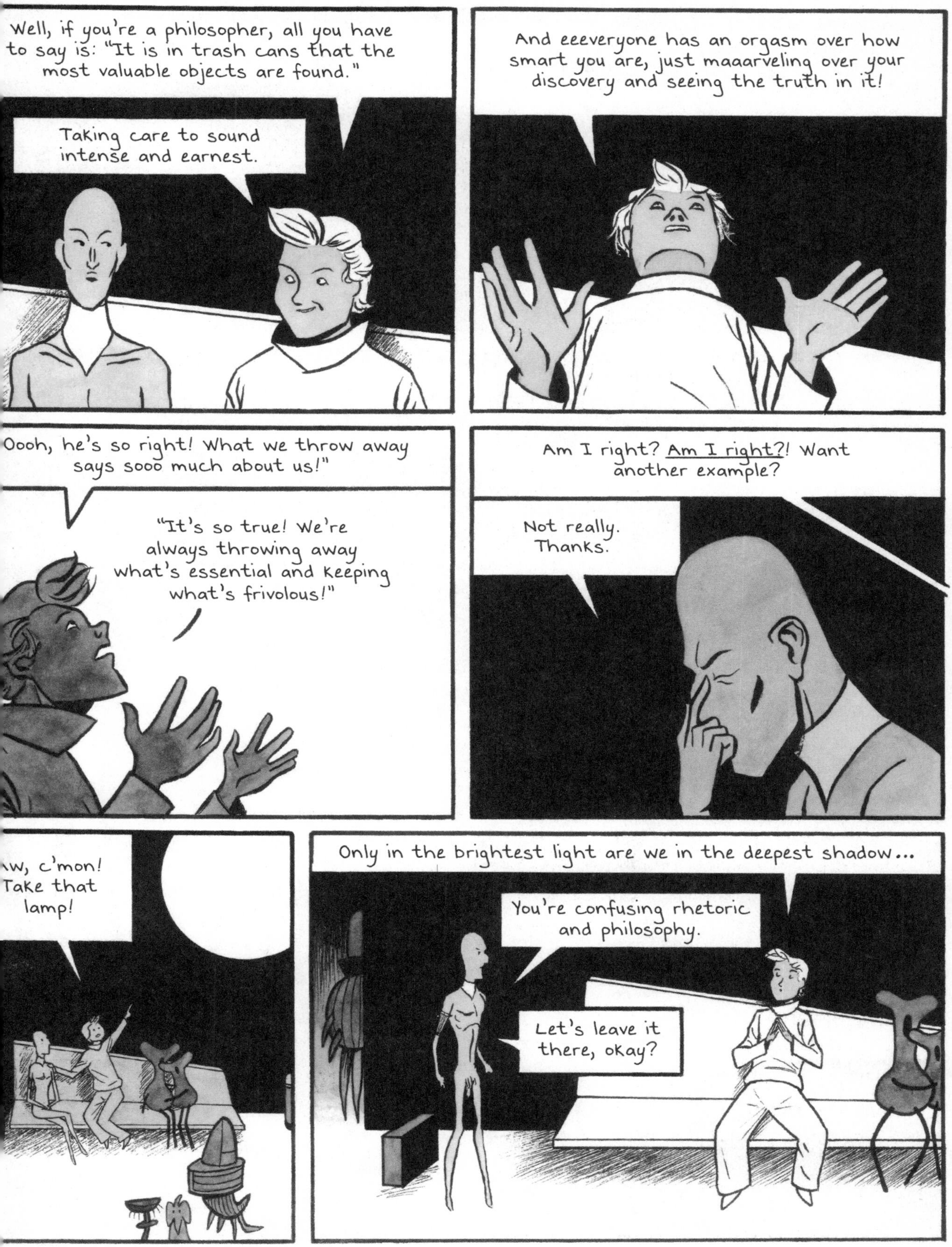

Well, if you're a philosopher, all you have to say is: "It is in trash cans that the most valuable objects are found."
Taking care to sound intense and earnest.
And eeeveryone has an orgasm over how smart you are, just maaarveling over your discovery and seeing the truth in it!
Oooh, he's so right! What we throw away says sooo much about us!"
"It's so true! We're always throwing away what's essential and keeping what's frivolous!"
Am I right? Am I right?! Want another example?
Not really. Thanks.
Aw, c'mon! Take that lamp!
Only in the brightest light are we in the deepest shadow...
You're confusing rhetoric and philosophy.
Let's leave it there, okay?

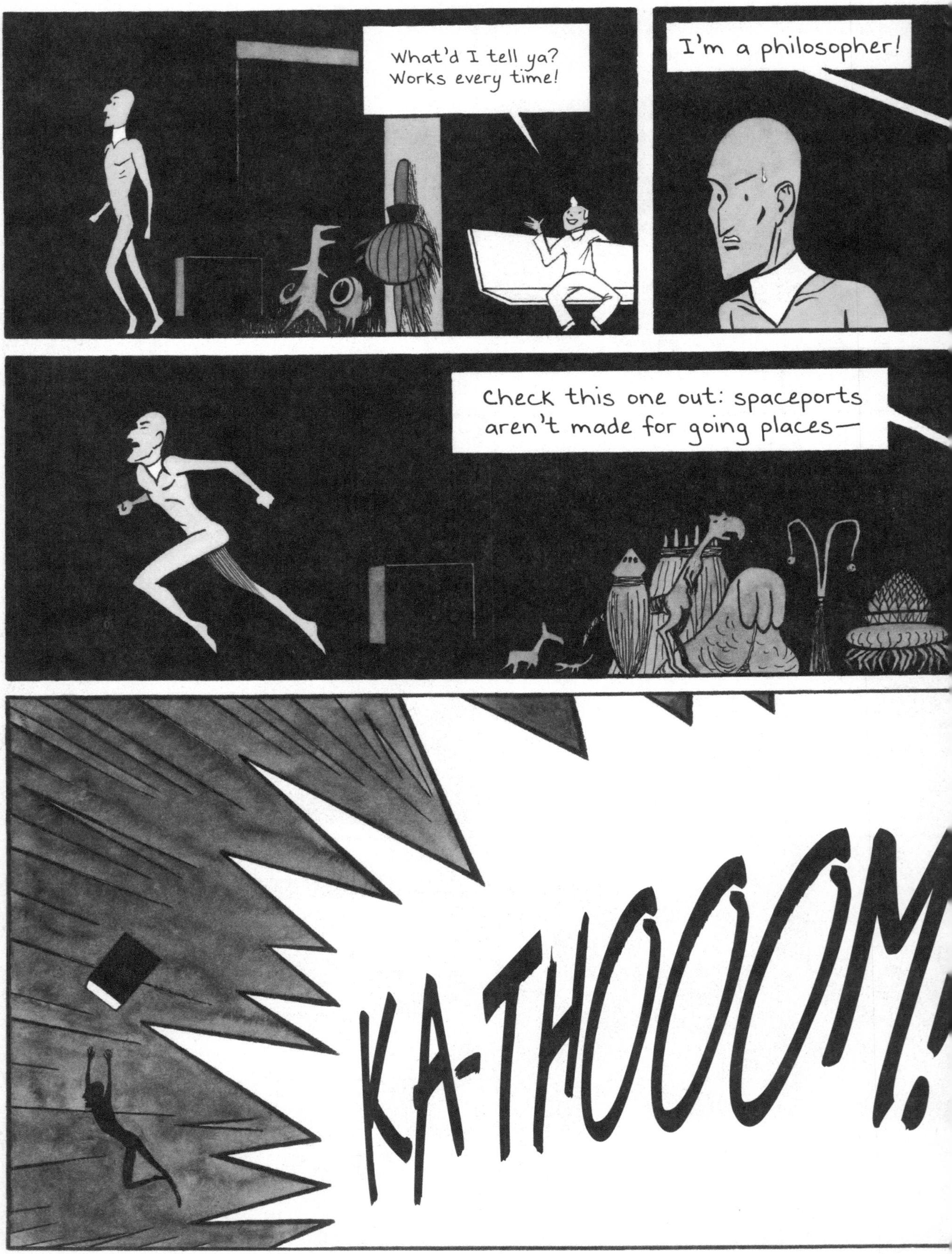
What'd I tell ya? Works every time!
I'm a philosopher!
Check this one out: spaceports aren't made for going places—
KA-THOOOM!

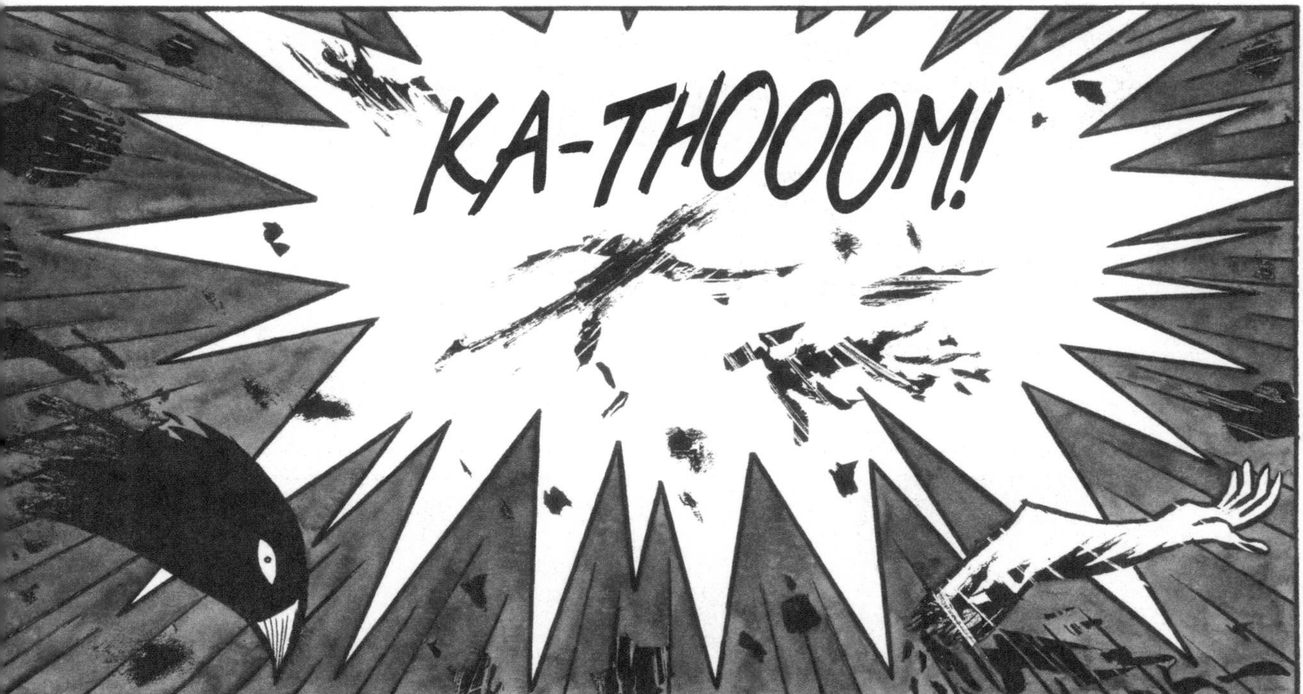
KA-THOOOM!

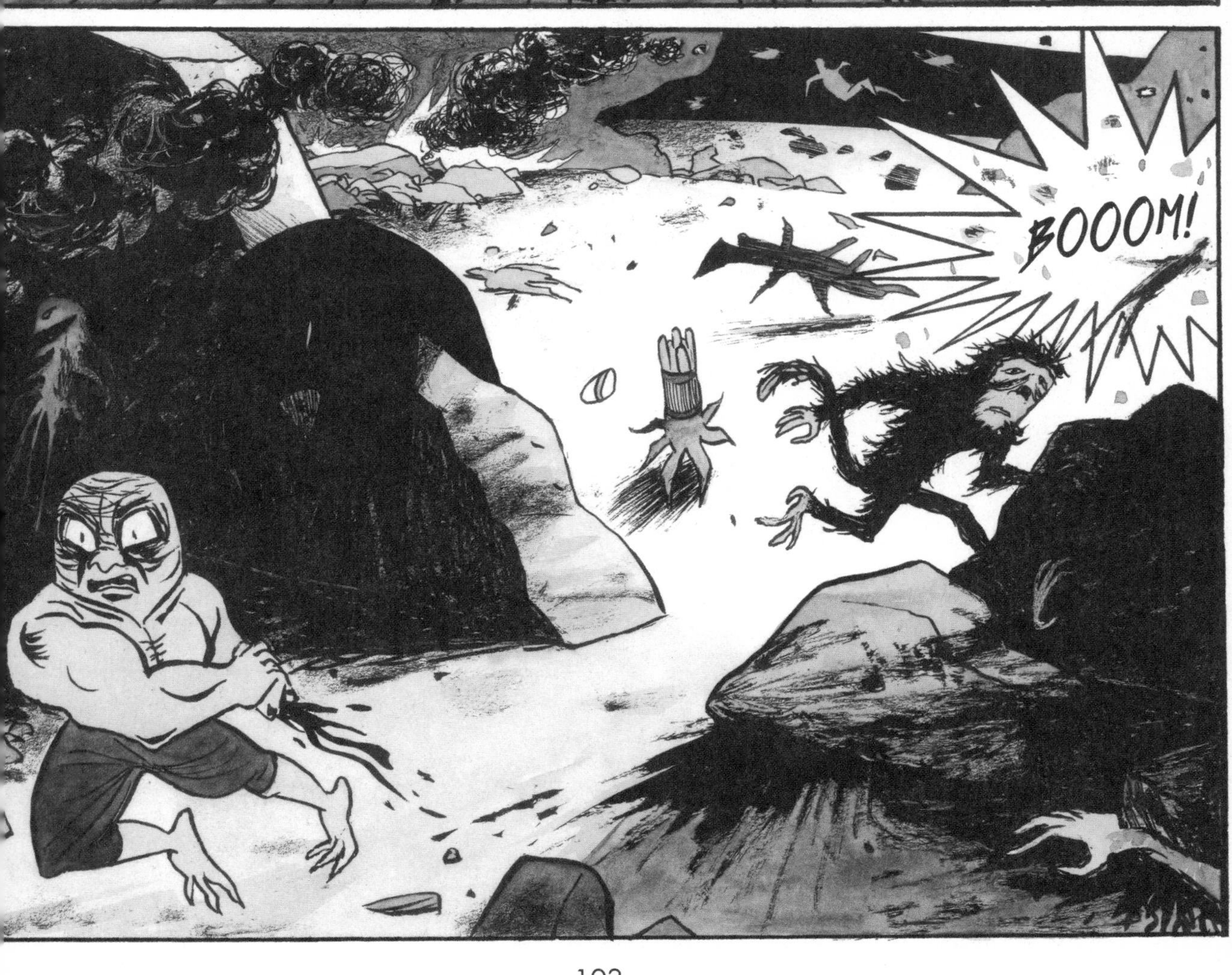
BOOOM!

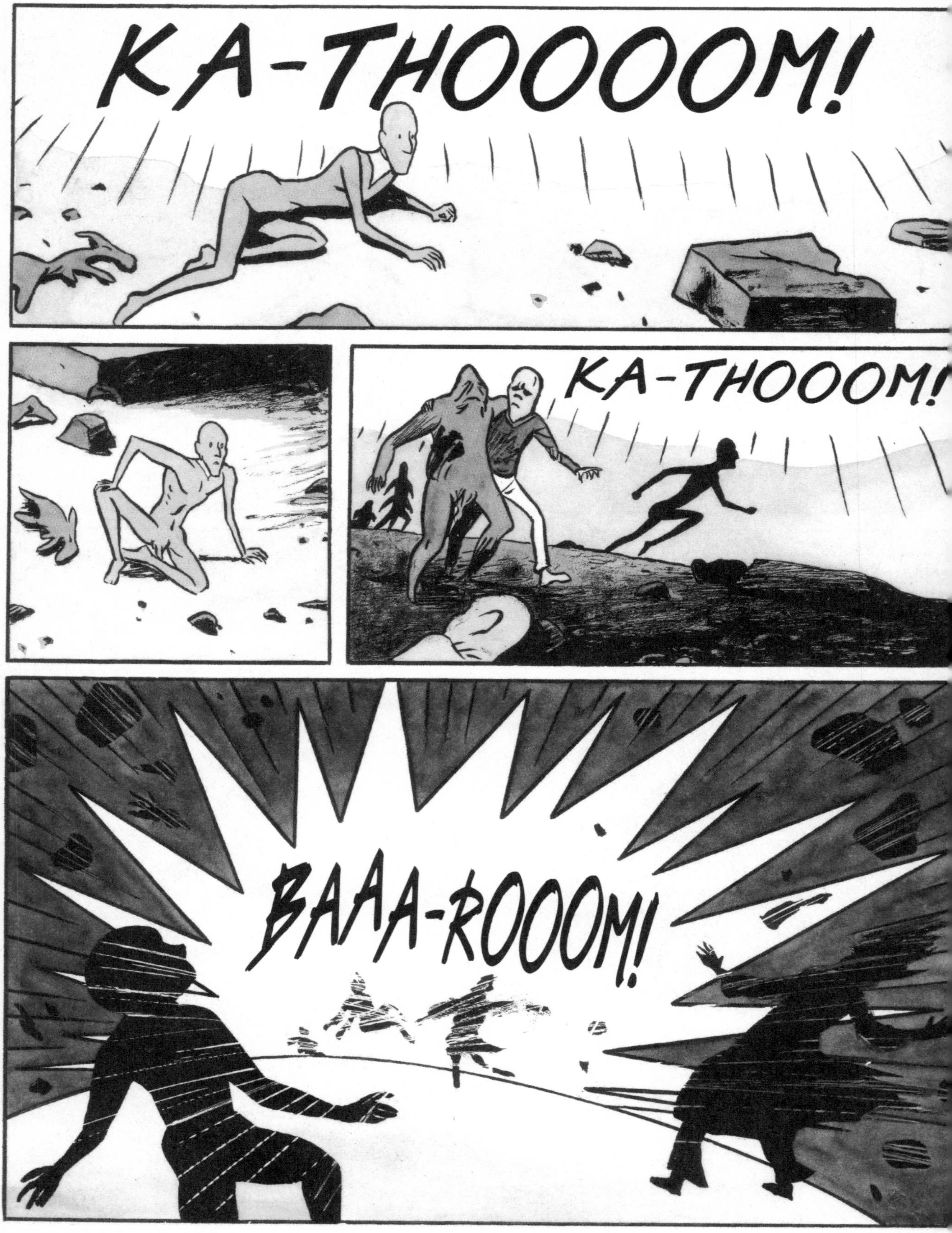
KA-THOOOOOM!
KA-THOOOM!
BAAA-ROOOM!

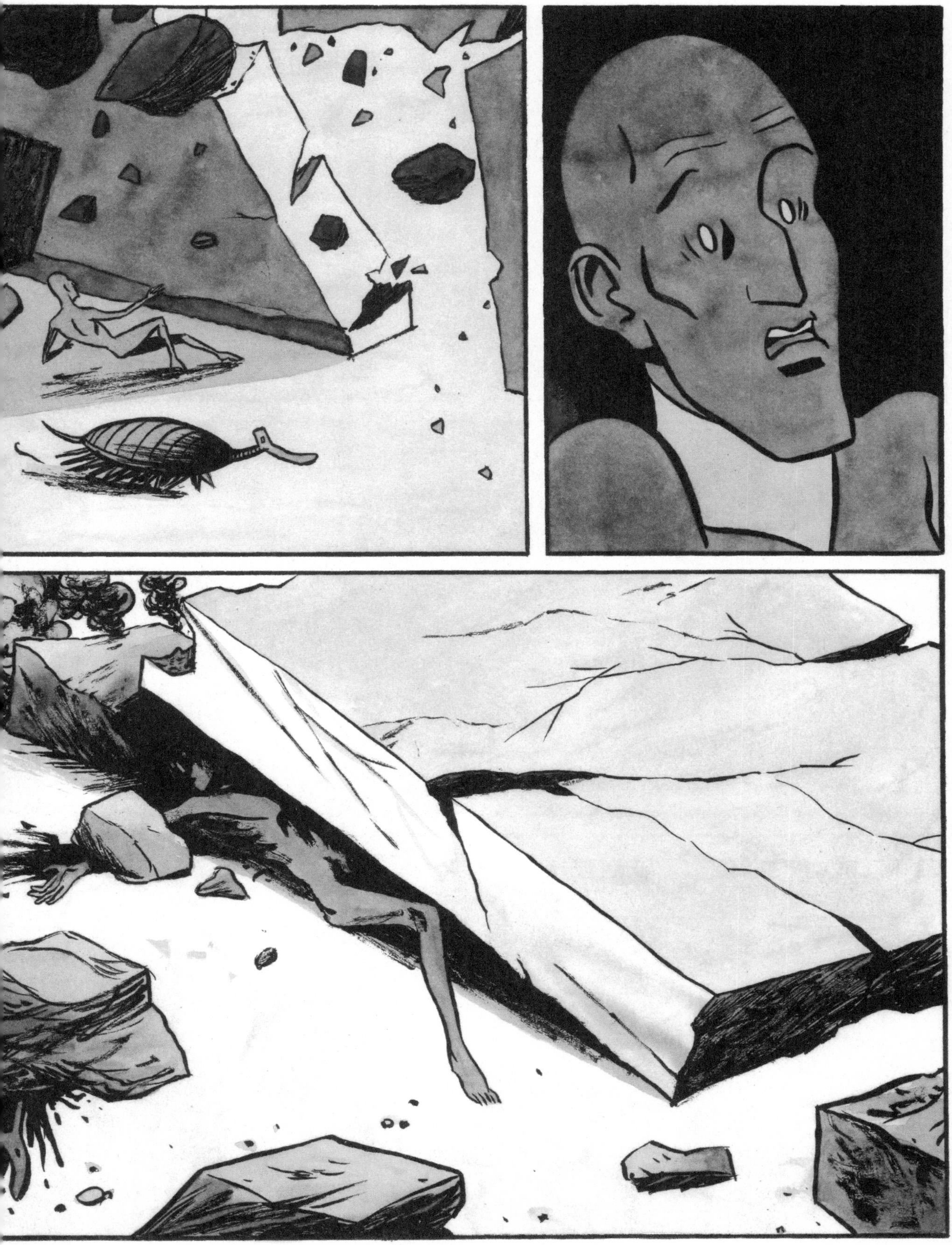

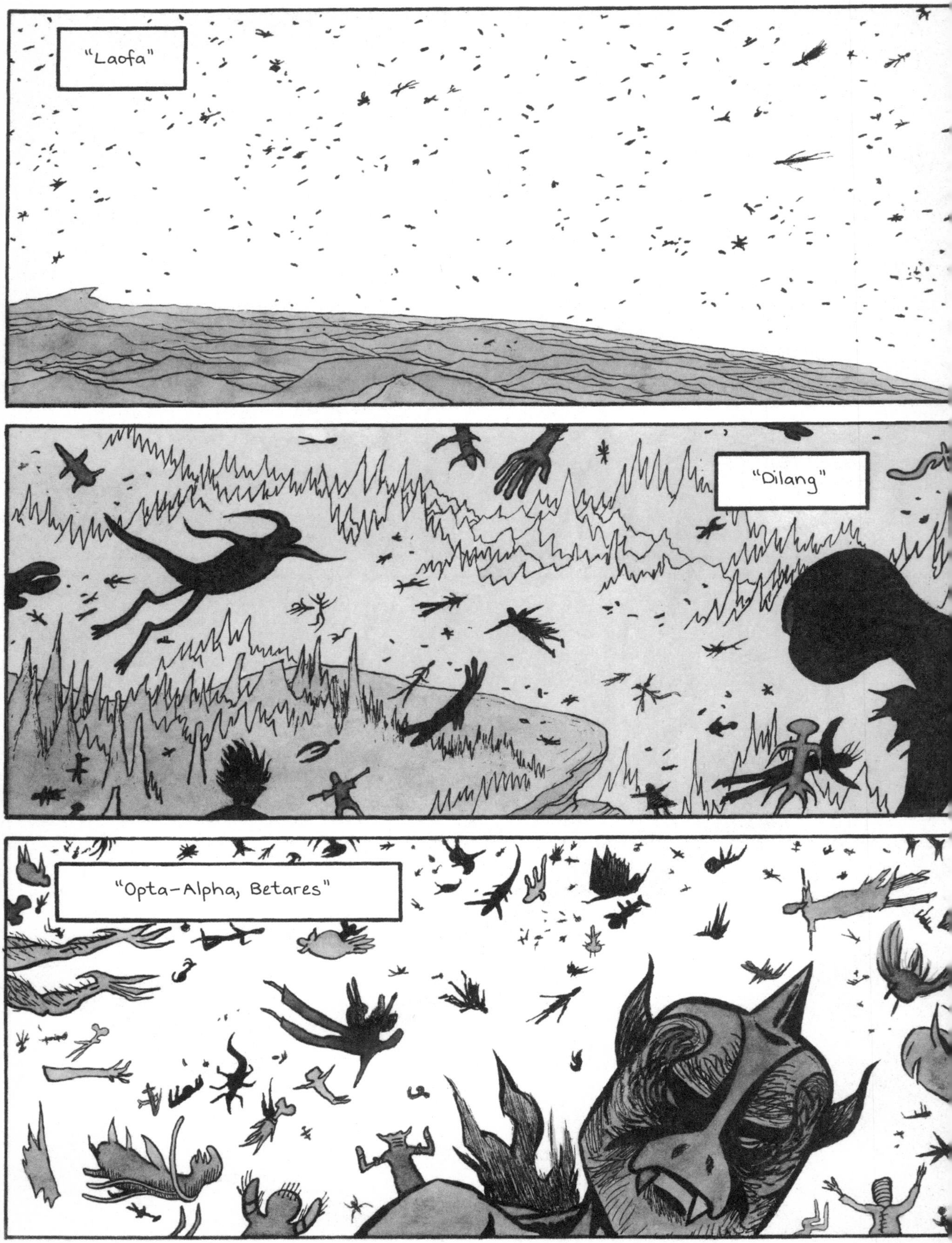
"Laofa"
"Dilang"
"Opta-Alpha, Betares"

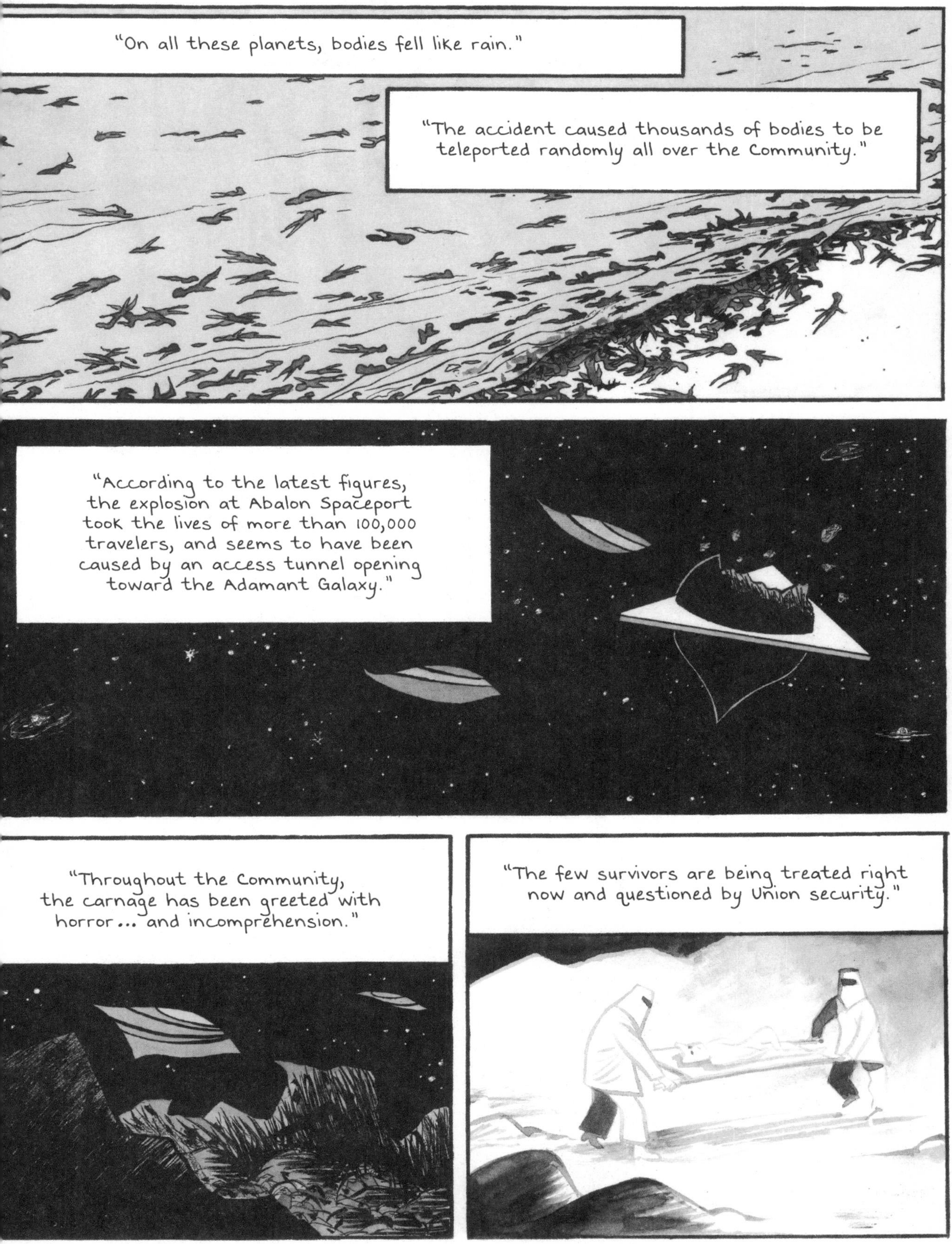
"On all these planets, bodies fell like rain."
"The accident caused thousands of bodies to be teleported randomly all over the Community."
"According to the latest figures, the explosion at Abalon Spaceport took the lives of more than 100,000 travelers, and seems to have been caused by an access tunnel opening toward the Adamant Galaxy."
"Throughout the Community, the carnage has been greeted with horror... and incomprehension."
"The few survivors are being treated right now and questioned by Union security."

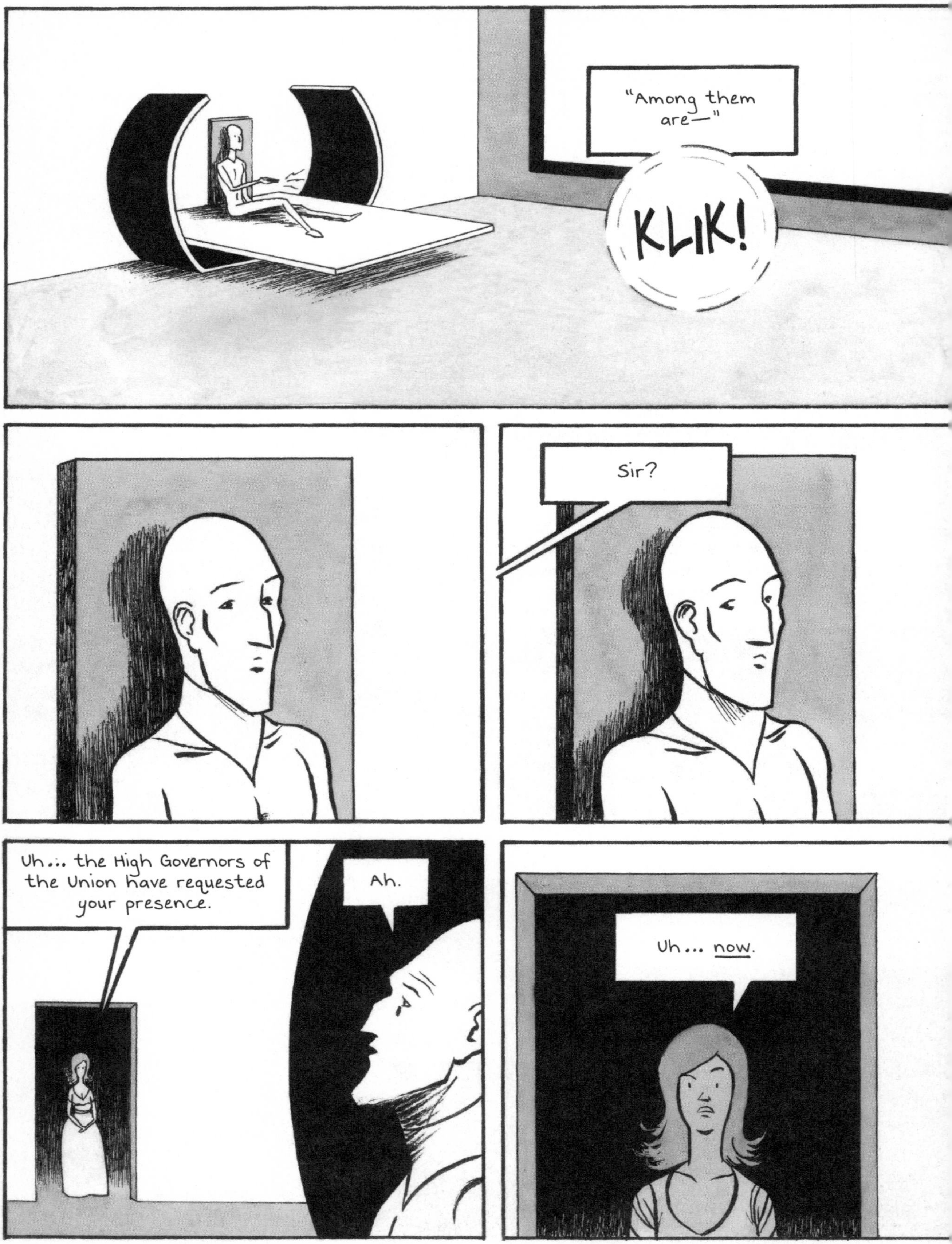
"Among them are—"
KLIK!
Sir?
Uh... the High Governors of the Union have requested your presence.
Ah.
Uh... now.

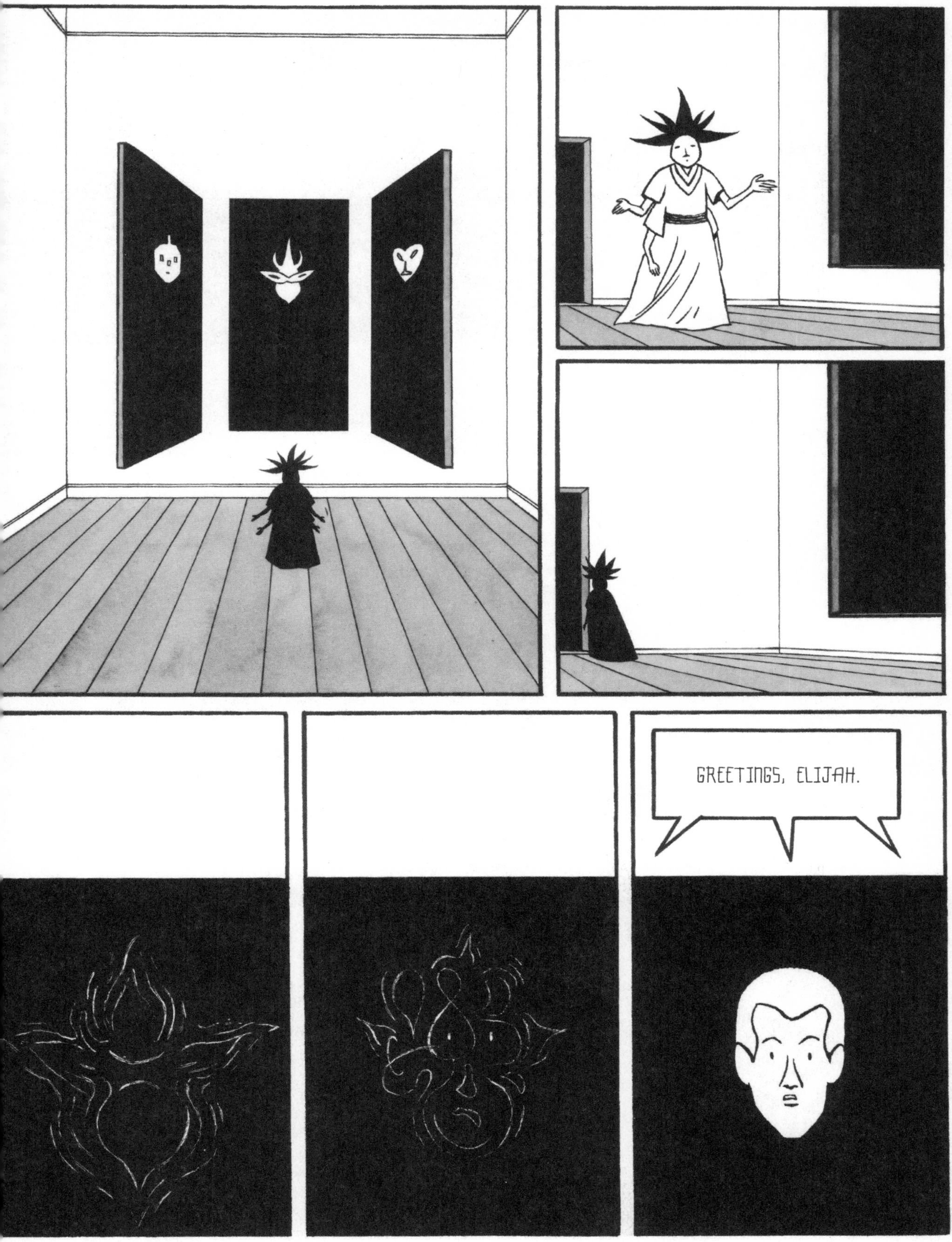
GREETINGS, ELIJAH.

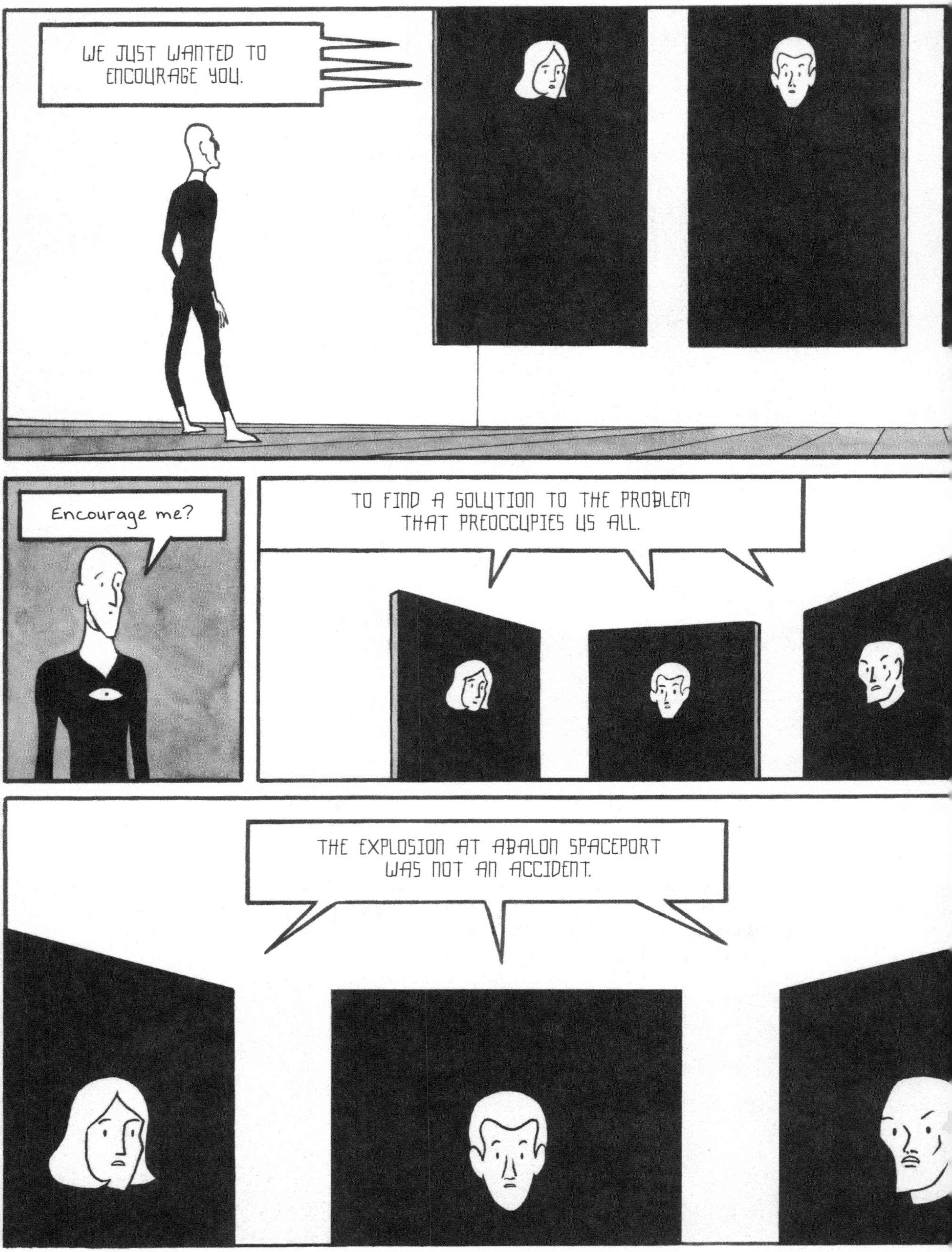
WE JUST WANTED TO ENCOURAGE YOU.
Encourage me?
TO FIND A SOLUTION TO THE PROBLEM THAT PREOCCUPIES US ALL.
THE EXPLOSION AT ABALON SPACEPORT WAS NOT AN ACCIDENT.

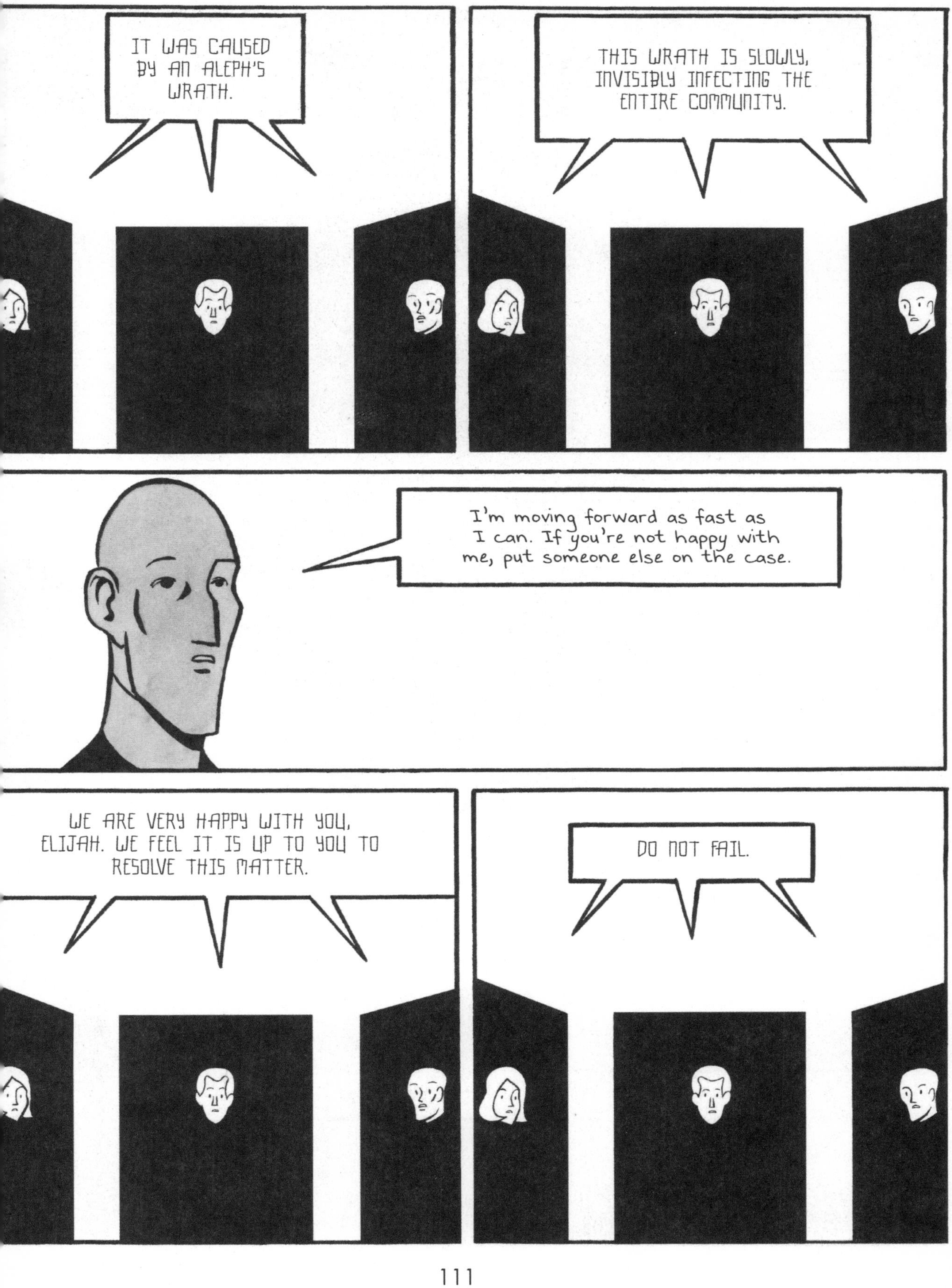
IT WAS CAUSED BY AN ALEPH'S WRATH.
THIS WRATH IS SLOWLY, INVISIBLY INFECTING THE ENTIRE COMMUNITY.
I'm moving forward as fast as I can. If you're not happy with me, put someone else on the case.
WE ARE VERY HAPPY WITH YOU, ELIJAH. WE FEEL IT IS UP TO YOU TO RESOLVE THIS MATTER.
DO NOT FAIL.

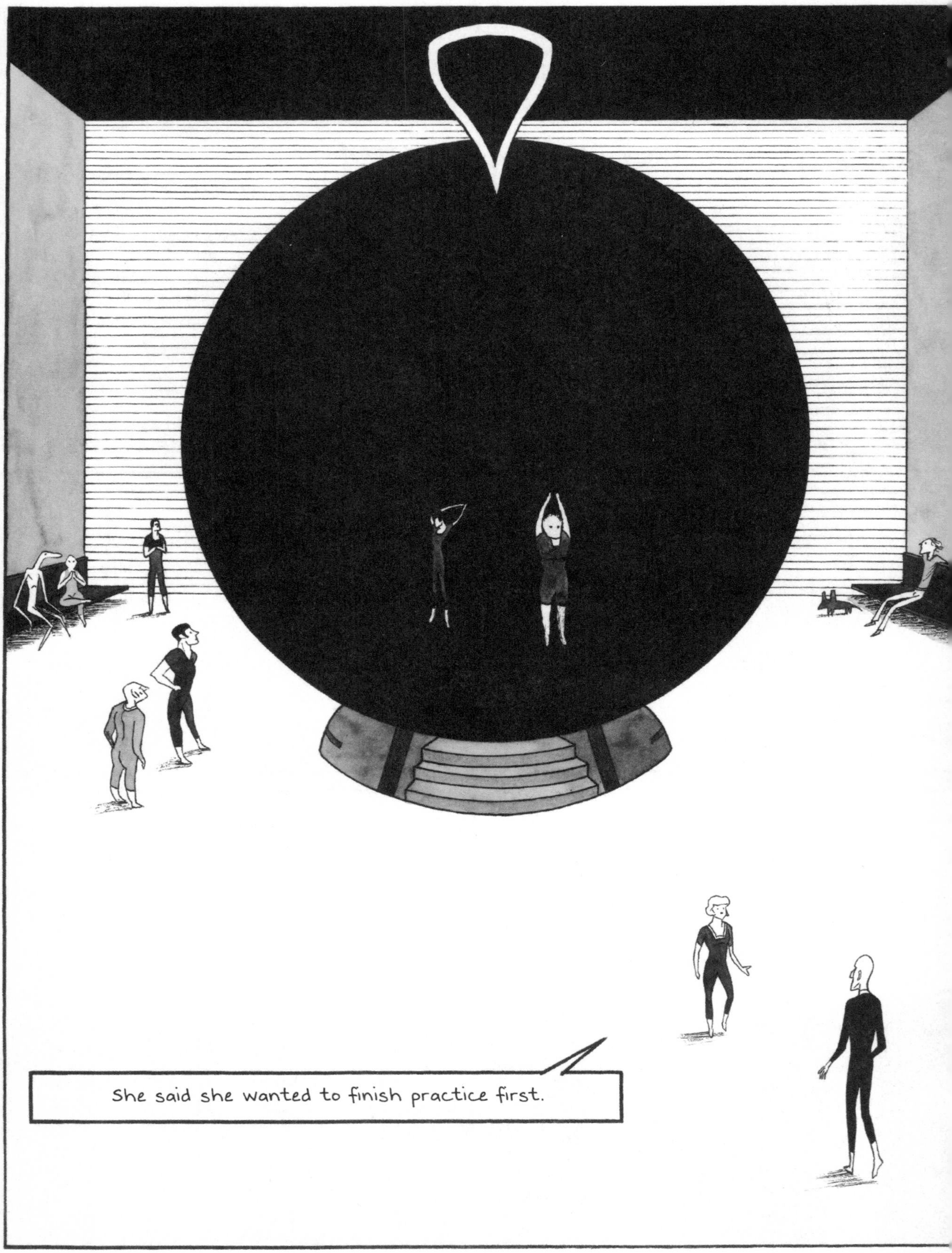
She said she wanted to finish practice first.

Fine. Tell her I'm leaving for Ganed with my echoes. It's an emergency.

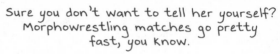

Sure you don't want to tell her yourself? Morphowrestling matches go pretty fast, you know.

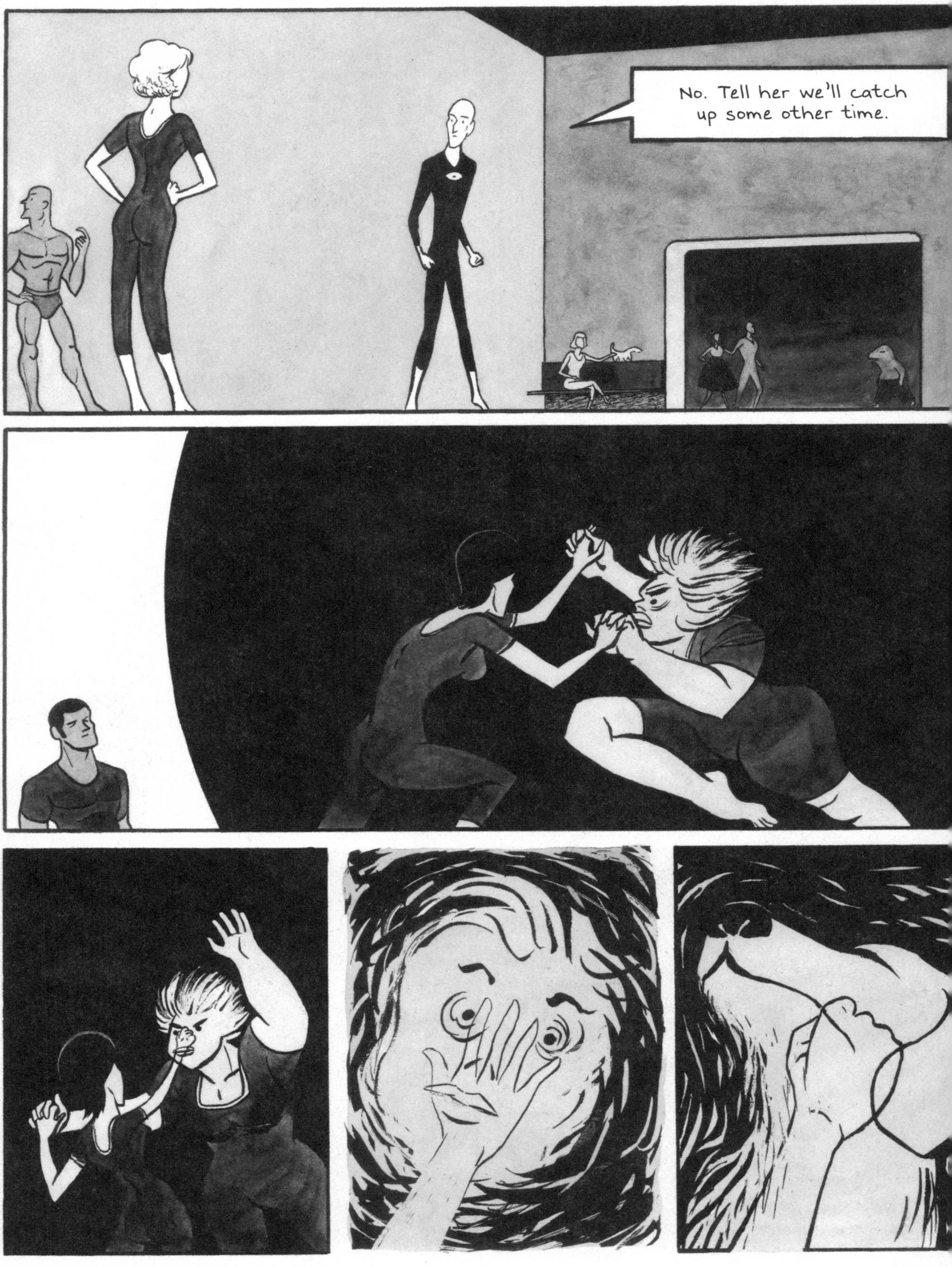
No. Tell her we'll catch up some other time.

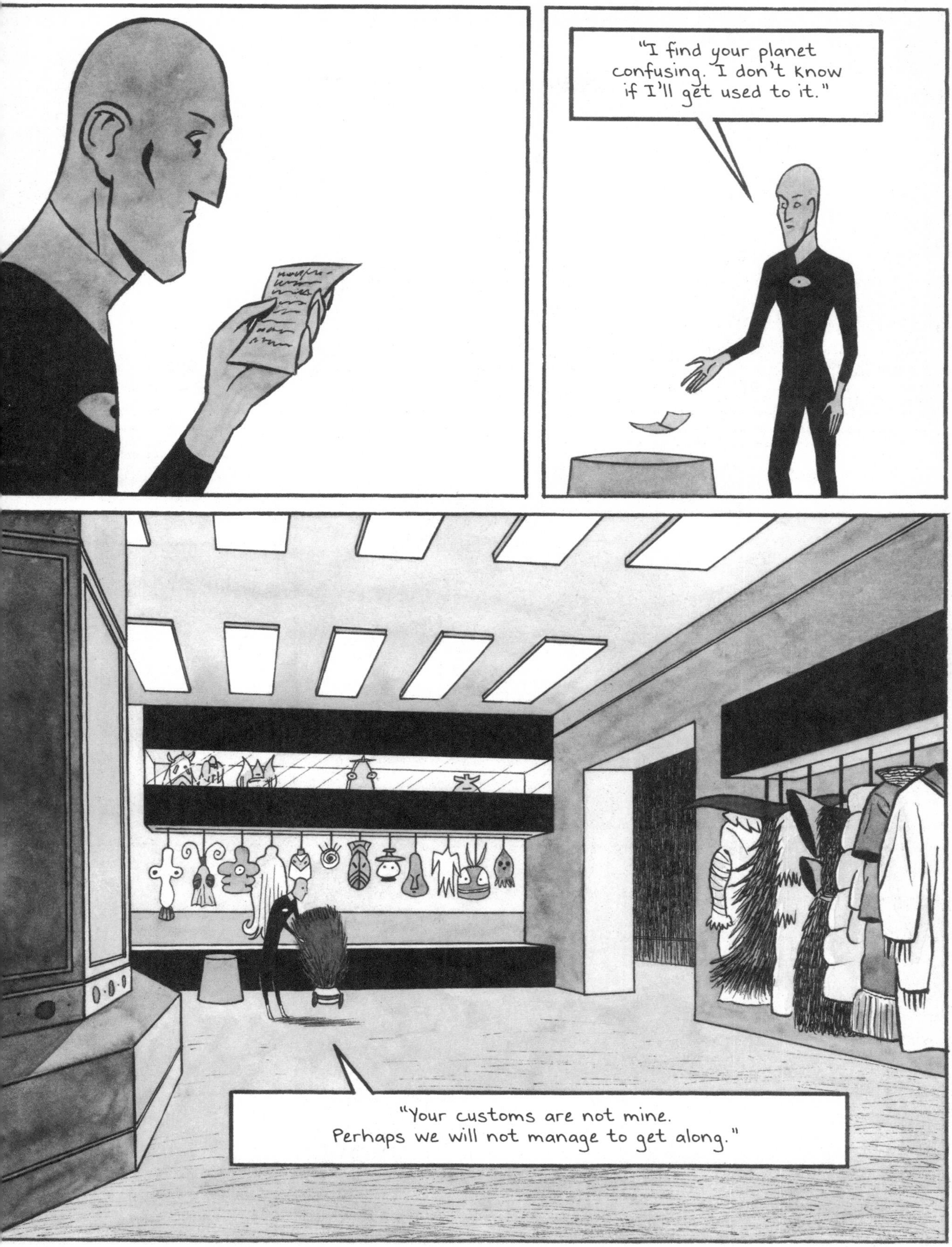
"I find your planet confusing. I don't know if I'll get used to it."
"Your customs are not mine. Perhaps we will not manage to get along."

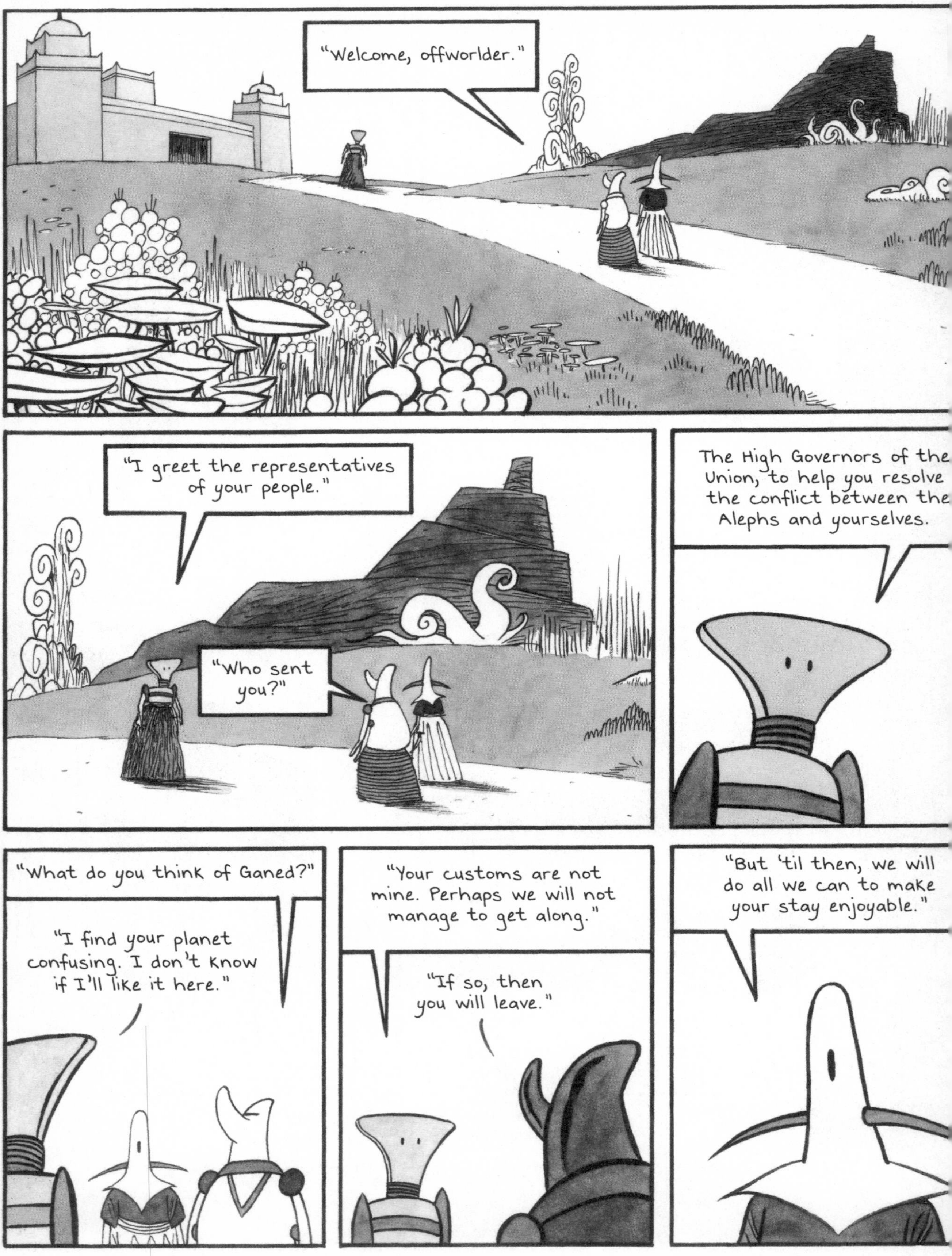
"Welcome, offworlder."
"I greet the representatives of your people."
"Who sent you?"
The High Governors of the Union, to help you resolve the conflict between the Alephs and yourselves.
"What do you think of Ganed?"
"I find your planet confusing. I don't know if I'll like it here."
"Your customs are not mine. Perhaps we will not manage to get along."
"If so, then you will leave."
"But 'til then, we will do all we can to make your stay enjoyable."

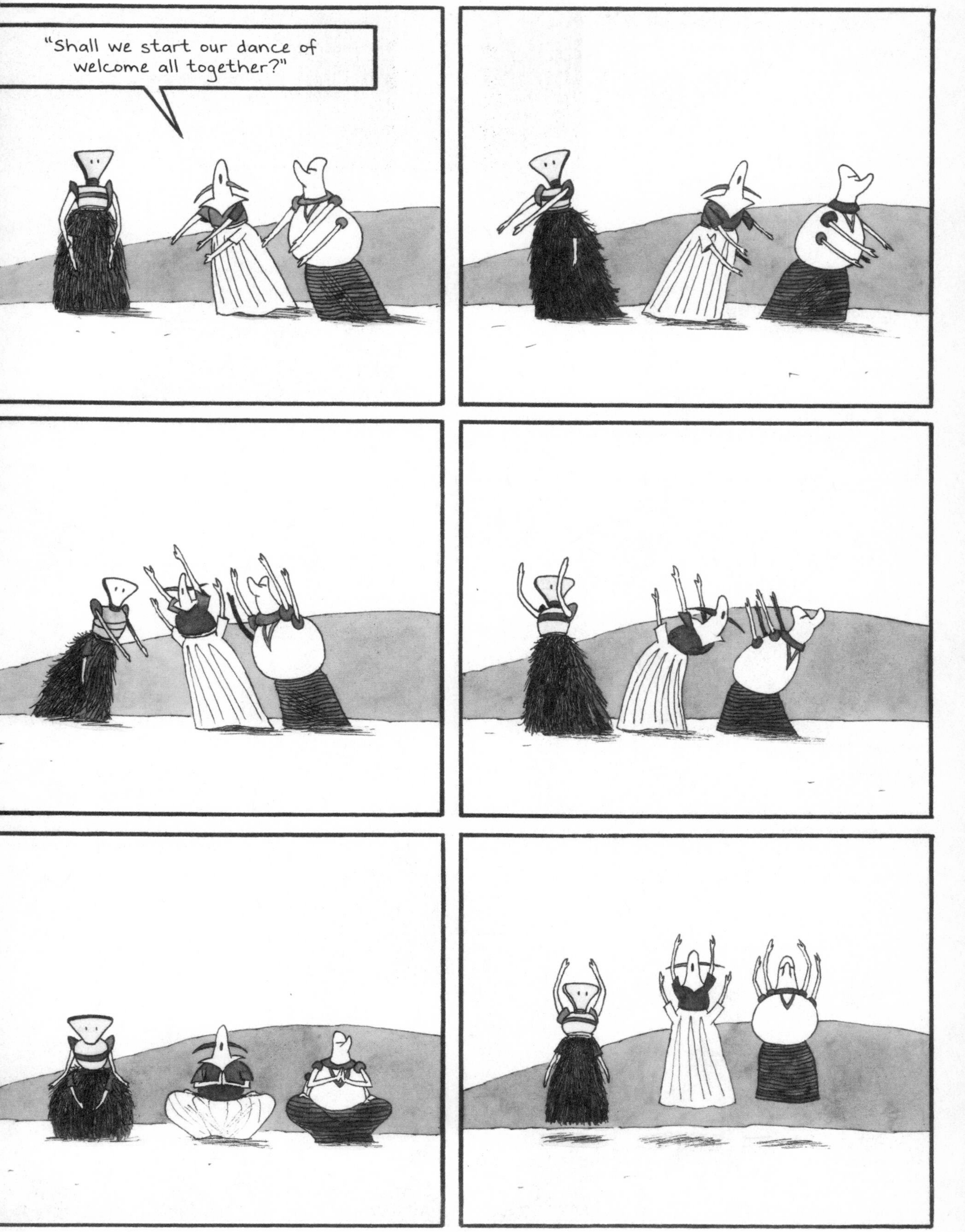
"Shall we start our dance of welcome all together?"

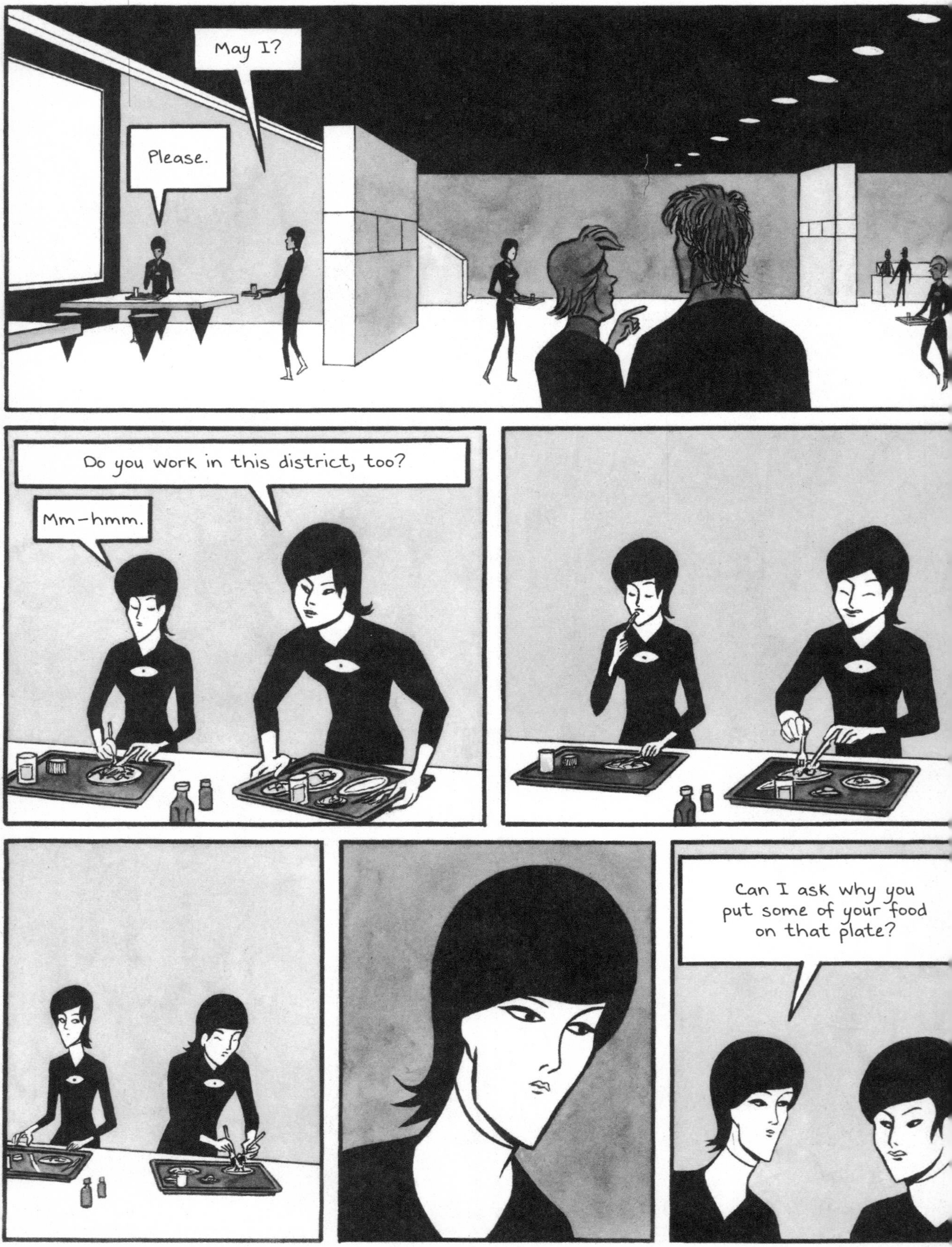
May I?
Please.
Do you work in this district, too?
Mm-hmm.
Can I ask why you put some of your food on that plate?

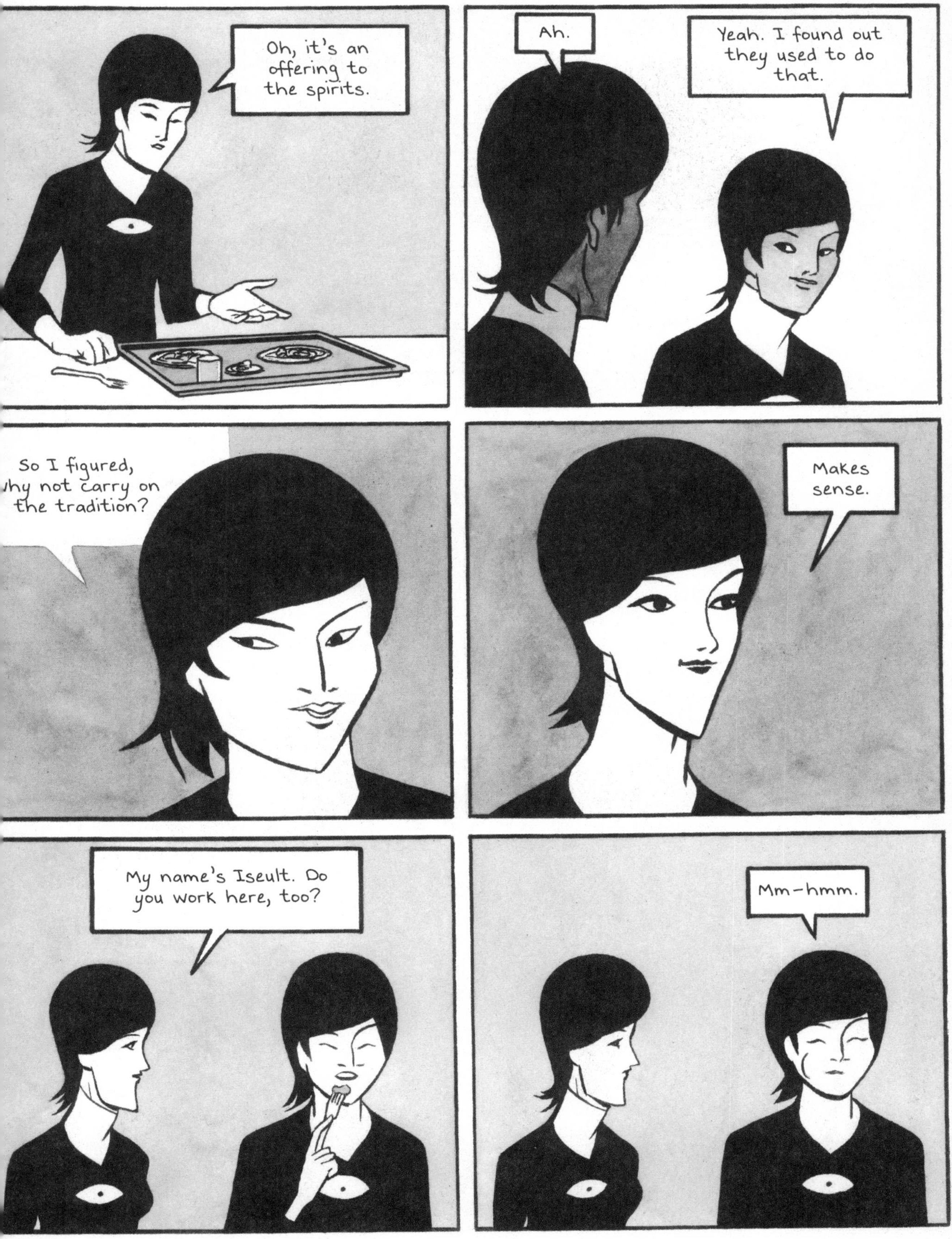
Oh, it's an offering to the spirits.
Ah.
Yeah. I found out they used to do that.
So I figured, why not carry on the tradition?
Makes sense.
My name's Iseult. Do you work here, too?
Mm-hmm.

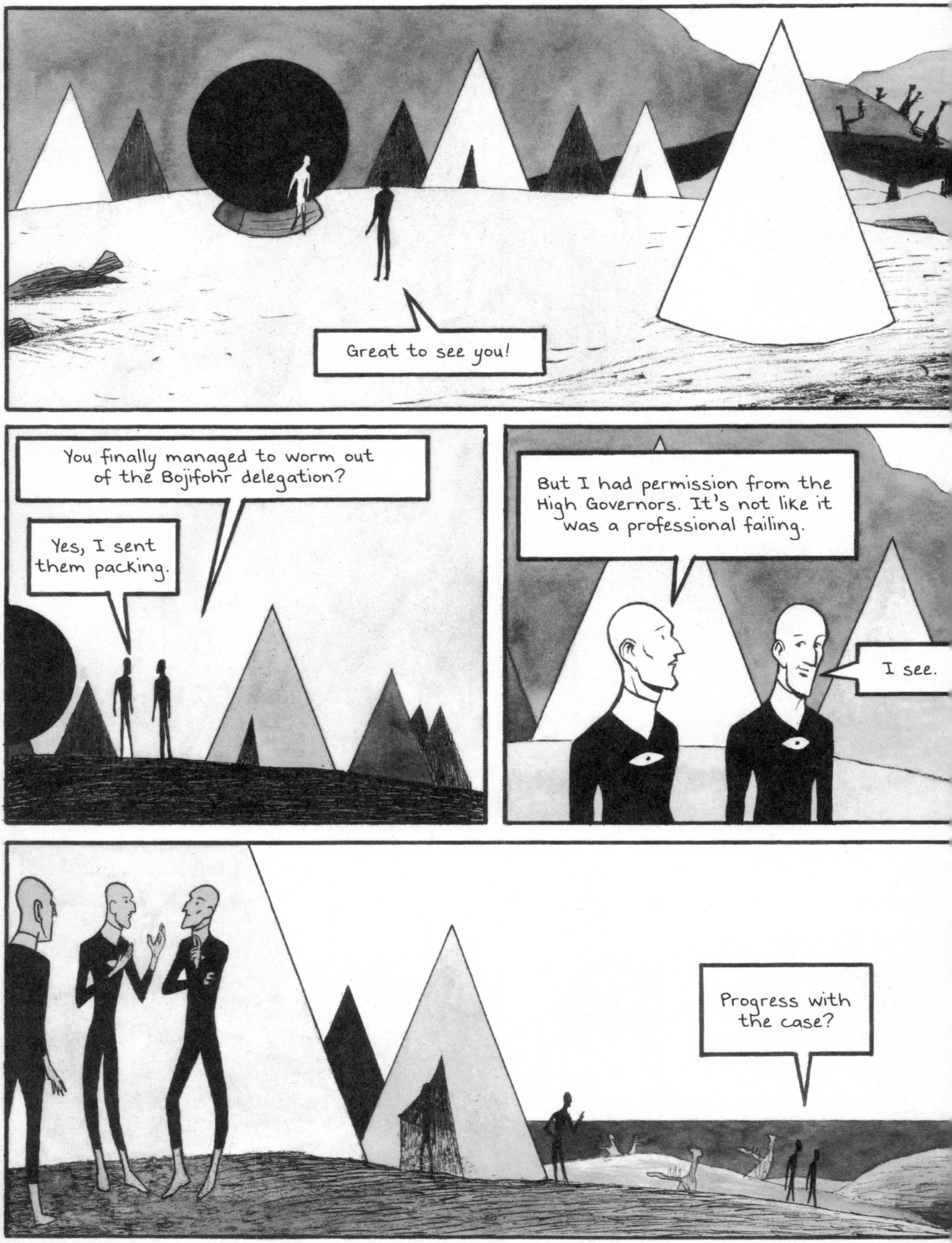
Great to see you!
You finally managed to worm out of the Bojifohr delegation?
Yes, I sent them packing.
But I had permission from the High Governors. It's not like it was a professional failing.
I see.
Progress with the case?

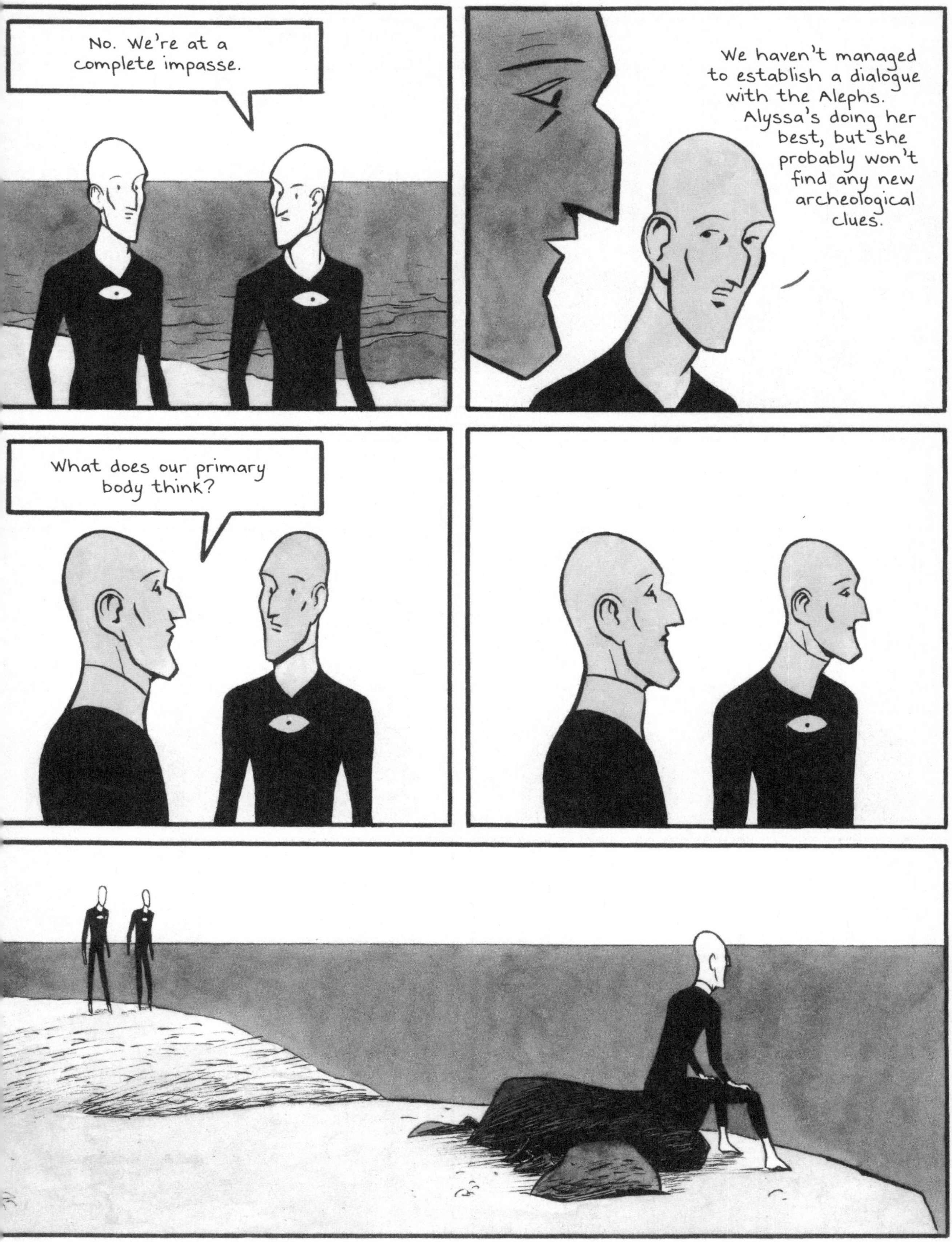
No. We're at a complete impasse.
We haven't managed to establish a dialogue with the Alephs. Alyssa's doing her best, but she probably won't find any new archeological clues.
What does our primary body think?

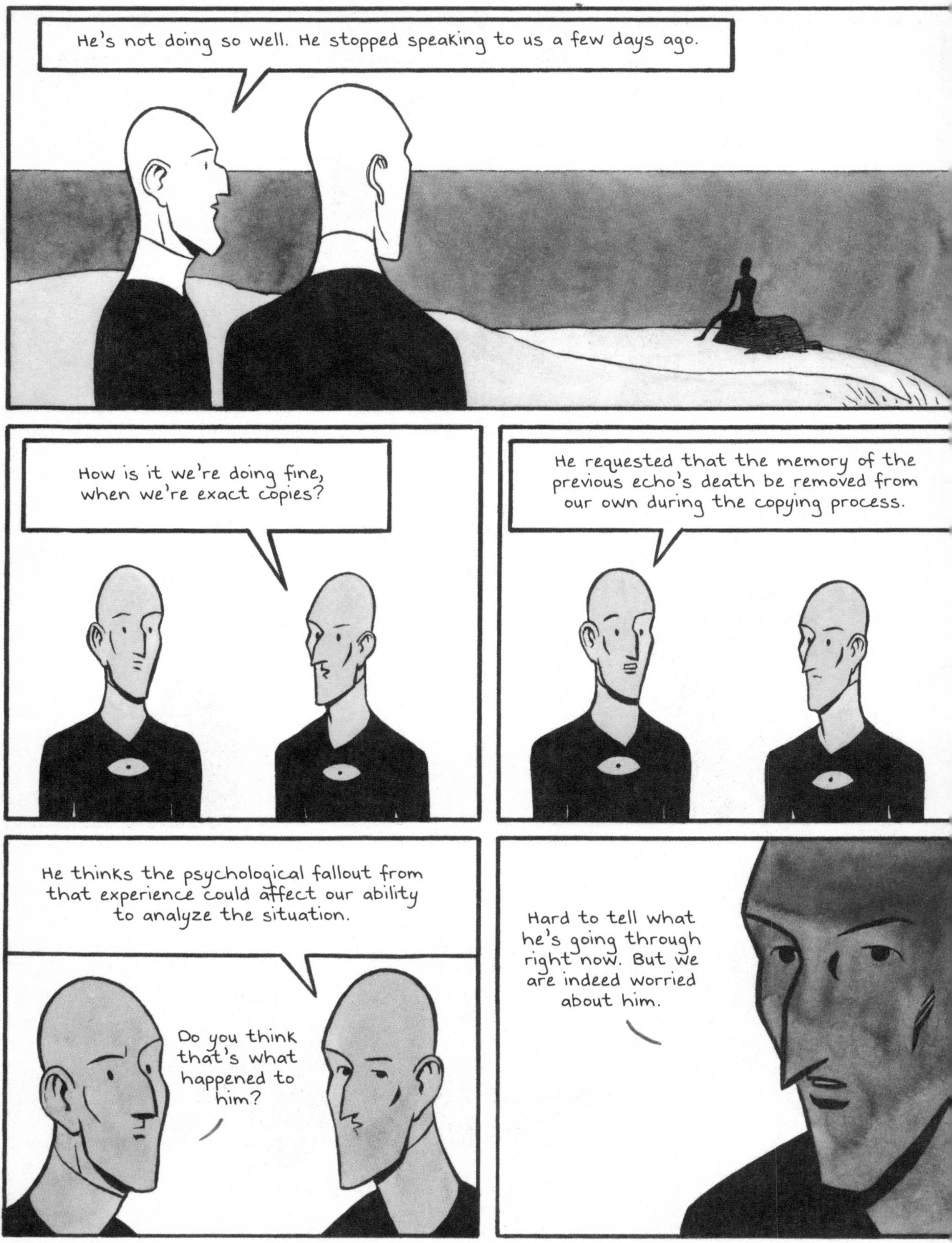
He's not doing so well. He stopped speaking to us a few days ago.
How is it we're doing fine, when we're exact copies?
He requested that the memory of the previous echo's death be removed from our own during the copying process.
He thinks the psychological fallout from that experience could affect our ability to analyze the situation.
Do you think that's what happened to him?
Hard to tell what he's going through right now. But we are indeed worried about him.

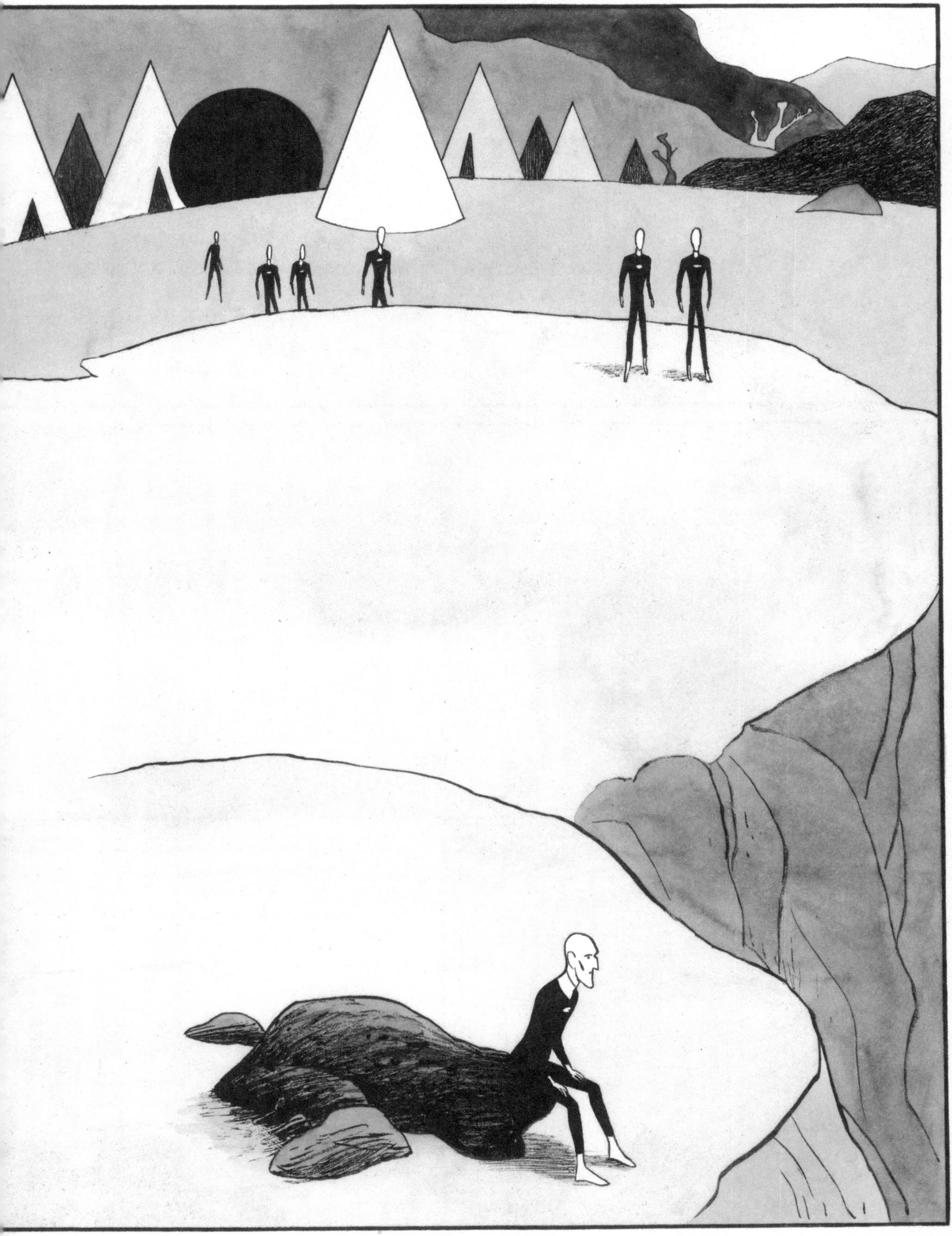

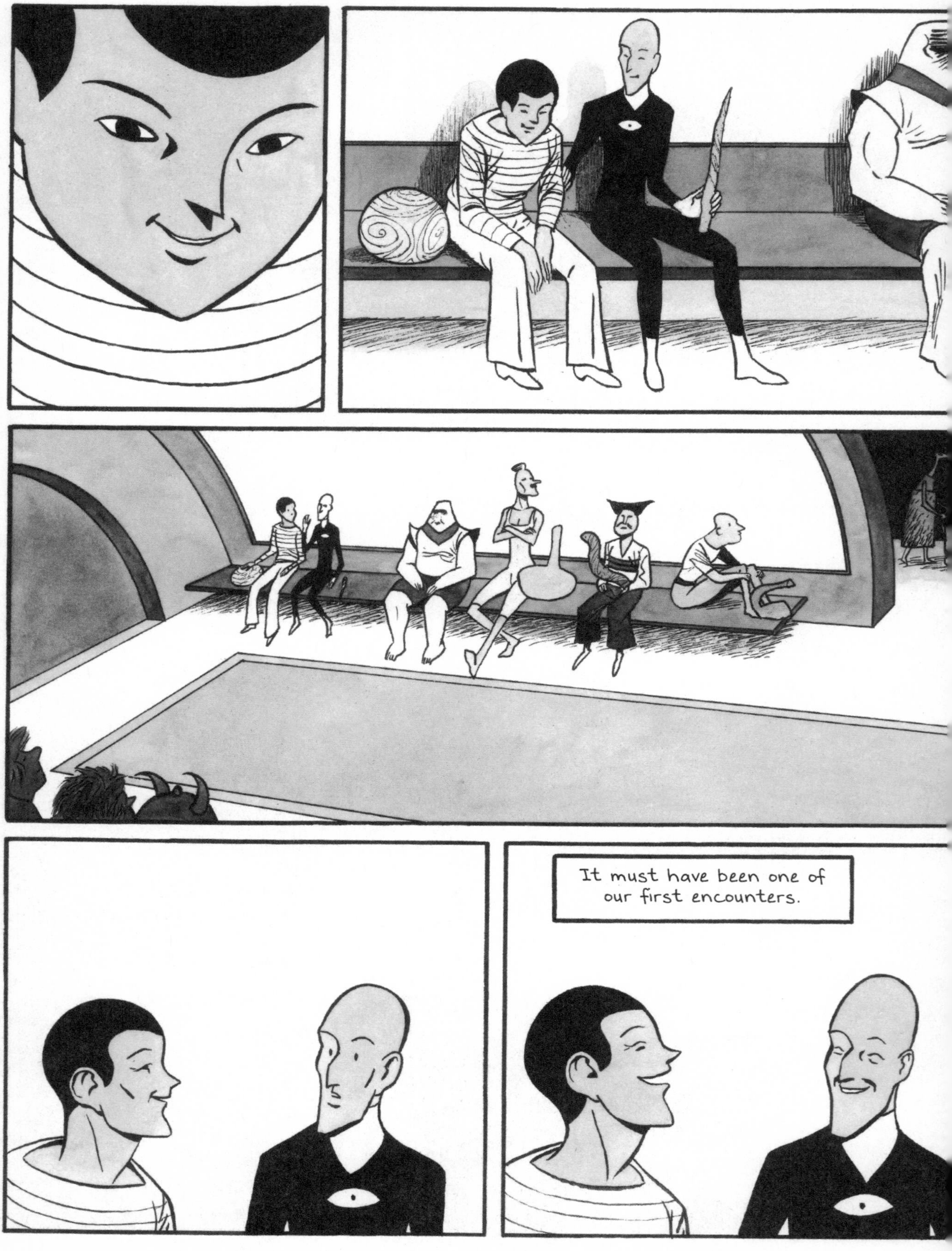
It must have been one of
our first encounters.

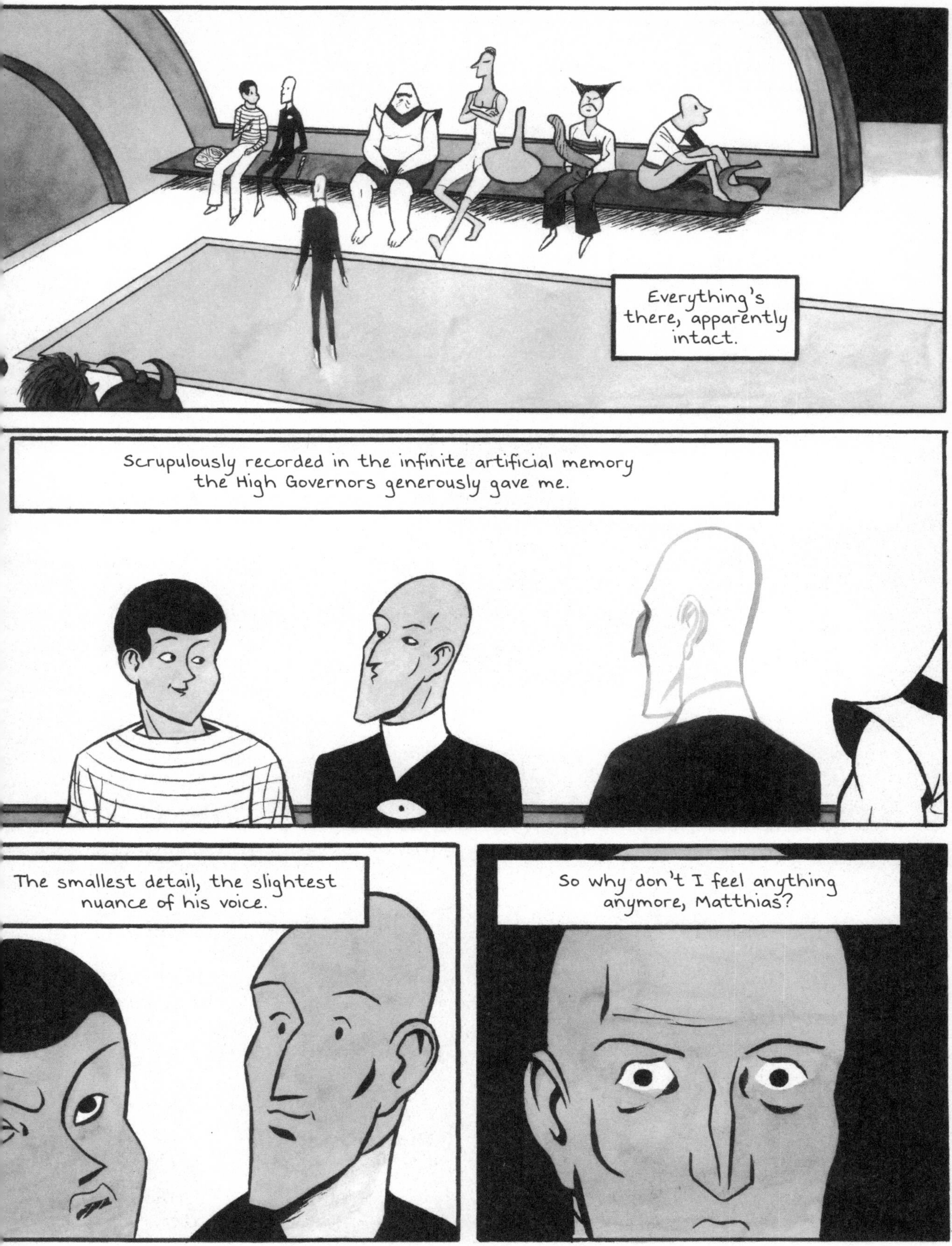
Everything's there, apparently intact.
Scrupulously recorded in the infinite artificial memory the High Governors generously gave me.
The smallest detail, the slightest nuance of his voice.
So why don't I feel anything anymore, Matthias?

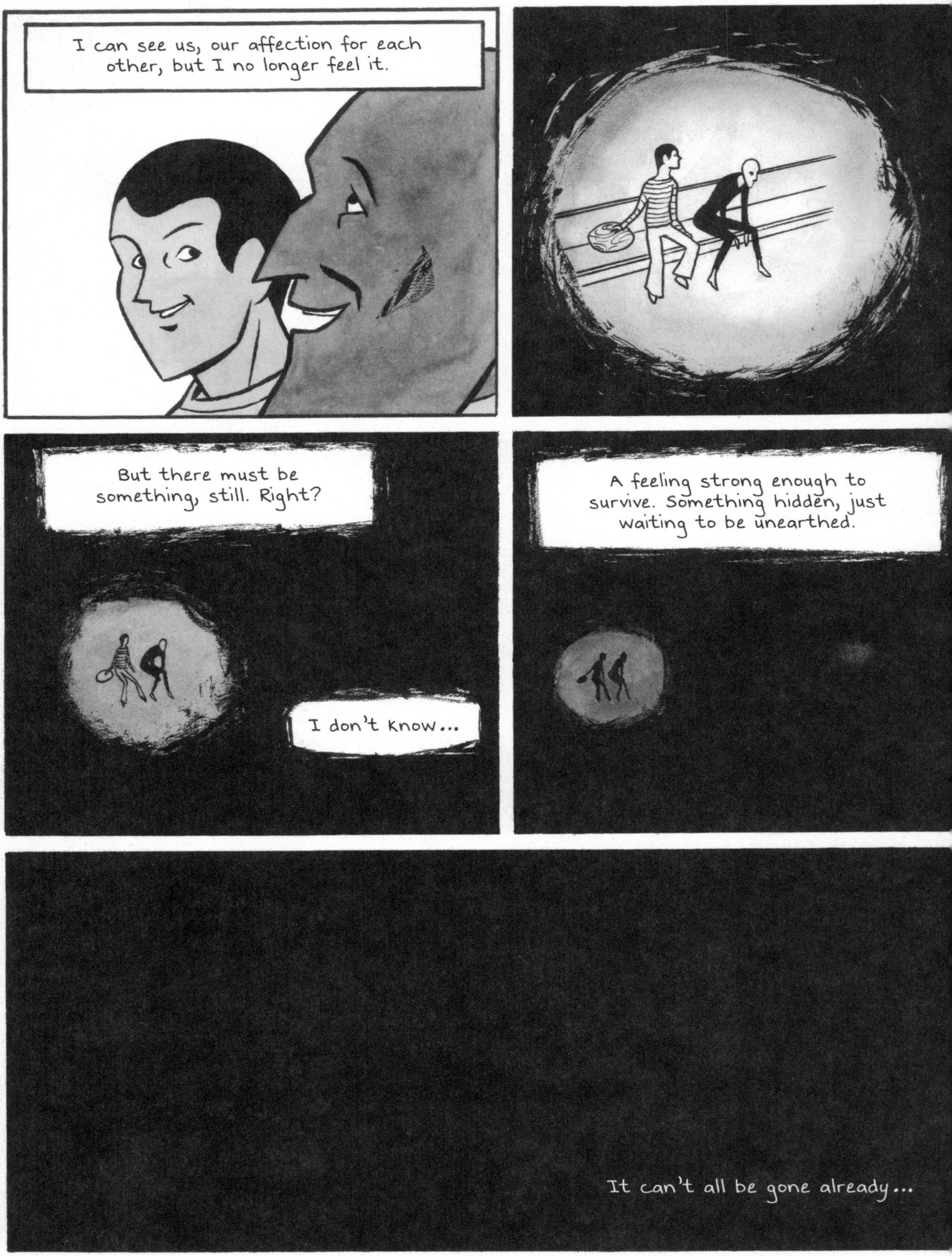

I can see us, our affection for each other, but I no longer feel it.
But there must be something, still. Right?
I don't know...
A feeling strong enough to survive. Something hidden, just waiting to be unearthed.
It can't all be gone already...

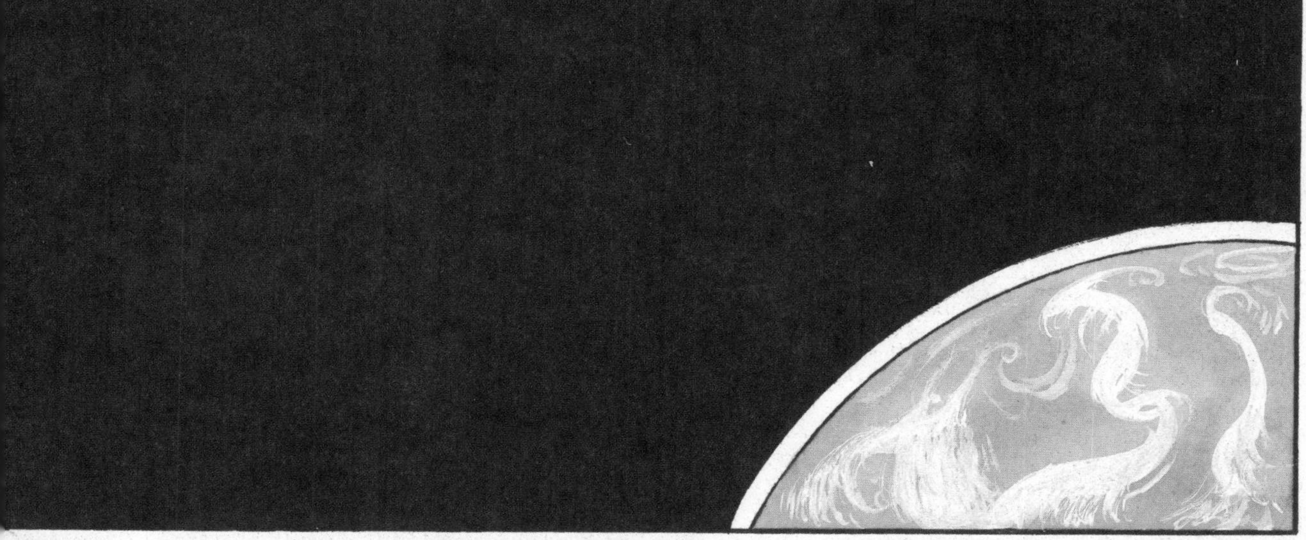

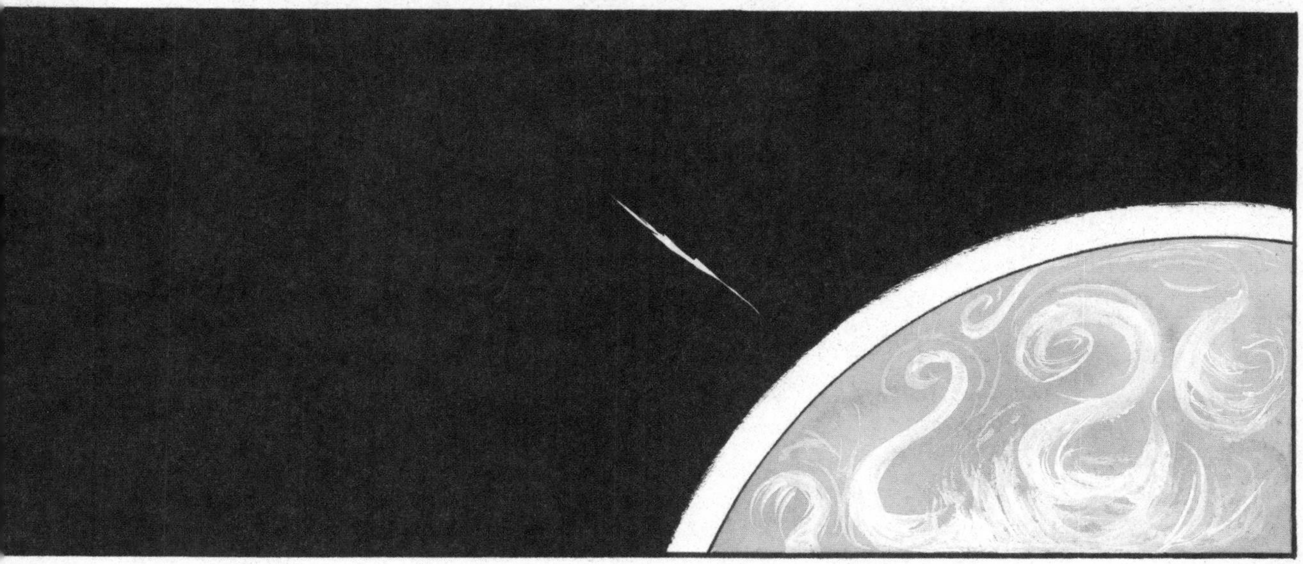

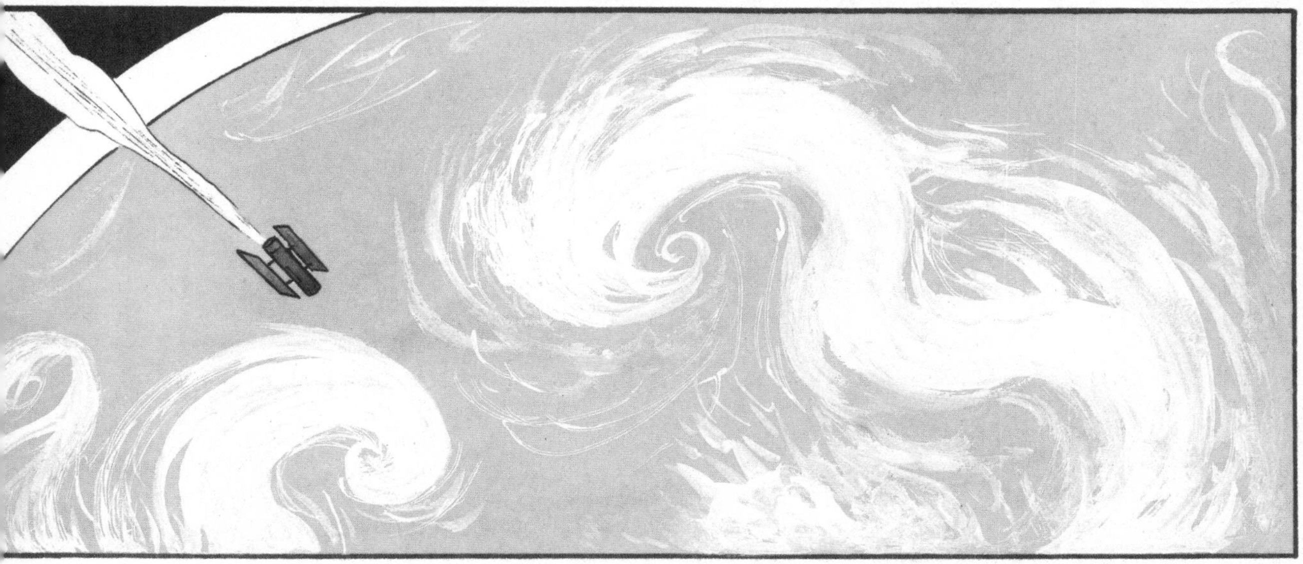

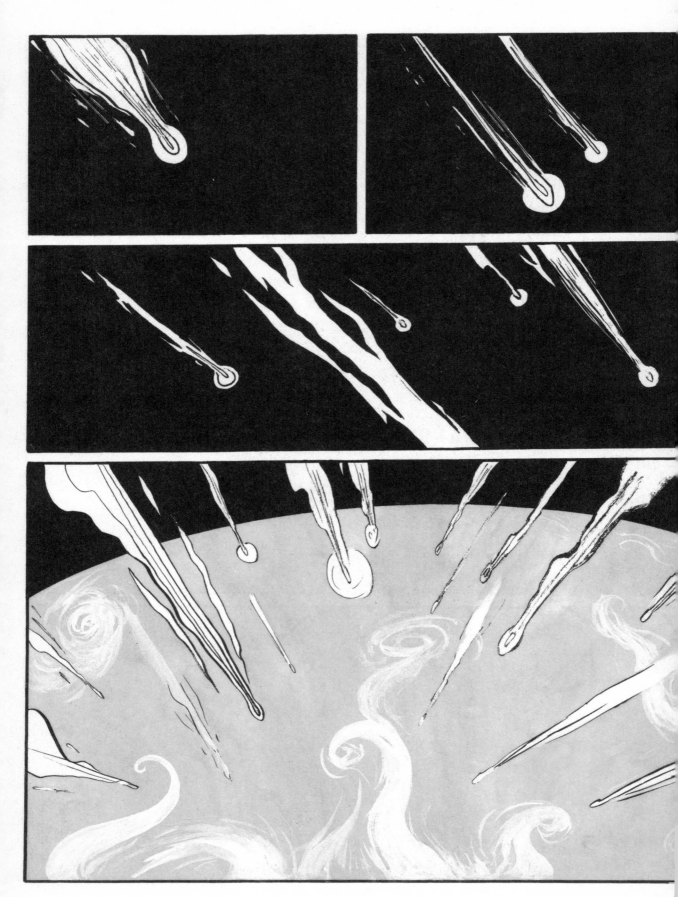

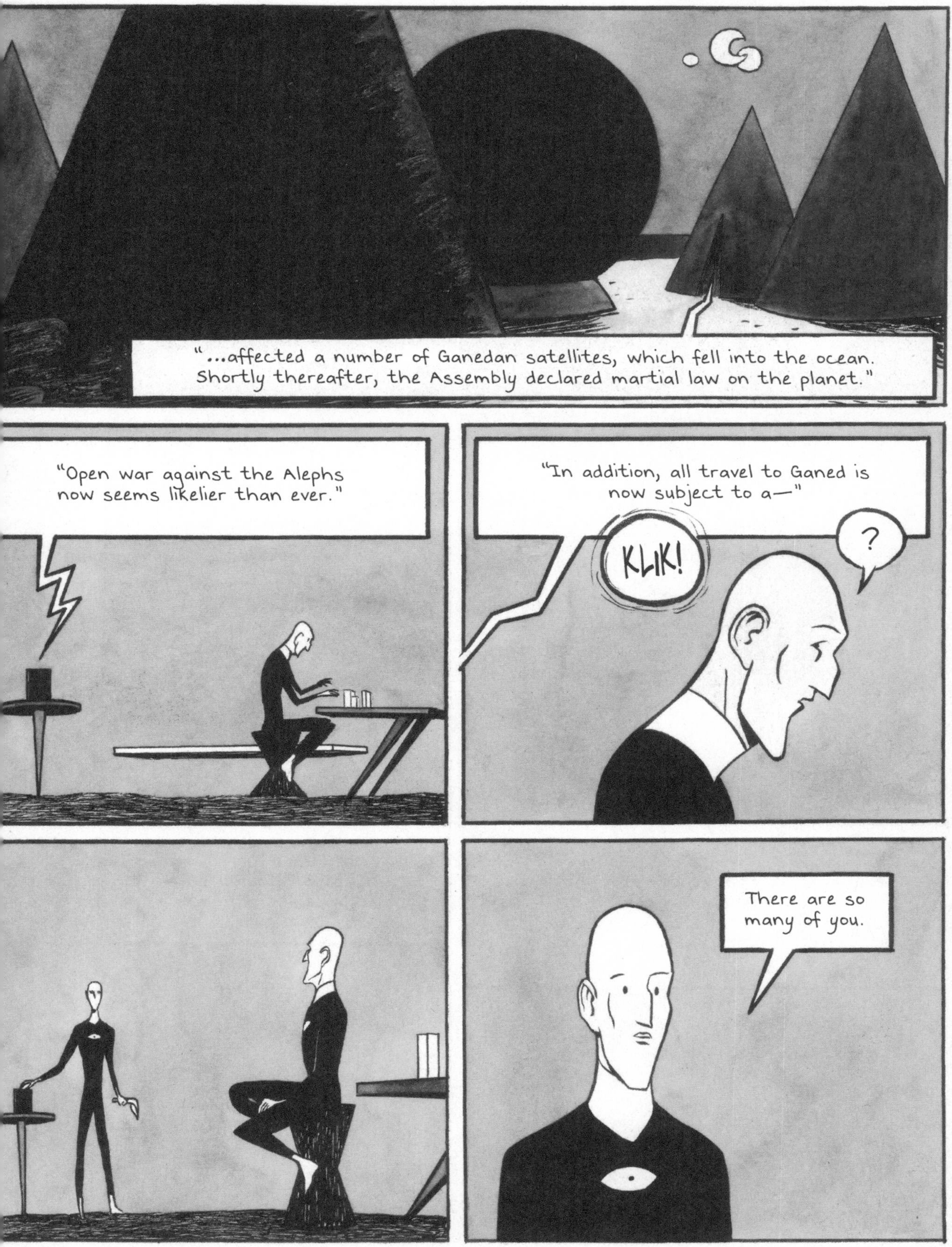
"...affected a number of Ganedan satellites, which fell into the ocean. Shortly thereafter, the Assembly declared martial law on the planet."
"Open war against the Alephs now seems likelier than ever."
"In addition, all travel to Ganed is now subject to a—"
KLIK!
?
There are so many of you.

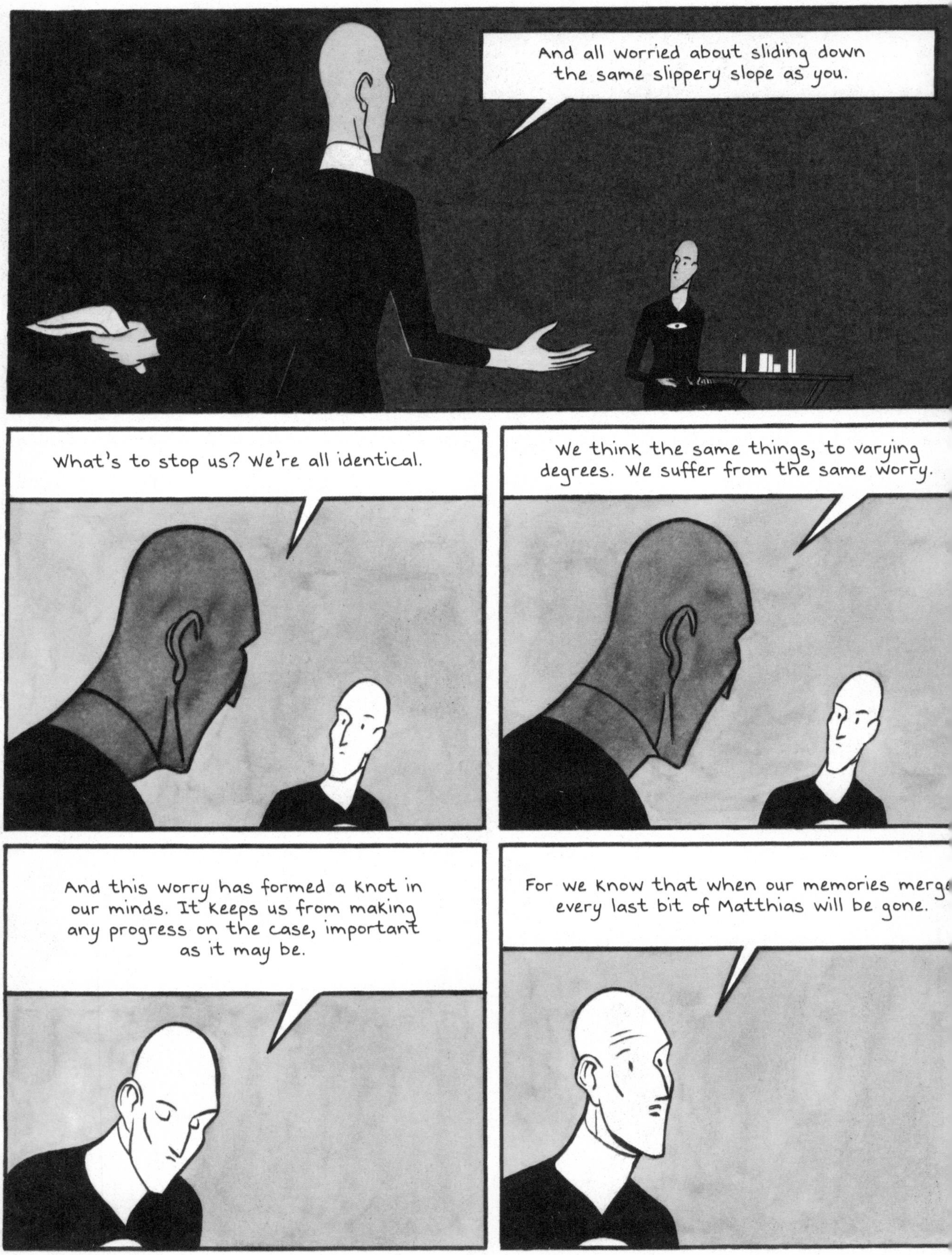
And all worried about sliding down the same slippery slope as you.
What's to stop us? We're all identical.
We think the same things, to varying degrees. We suffer from the same worry.
And this worry has formed a knot in our minds. It keeps us from making any progress on the case, important as it may be.
For we know that when our memories merge every last bit of Matthias will be gone.

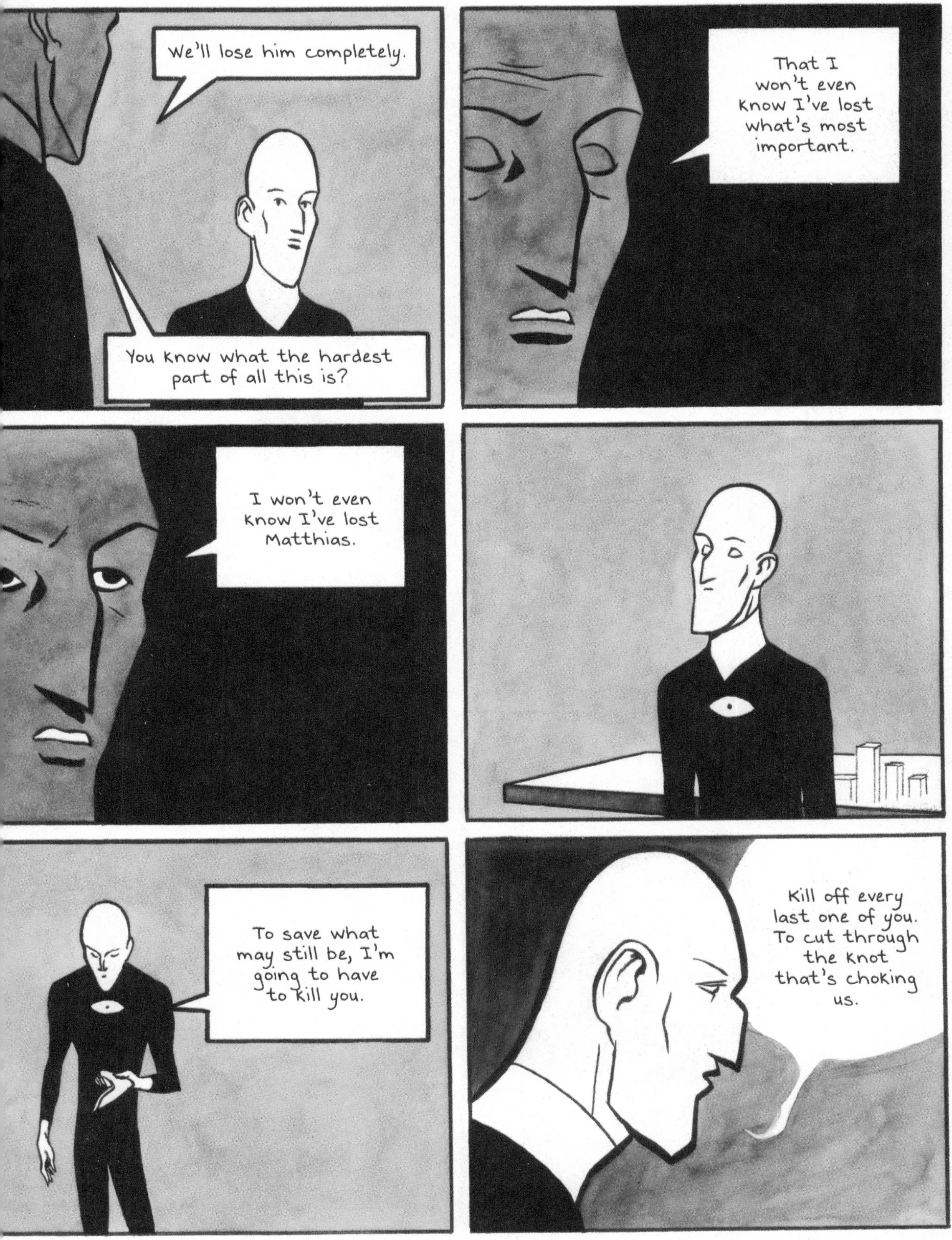
We'll lose him completely.
You know what the hardest part of all this is?
That I won't even know I've lost what's most important.
I won't even know I've lost Matthias.
To save what may still be, I'm going to have to kill you.
Kill off every last one of you. To cut through the knot that's choking us.

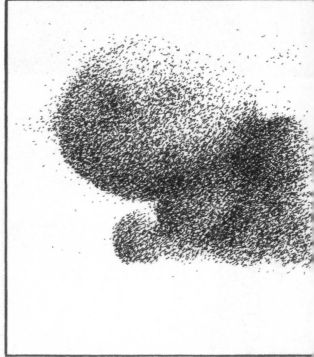

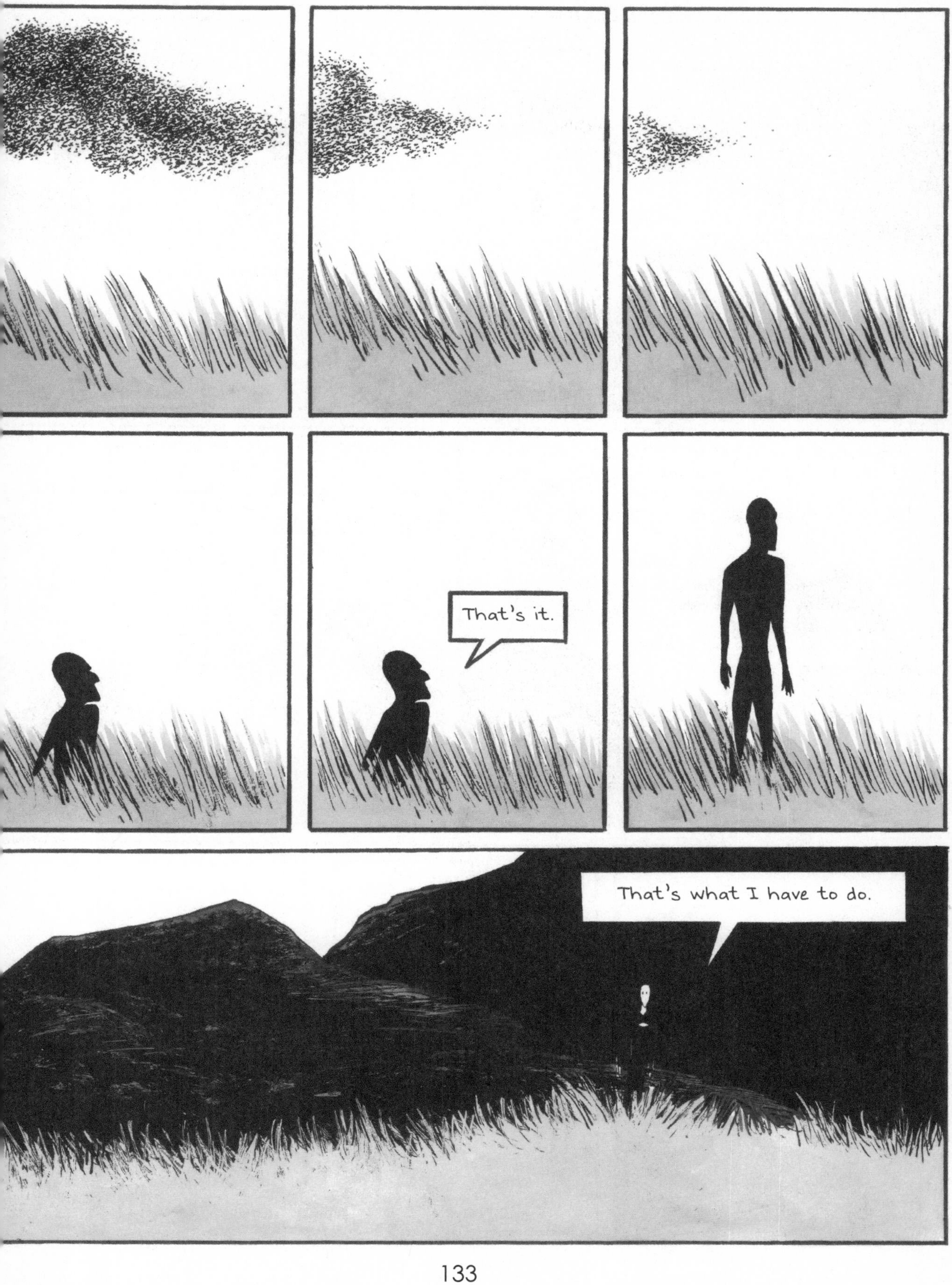
That's it.
That's what I have to do.

Hello, Alyssa.

Why, hello there, Elijah!

I finished up in the city archives and was on my way back to camp. I'm sick of wearing that costume.

Walk with me a bit?

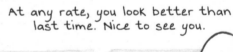

Not now. I have something important to finish.

At any rate, you look better than last time. Nice to see you.

See you later, then!

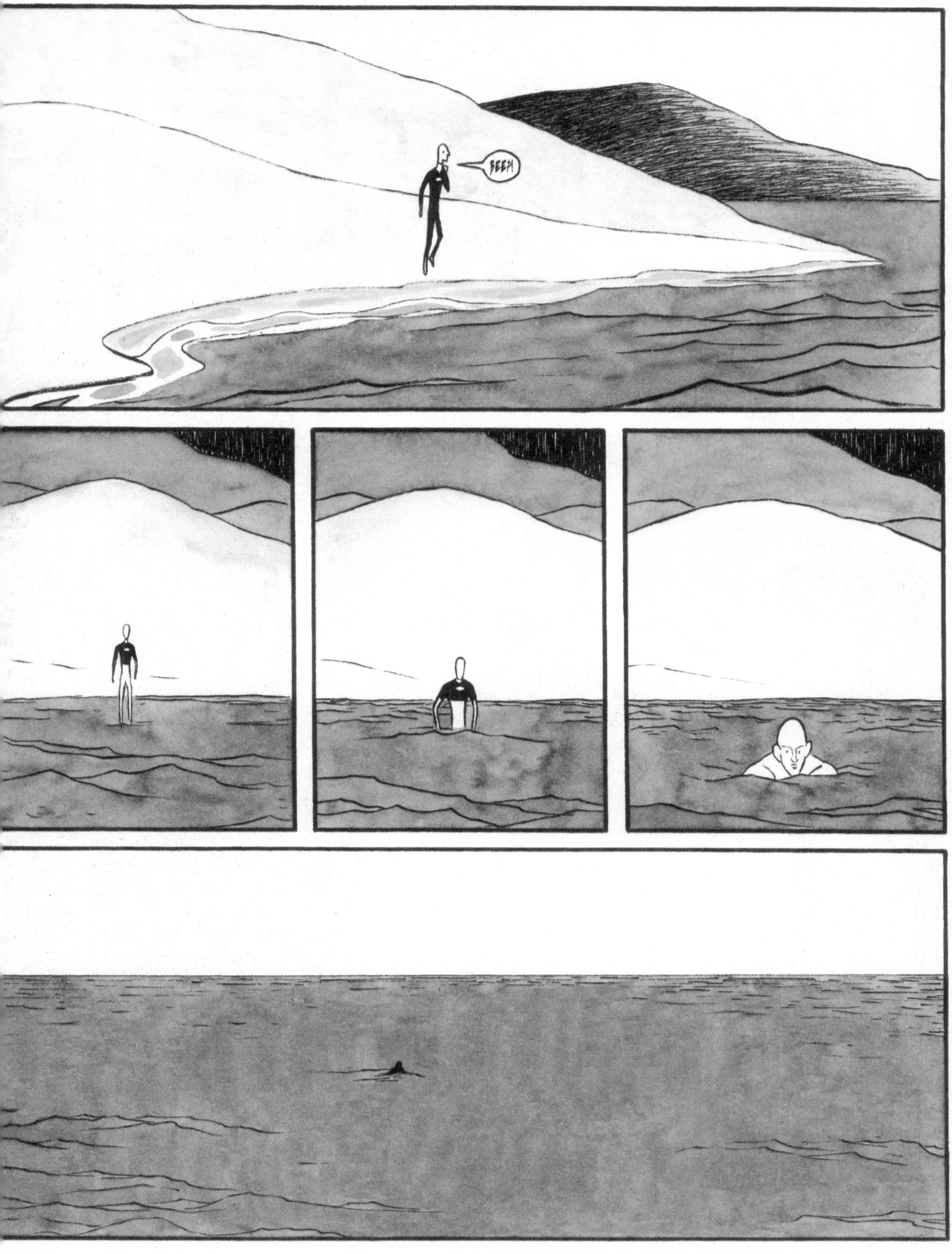
BEEP!

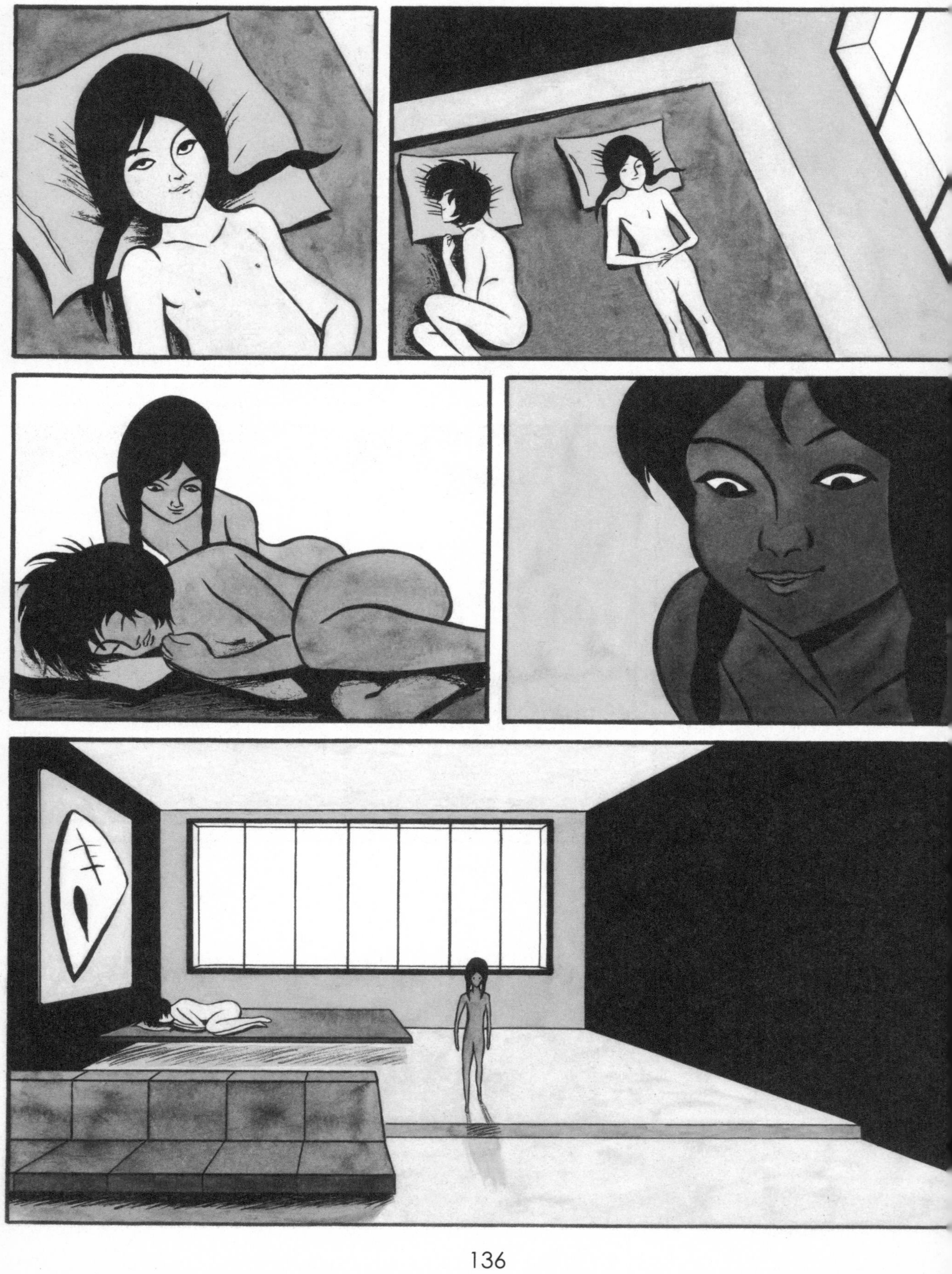

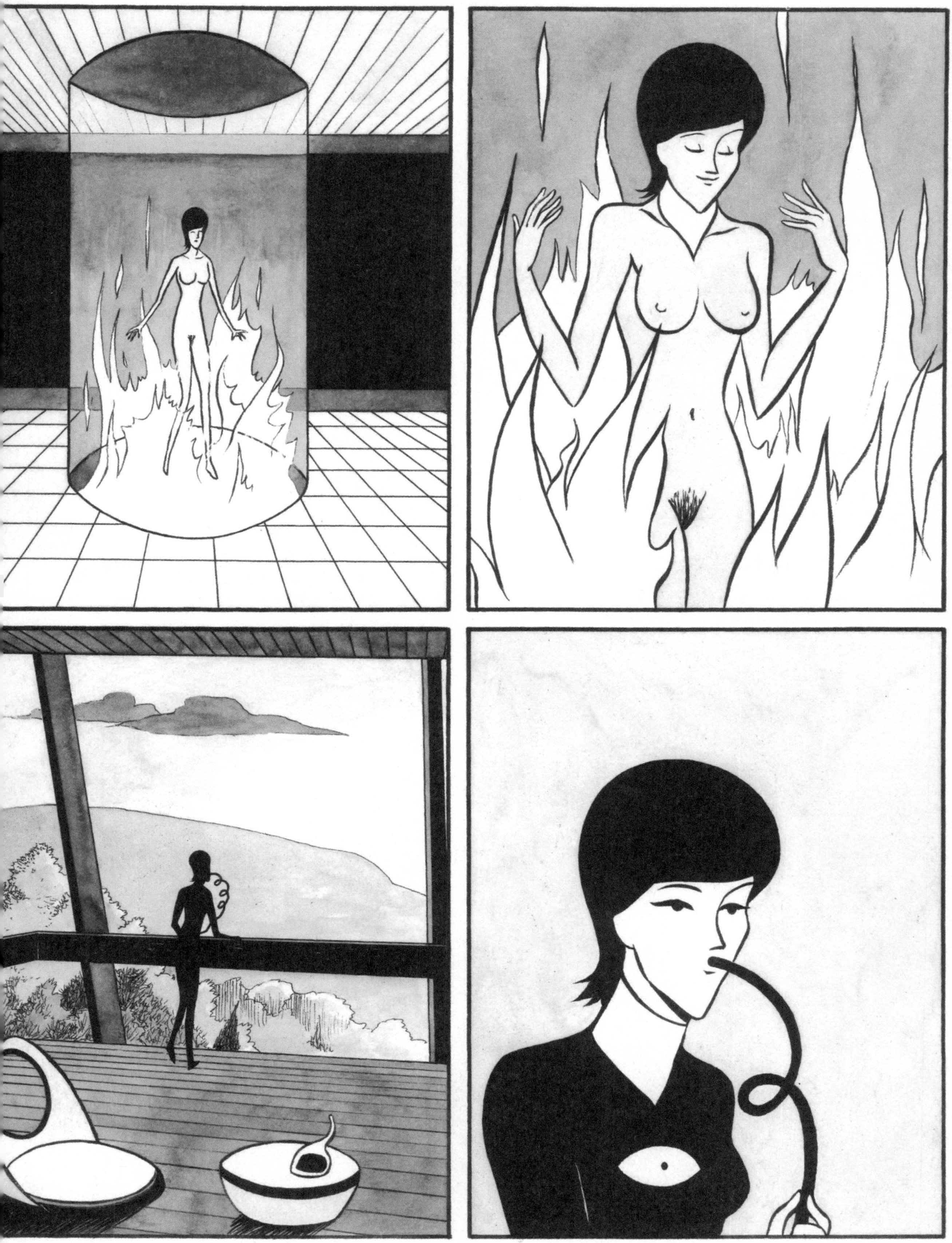

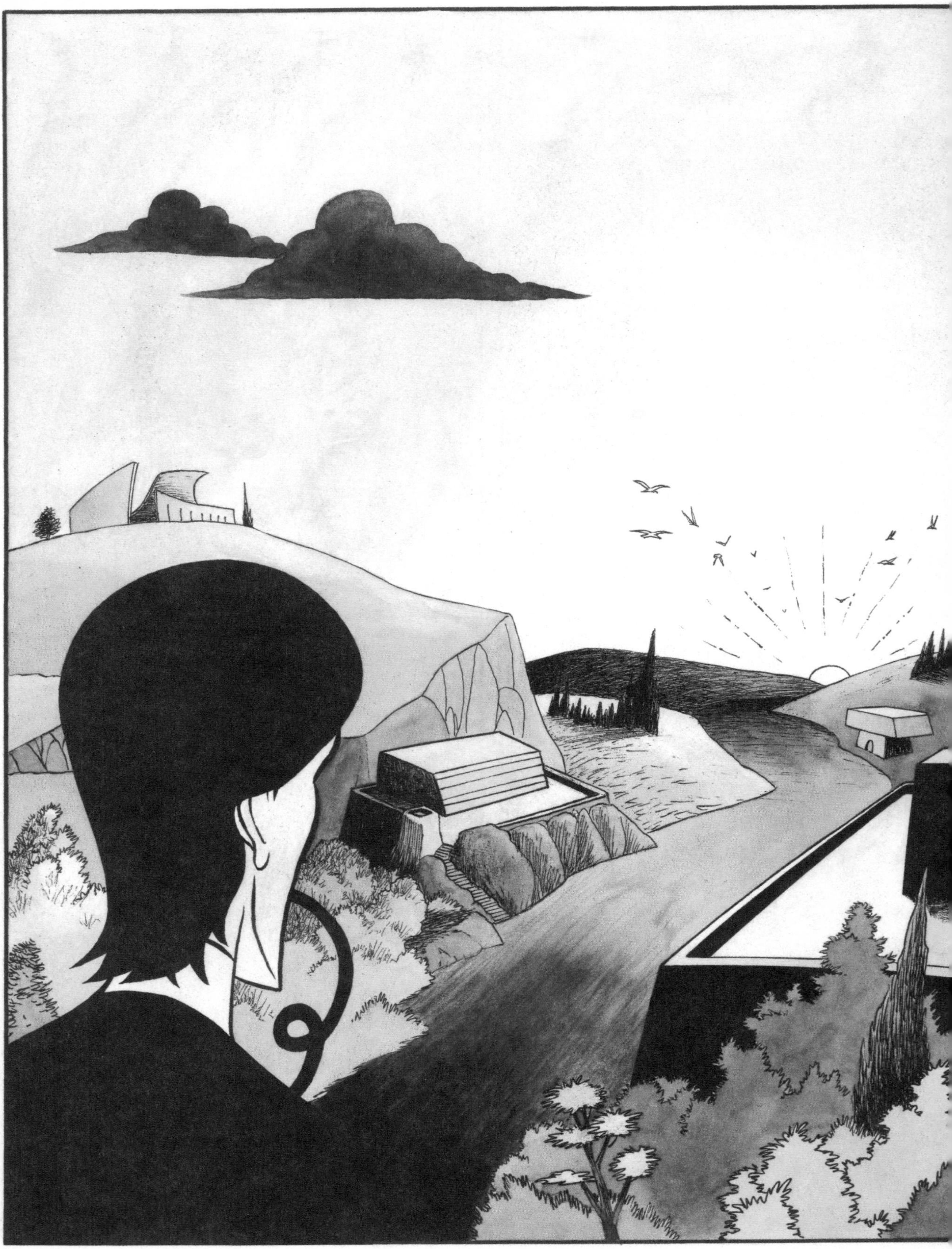

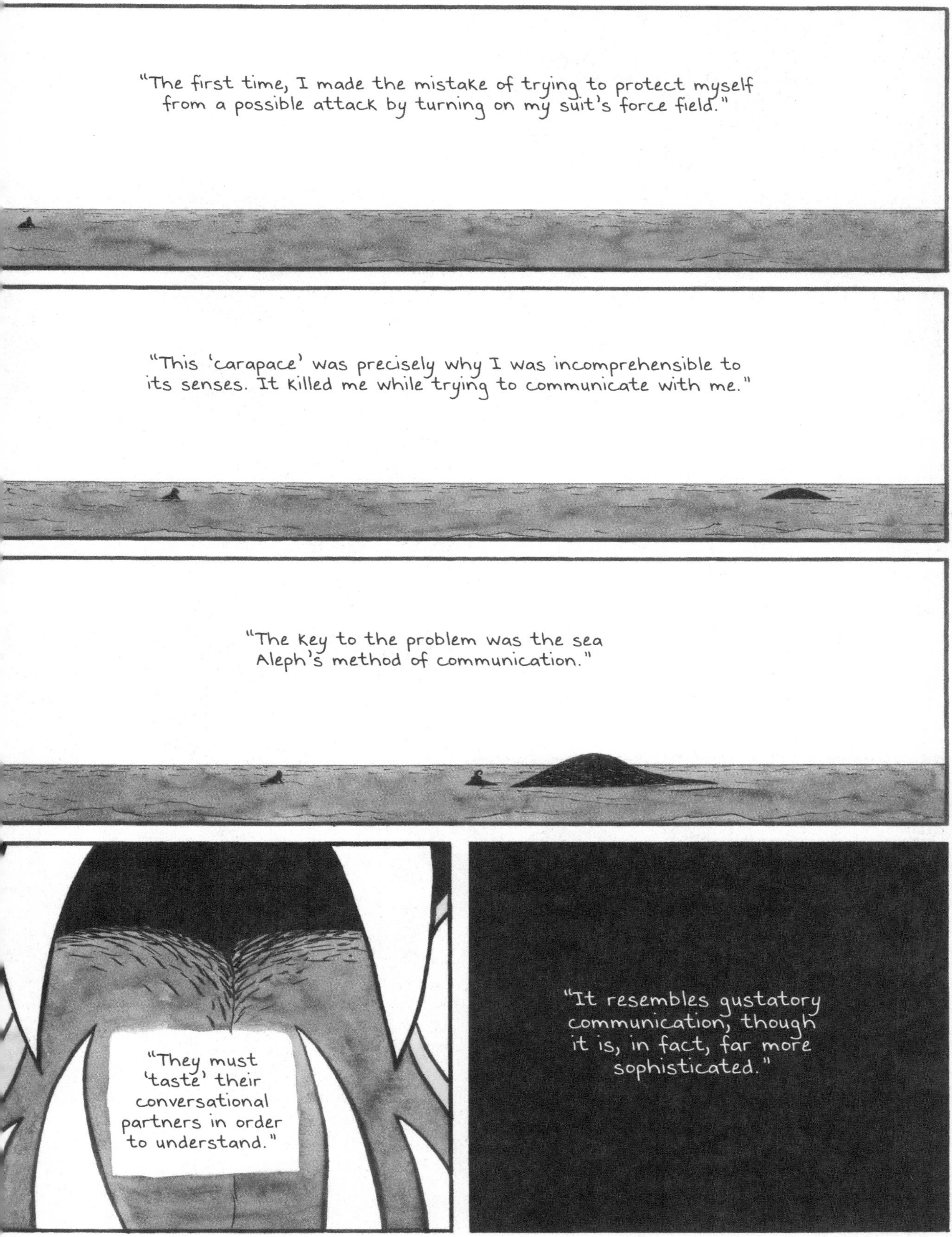

"The first time, I made the mistake of trying to protect myself from a possible attack by turning on my suit's force field."

"This 'carapace' was precisely why I was incomprehensible to its senses. It killed me while trying to communicate with me."

"The key to the problem was the sea Aleph's method of communication."

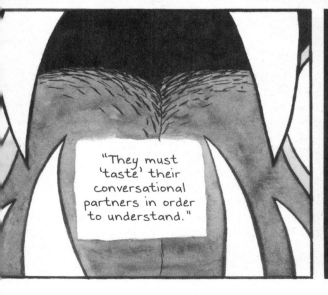

"They must 'taste' their conversational partners in order to understand."

"It resembles gustatory communication, though it is, in fact, far more sophisticated."

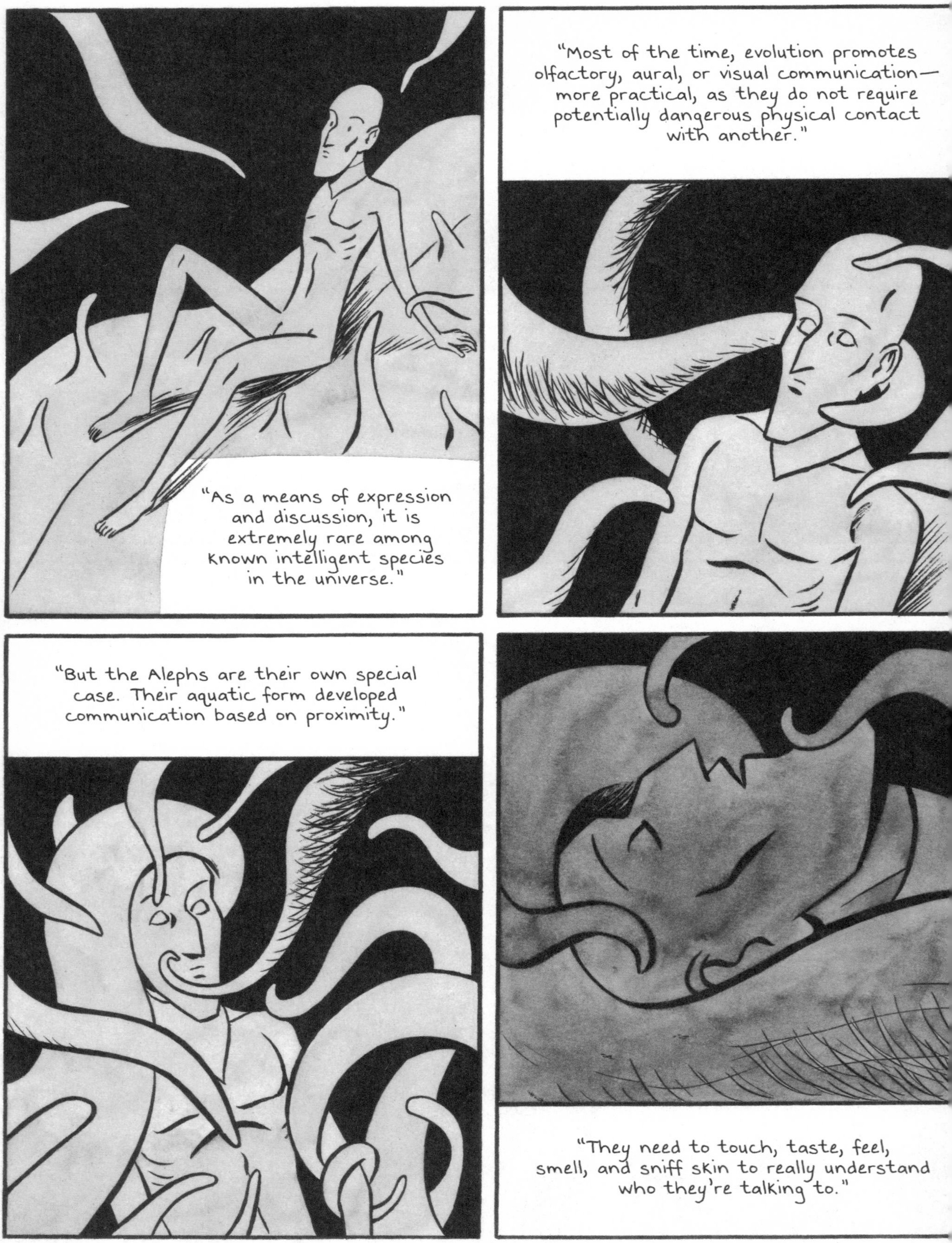
"As a means of expression and discussion, it is extremely rare among known intelligent species in the universe."
"Most of the time, evolution promotes olfactory, aural, or visual communication— more practical, as they do not require potentially dangerous physical contact with another."
"But the Alephs are their own special case. Their aquatic form developed communication based on proximity."
"They need to touch, taste, feel, smell, and sniff skin to really understand who they're talking to."

"It's a kind of tactile telepathy, purely of the flesh."

"It's not unpleasant, either. A bit weird, of course. But above all, it takes time, for the Alephs are never in a hurry."

"That's why King Faerela thought his son had been devoured."

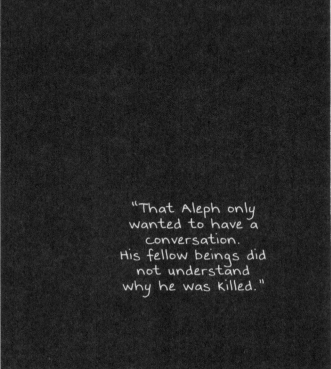

"That Aleph only wanted to have a conversation. His fellow beings did not understand why he was killed."

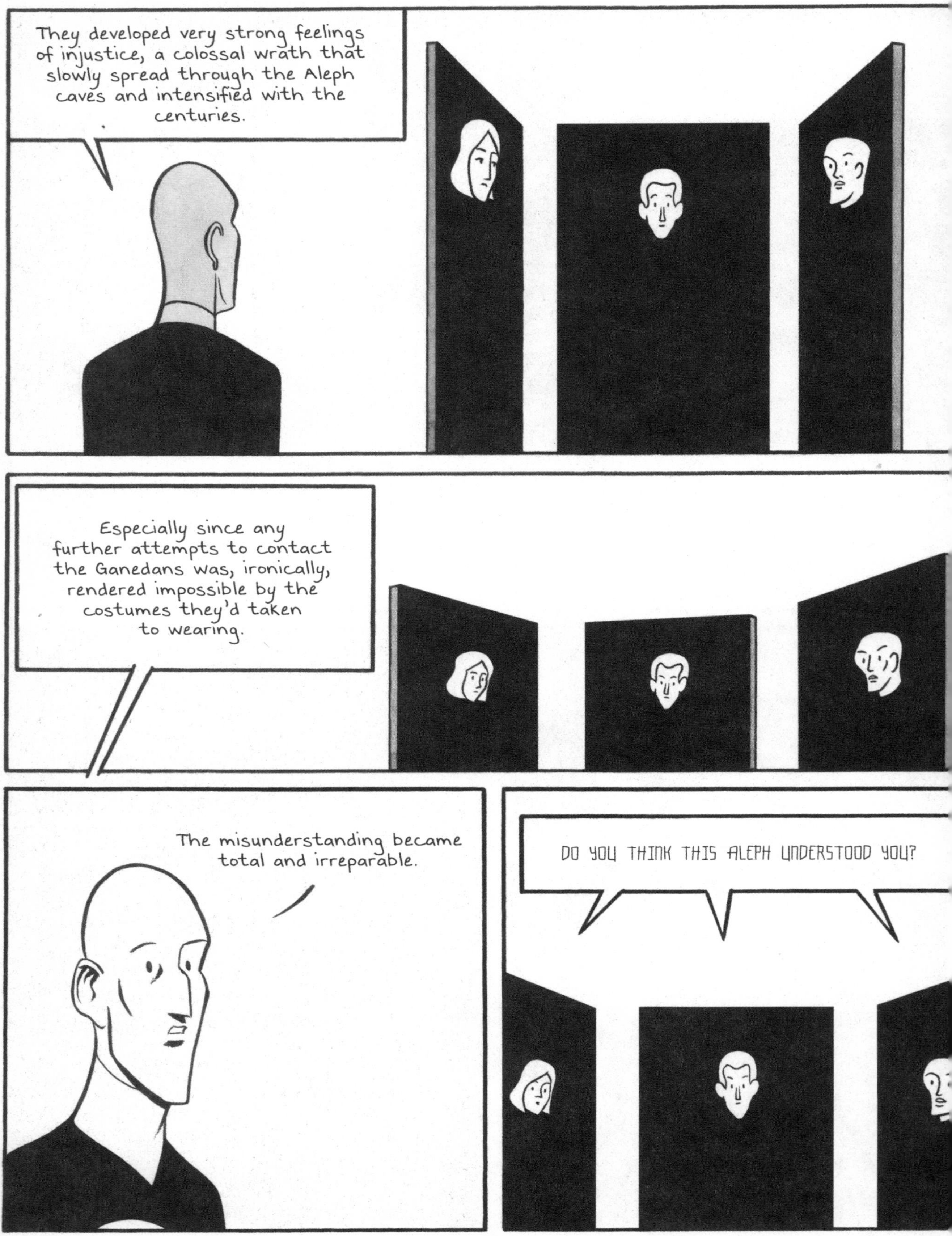
They developed very strong feelings of injustice, a colossal wrath that slowly spread through the Aleph caves and intensified with the centuries.
Especially since any further attempts to contact the Ganedans was, ironically, rendered impossible by the costumes they'd taken to wearing.
The misunderstanding became total and irreparable.
DO YOU THINK THIS ALEPH UNDERSTOOD YOU?

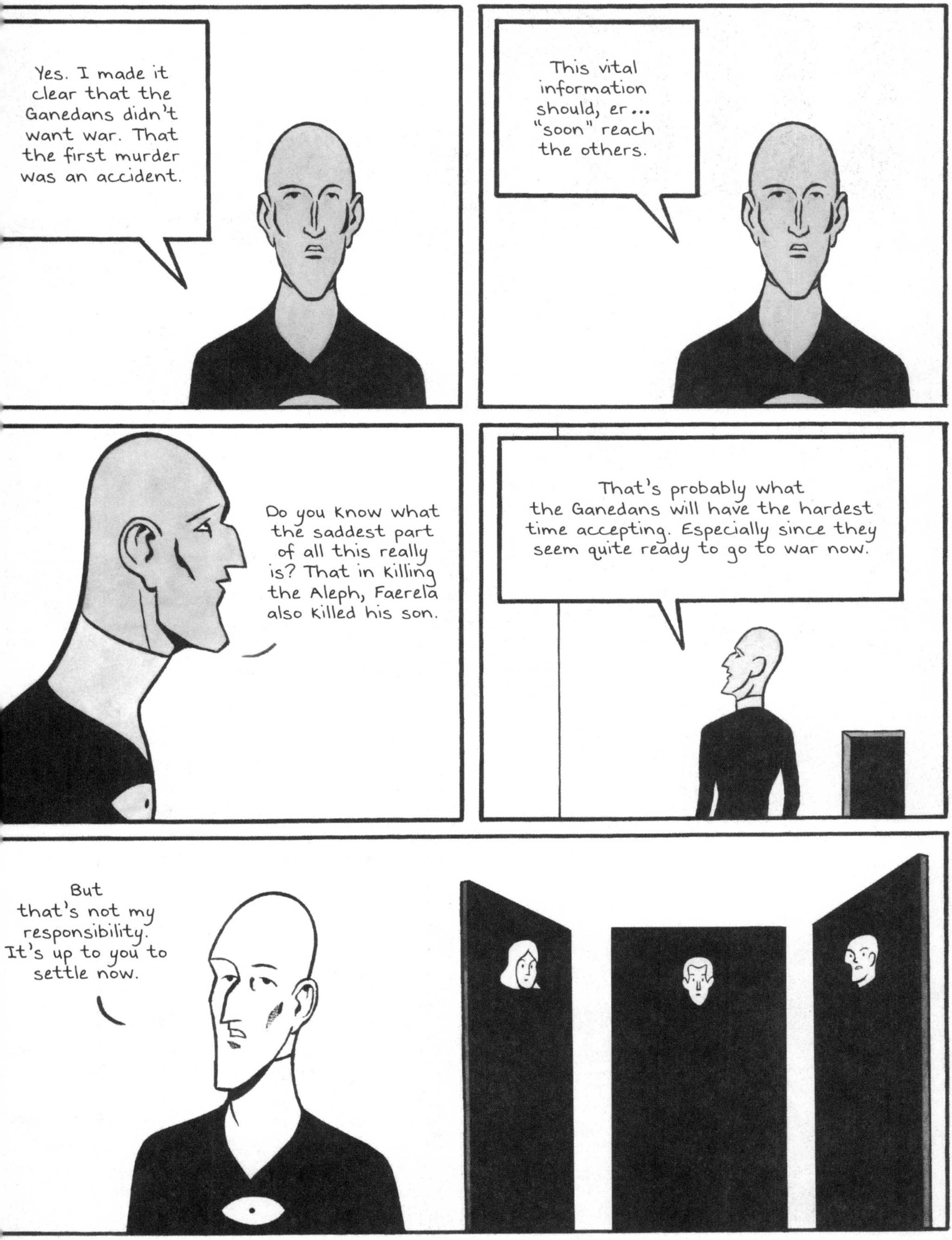
Yes. I made it clear that the Ganedans didn't want war. That the first murder was an accident.
This vital information should, er... "soon" reach the others.
Do you know what the saddest part of all this really is? That in killing the Aleph, Faerela also killed his son.
That's probably what the Ganedans will have the hardest time accepting. Especially since they seem quite ready to go to war now.
But that's not my responsibility. It's up to you to settle now.

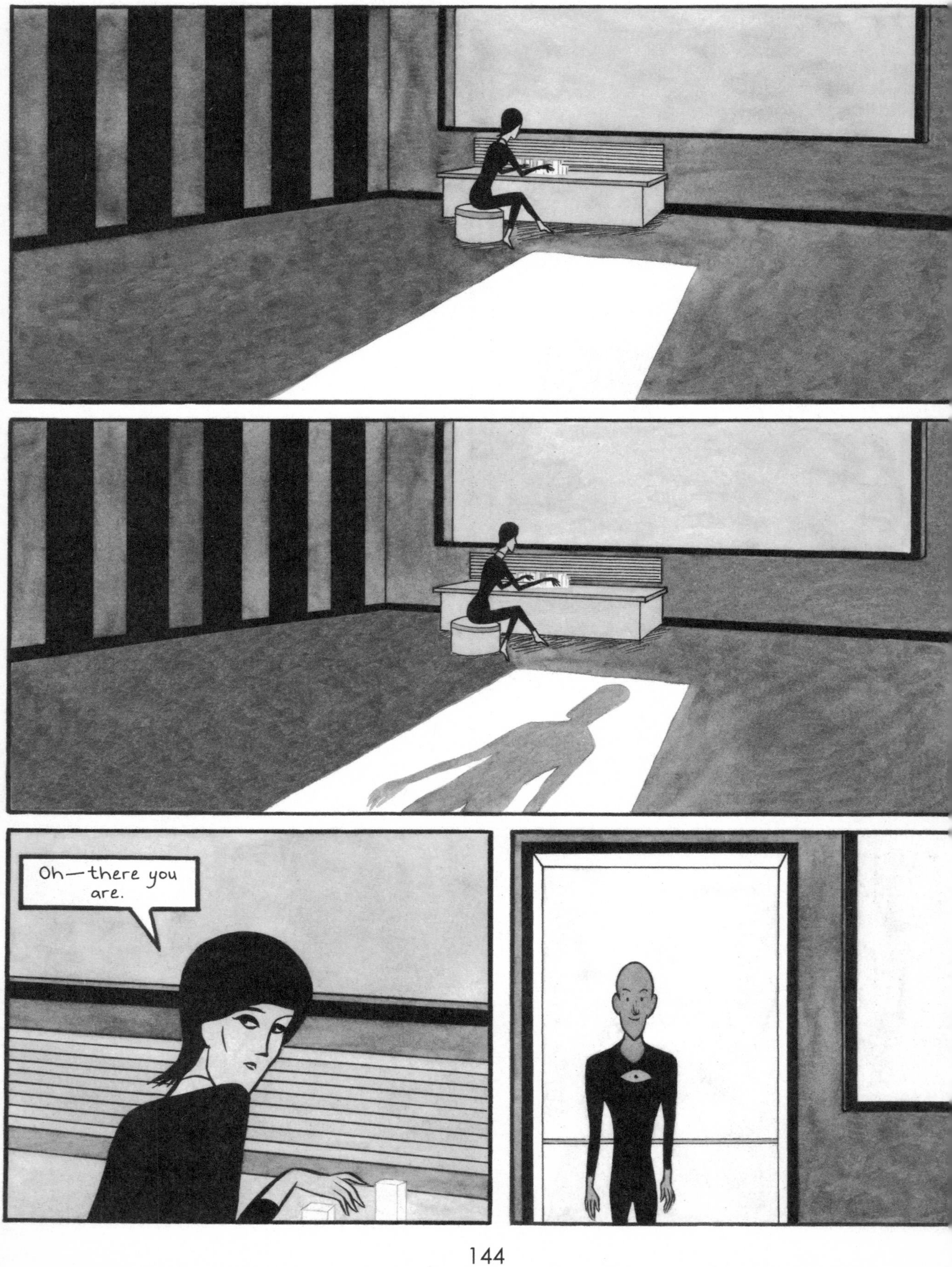
Oh—there you are.

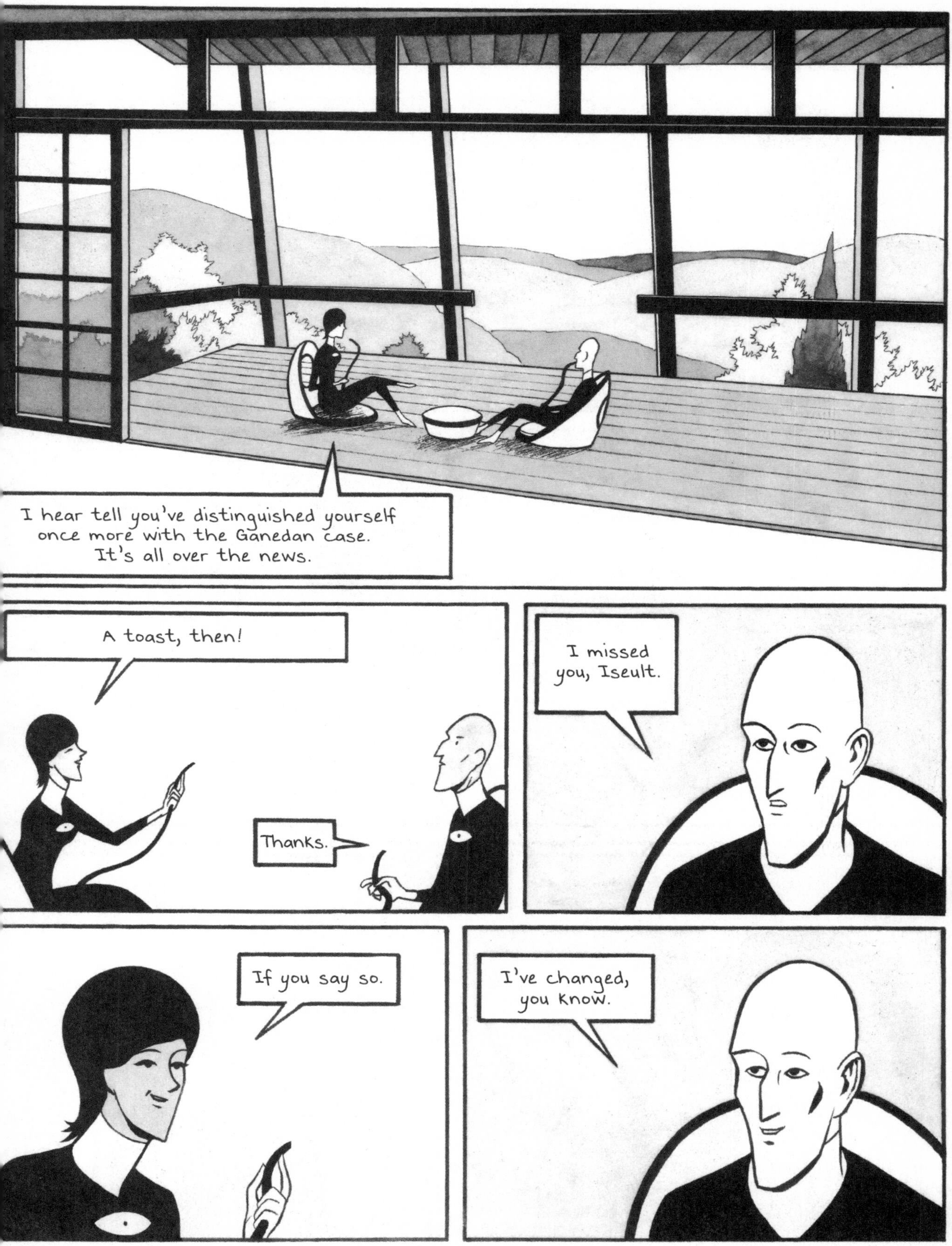
I hear tell you've distinguished yourself once more with the Ganedan case. It's all over the news.
A toast, then!
Thanks.
I missed you, Iseult.
If you say so.
I've changed, you know.

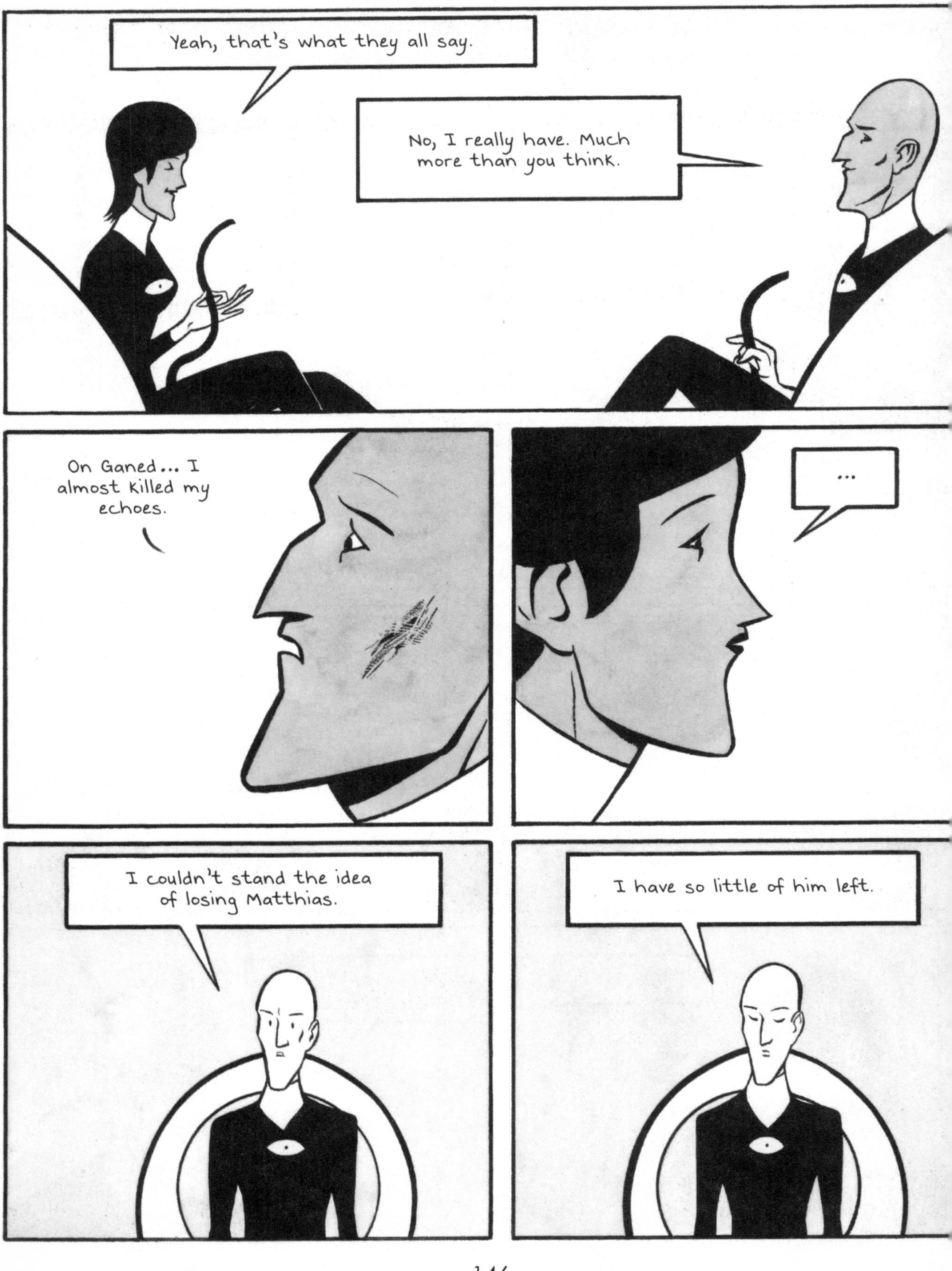
Yeah, that's what they all say.
No, I really have. Much more than you think.
On Ganed... I almost killed my echoes.
...
I couldn't stand the idea of losing Matthias.
I have so little of him left.

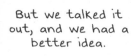
But we talked it out, and we had a better idea.

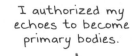
I authorized my echoes to become primary bodies.

...You what?

They're not my echoes anymore. They're other Elijahs, completely independent of me, with no predetermined lifespan.

But wait, Elijah... if you don't have any more echoes, what happens if—

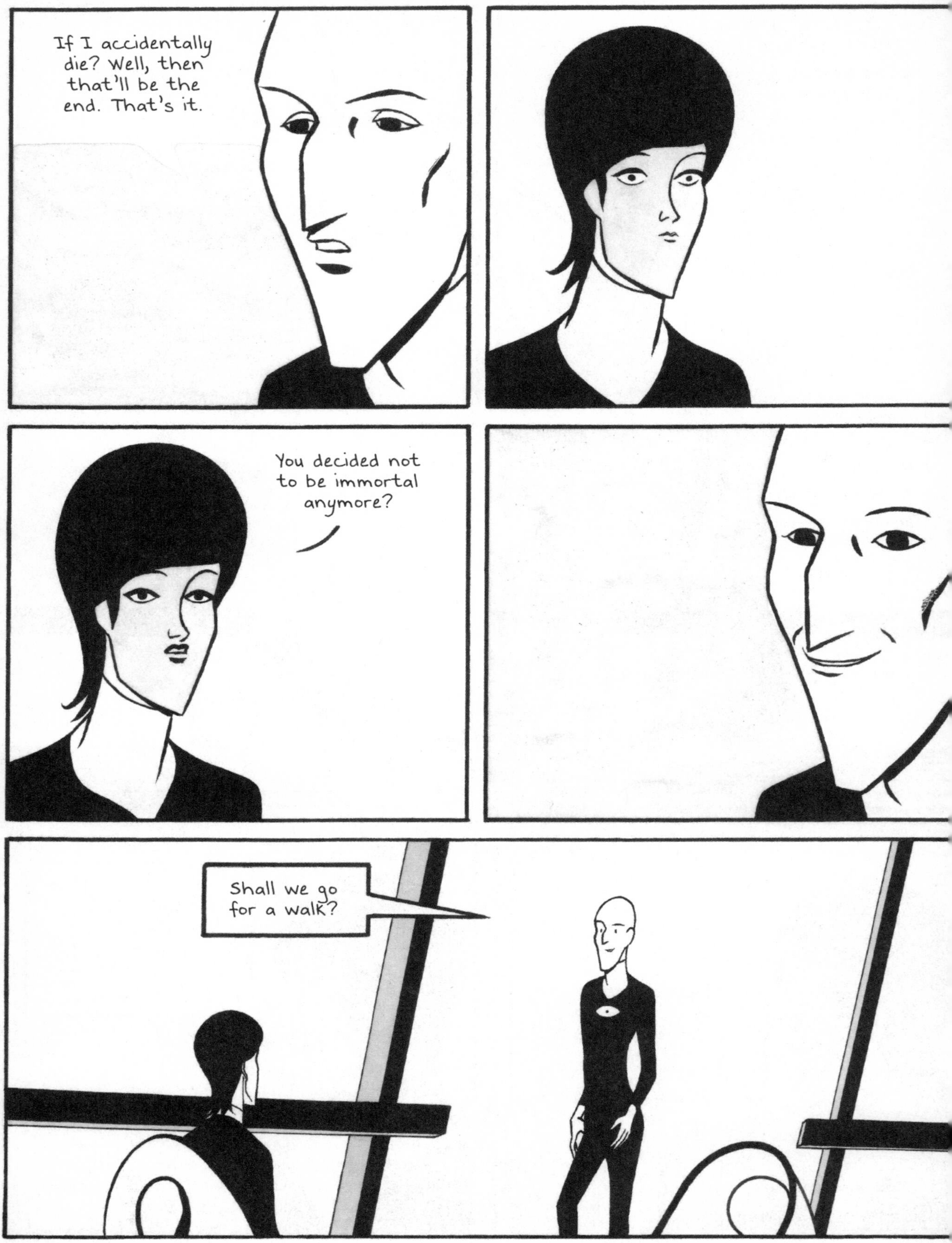
If I accidentally die? Well, then that'll be the end. That's it.
You decided not to be immortal anymore?
Shall we go for a walk?

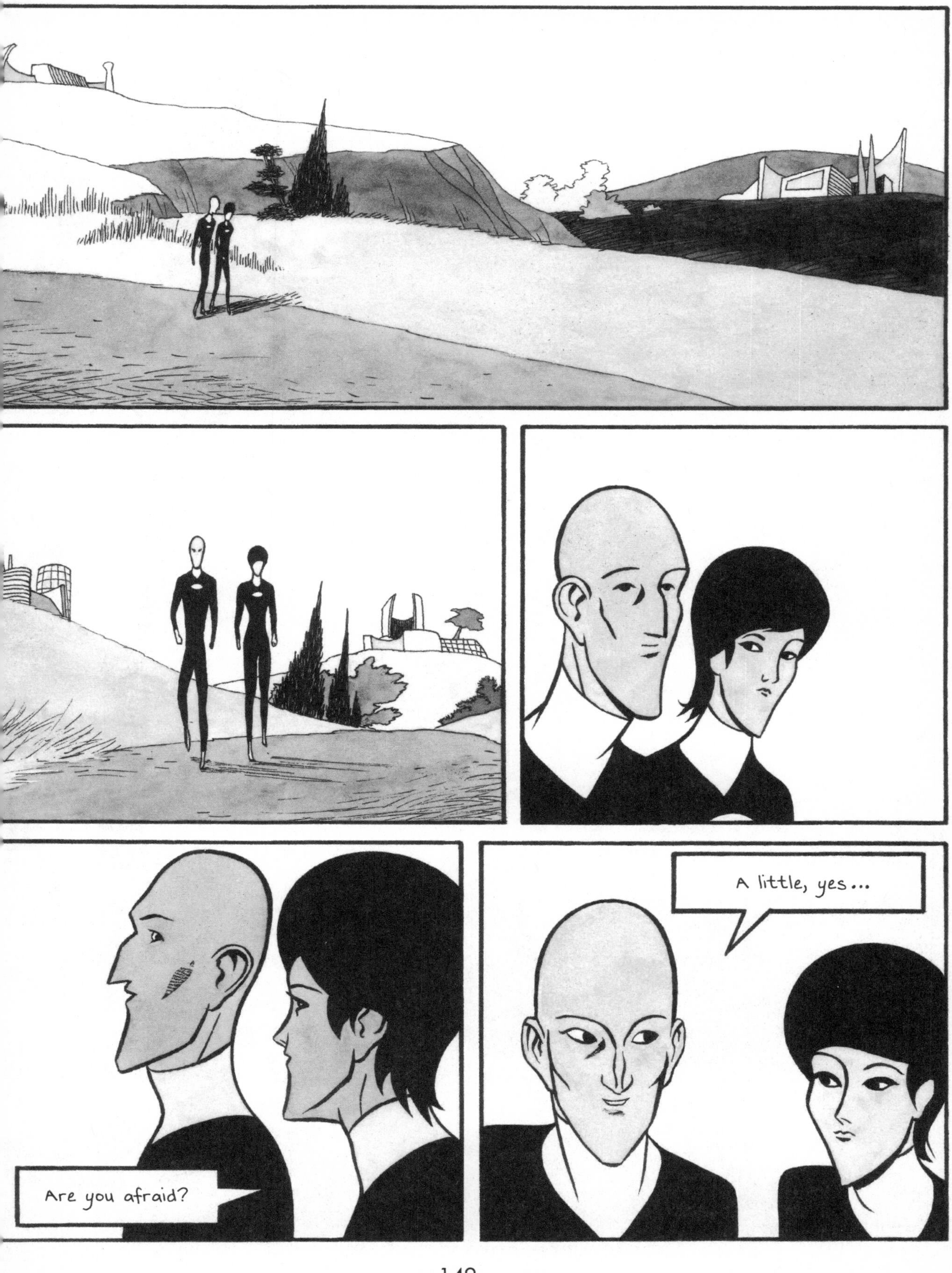
Are you afraid?
A little, yes...

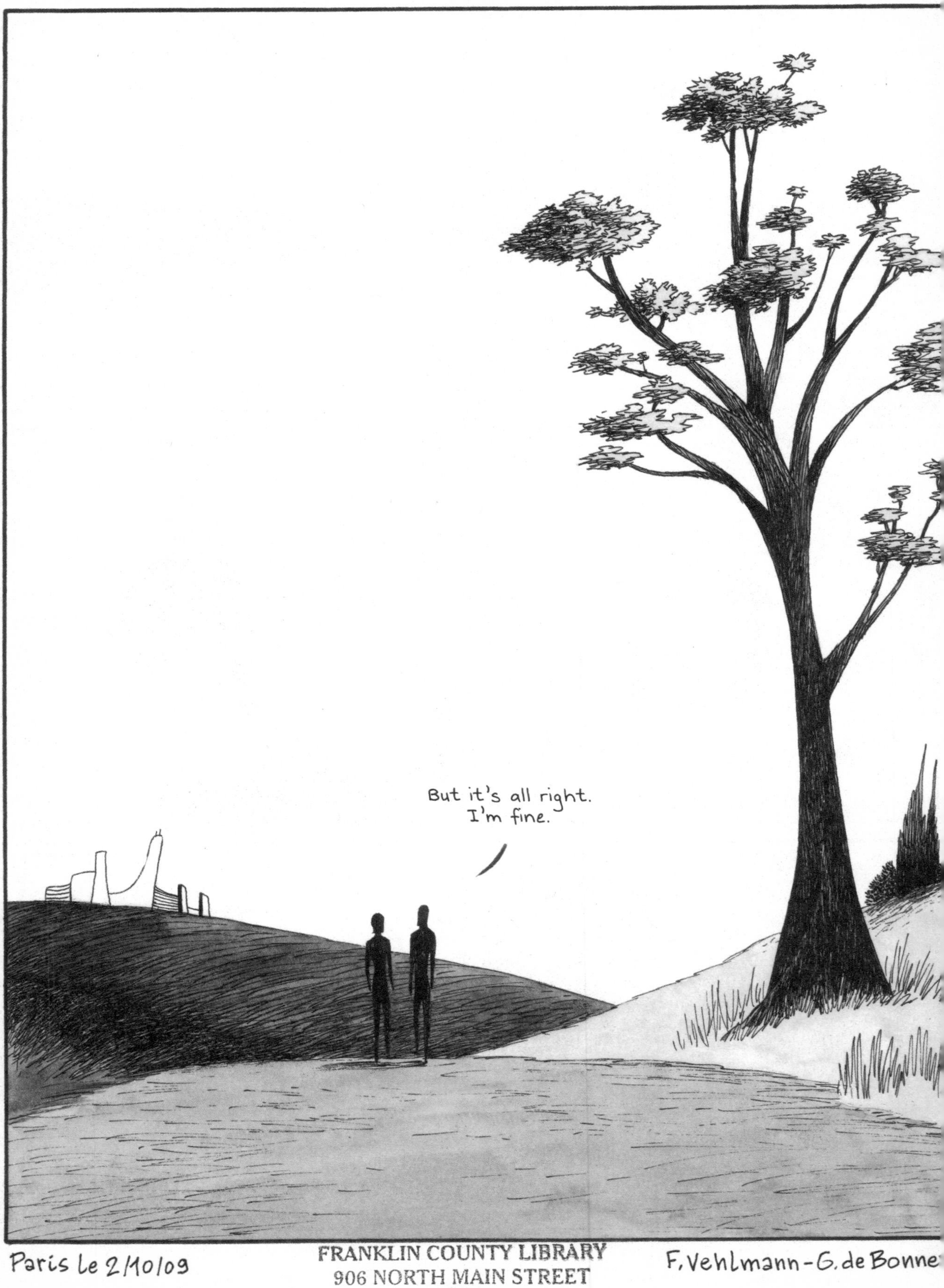
But it's all right.
I'm fine.

Paris le 2/10/09

F. Vehlmann - G. de Bonne

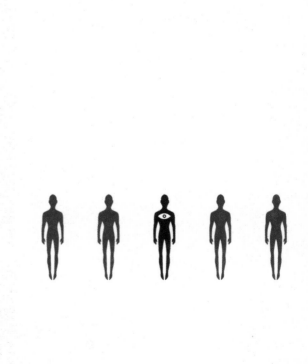

ABOUT THE **AUTHORS**

Fabien Vehlmann was born in 1972 in Mont de Marsan, France. After studying at l'École Supérieure de Commerce in Nantes, he turned to comics as a writer and has published many graphic novels including ***Les Cinq Conteurs de Baghdad***, winner of the 2007 Booksellers Prize, and ***Jolies Ténèbres***, an official selection of the Angoulême International Comics Festival in 2009.

Gwen De Bonneval was born in 1973 in Nantes, France. He has illustrated and written a number of award-winning graphic novels, including ***La Vierge Froide et Autres Racontars*** (an official selection of the Angoulême International Comics Festival) and ***L'Esprit Perdu*** (winner of the Prix Essentiels at Angoulême in 2010).

From the Same Authors

From Dargaud Editions

Samedi et Dimanche:
4 volumes and a collected omnibus

From Gwen De Bonneval

From Delcourt Editions

Basile Bonjour
3 collected volumes

Monsieur Forme

From Dupuis Editions

Messire Guillaume
3 volumes and a collected omnibus
Art by Mattieu Bonhomme

From Dargaud Editions

Gilgamesh
2 volumes and a collected omnibus
Art by Frantz Duchazeau

From Milan Editions

Vladimir sur les toits
Art by Nicolas Hubesch

From Sarbacane Editions

La Vierge froide et autres racontars
Aftewords by Jørn Riel
Art by Hervé Tanquerelle

From Fabien Vehlmann

From Dupuis Editions

Les aventures de Spirou et Fant
3 collected volumes
Art by Yoann

Green manor
3 collected volumes
Art by Denis Bodart

Jolies ténèbres
In collaboration with Marie Pommep
Art by Kerascoët

Seuls
4 collected volumes
Art by Bruno Gazzotti

Wondertown
2 collected volumes
Art by Benoît Féroumont

From Dargaud Editions

Le Marquis d'Anaon
5 collected volumes
Art by Matthieu Bonhomme

Les Cinq Conteurs de Bagdad
Art by Frantz Duchazeau

La Nuit de l'Inca
2 volumes and a collected omnibus
Art by Frantz Duchazeau

IAN
4 collected volumes
Art by Ralph Meyer

From Delecourt Editions

Sept psychopathes
Art by Sean Phillips

From Milan Editions

Dieu qui pue Dieu qui pète
Art by Frantz Duchazeau

From Lombard Editions

Des lendemains sans nuage
Art by Bruno Gazotti and Ralph Meye

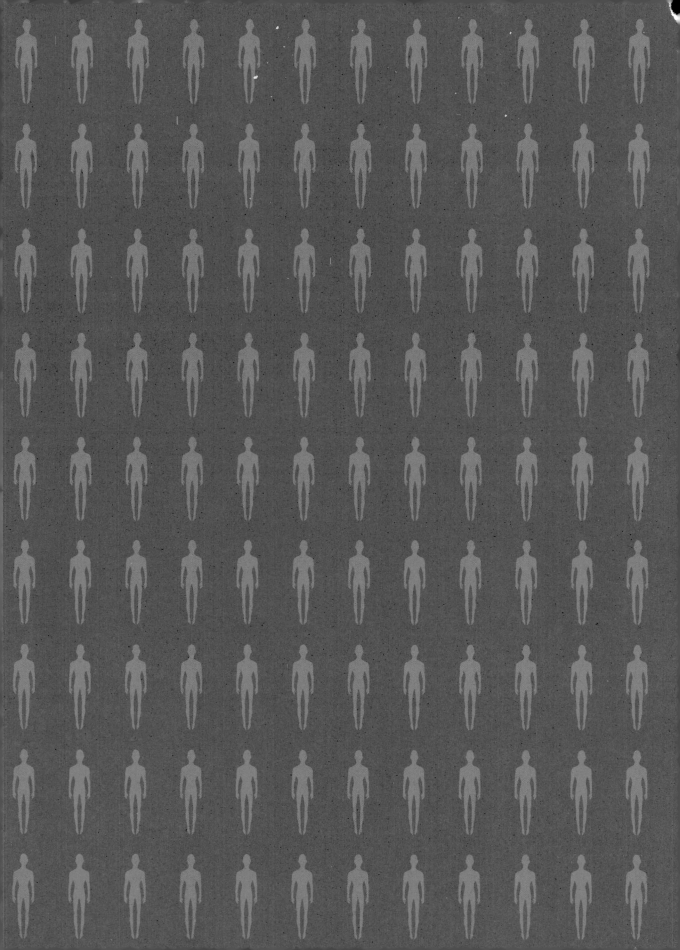